GNU gettext tools

A catalogue record for this book is available from the Hong Kong Public Libraries.

Published in Hong Kong by Samurai Media Limited.

Email: info@samuraimedia.org

ISBN 978-988-8381-56-2

Table of Contents

11   The Programmer's View 113

12   The Translator's View 131

1 Introduction

This chapter explains the goals sought in the creation of GNU `gettext` and the free Translation Project. Then, it explains a few broad concepts around Native Language Support, and positions message translation with regard to other aspects of national and cultural variance, as they apply to programs. It also surveys those files used to convey the translations. It explains how the various tools interact in the initial generation of these files, and later, how the maintenance cycle should usually operate.

In this manual, we use *he* when speaking of the programmer or maintainer, *she* when speaking of the translator, and *they* when speaking of the installers or end users of the translated program. This is only a convenience for clarifying the documentation. It is *absolutely* not meant to imply that some roles are more appropriate to males or females. Besides, as you might guess, GNU `gettext` is meant to be useful for people using computers, whatever their sex, race, religion or nationality!

Please send suggestions and corrections to:

Internet address:
       `bug-gnu-gettext@gnu.org`

Please include the manual's edition number and update date in your messages.

1.1 The Purpose of GNU `gettext`

Usually, programs are written and documented in English, and use English at execution time to interact with users. This is true not only of GNU software, but also of a great deal of proprietary and free software. Using a common language is quite handy for communication between developers, maintainers and users from all countries. On the other hand, most people are less comfortable with English than with their own native language, and would prefer to use their mother tongue for day to day's work, as far as possible. Many would simply *love* to see their computer screen showing a lot less of English, and far more of their own language.

However, to many people, this dream might appear so far fetched that they may believe it is not even worth spending time thinking about it. They have no confidence at all that the dream might ever become true. Yet some have not lost hope, and have organized themselves. The Translation Project is a formalization of this hope into a workable structure, which has a good chance to get all of us nearer the achievement of a truly multi-lingual set of programs.

GNU `gettext` is an important step for the Translation Project, as it is an asset on which we may build many other steps. This package offers to programmers, translators and even users, a well integrated set of tools and documentation. Specifically, the GNU `gettext` utilities are a set of tools that provides a framework within which other free packages may produce multi-lingual messages. These tools include

- A set of conventions about how programs should be written to support message catalogs.
- A directory and file naming organization for the message catalogs themselves.
- A runtime library supporting the retrieval of translated messages.
- A few stand-alone programs to massage in various ways the sets of translatable strings, or already translated strings.

- A library supporting the parsing and creation of files containing translated messages.
- A special mode for Emacs[1] which helps preparing these sets and bringing them up to date.

GNU `gettext` is designed to minimize the impact of internationalization on program sources, keeping this impact as small and hardly noticeable as possible. Internationalization has better chances of succeeding if it is very light weighted, or at least, appear to be so, when looking at program sources.

The Translation Project also uses the GNU `gettext` distribution as a vehicle for documenting its structure and methods. This goes beyond the strict technicalities of documenting the GNU `gettext` proper. By so doing, translators will find in a single place, as far as possible, all they need to know for properly doing their translating work. Also, this supplemental documentation might also help programmers, and even curious users, in understanding how GNU `gettext` is related to the remainder of the Translation Project, and consequently, have a glimpse at the *big picture*.

1.2 I18n, L10n, and Such

Two long words appear all the time when we discuss support of native language in programs, and these words have a precise meaning, worth being explained here, once and for all in this document. The words are *internationalization* and *localization*. Many people, tired of writing these long words over and over again, took the habit of writing *i18n* and *l10n* instead, quoting the first and last letter of each word, and replacing the run of intermediate letters by a number merely telling how many such letters there are. But in this manual, in the sake of clarity, we will patiently write the names in full, each time...

By *internationalization*, one refers to the operation by which a program, or a set of programs turned into a package, is made aware of and able to support multiple languages. This is a generalization process, by which the programs are untied from calling only English strings or other English specific habits, and connected to generic ways of doing the same, instead. Program developers may use various techniques to internationalize their programs. Some of these have been standardized. GNU `gettext` offers one of these standards. See Chapter 11 [Programmers], page 113.

By *localization*, one means the operation by which, in a set of programs already internationalized, one gives the program all needed information so that it can adapt itself to handle its input and output in a fashion which is correct for some native language and cultural habits. This is a particularisation process, by which generic methods already implemented in an internationalized program are used in specific ways. The programming environment puts several functions to the programmers disposal which allow this runtime configuration. The formal description of specific set of cultural habits for some country, together with all associated translations targeted to the same native language, is called the *locale* for this language or country. Users achieve localization of programs by setting proper values to special environment variables, prior to executing those programs, identifying which locale should be used.

In fact, locale message support is only one component of the cultural data that makes up a particular locale. There are a whole host of routines and functions provided to aid

---

[1] In this manual, all mentions of Emacs refers to either GNU Emacs or to XEmacs, which people sometimes call FSF Emacs and Lucid Emacs, respectively.

programmers in developing internationalized software and which allow them to access the data stored in a particular locale. When someone presently refers to a particular locale, they are obviously referring to the data stored within that particular locale. Similarly, if a programmer is referring to "accessing the locale routines", they are referring to the complete suite of routines that access all of the locale's information.

One uses the expression *Native Language Support*, or merely NLS, for speaking of the overall activity or feature encompassing both internationalization and localization, allowing for multi-lingual interactions in a program. In a nutshell, one could say that internationalization is the operation by which further localizations are made possible.

Also, very roughly said, when it comes to multi-lingual messages, internationalization is usually taken care of by programmers, and localization is usually taken care of by translators.

1.3 Aspects in Native Language Support

For a totally multi-lingual distribution, there are many things to translate beyond output messages.

- As of today, GNU `gettext` offers a complete toolset for translating messages output by C programs. Perl scripts and shell scripts will also need to be translated. Even if there are today some hooks by which this can be done, these hooks are not integrated as well as they should be.

- Some programs, like `autoconf` or `bison`, are able to produce other programs (or scripts). Even if the generating programs themselves are internationalized, the generated programs they produce may need internationalization on their own, and this indirect internationalization could be automated right from the generating program. In fact, quite usually, generating and generated programs could be internationalized independently, as the effort needed is fairly orthogonal.

- A few programs include textual tables which might need translation themselves, independently of the strings contained in the program itself. For example, RFC 1345 gives an English description for each character which the `recode` program is able to reconstruct at execution. Since these descriptions are extracted from the RFC by mechanical means, translating them properly would require a prior translation of the RFC itself.

- Almost all programs accept options, which are often worded out so to be descriptive for the English readers; one might want to consider offering translated versions for program options as well.

- Many programs read, interpret, compile, or are somewhat driven by input files which are texts containing keywords, identifiers, or replies which are inherently translatable. For example, one may want `gcc` to allow diacriticized characters in identifiers or use translated keywords; 'rm -i' might accept something else than 'y' or 'n' for replies, etc. Even if the program will eventually make most of its output in the foreign languages, one has to decide whether the input syntax, option values, etc., are to be localized or not.

- The manual accompanying a package, as well as all documentation files in the distribution, could surely be translated, too. Translating a manual, with the intent of later keeping up with updates, is a major undertaking in itself, generally.

As we already stressed, translation is only one aspect of locales. Other internationalization aspects are system services and are handled in GNU `libc`. There are many attributes that are needed to define a country's cultural conventions. These attributes include beside the country's native language, the formatting of the date and time, the representation of numbers, the symbols for currency, etc. These local *rules* are termed the country's locale. The locale represents the knowledge needed to support the country's native attributes.

There are a few major areas which may vary between countries and hence, define what a locale must describe. The following list helps putting multi-lingual messages into the proper context of other tasks related to locales. See the GNU `libc` manual for details.

Characters and Codesets

The codeset most commonly used through out the USA and most English speaking parts of the world is the ASCII codeset. However, there are many characters needed by various locales that are not found within this codeset. The 8-bit ISO 8859-1 code set has most of the special characters needed to handle the major European languages. However, in many cases, choosing ISO 8859-1 is nevertheless not adequate: it doesn't even handle the major European currency. Hence each locale will need to specify which codeset they need to use and will need to have the appropriate character handling routines to cope with the codeset.

Currency

The symbols used vary from country to country as does the position used by the symbol. Software needs to be able to transparently display currency figures in the native mode for each locale.

Dates

The format of date varies between locales. For example, Christmas day in 1994 is written as 12/25/94 in the USA and as 25/12/94 in Australia. Other countries might use ISO 8601 dates, etc.

Time of the day may be noted as *hh:mm*, *hh.mm*, or otherwise. Some locales require time to be specified in 24-hour mode rather than as AM or PM. Further, the nature and yearly extent of the Daylight Saving correction vary widely between countries.

Numbers

Numbers can be represented differently in different locales. For example, the following numbers are all written correctly for their respective locales:

```
12,345.67       English
12.345,67       German
 12345,67       French
1,2345.67       Asia
```

Some programs could go further and use different unit systems, like English units or Metric units, or even take into account variants about how numbers are spelled in full.

Messages

The most obvious area is the language support within a locale. This is where GNU `gettext` provides the means for developers and users to easily change the language that the software uses to communicate to the user.

These areas of cultural conventions are called *locale categories*. It is an unfortunate term; *locale aspects* or *locale feature categories* would be a better term, because each "locale category" describes an area or task that requires localization. The concrete data that describes the cultural conventions for such an area and for a particular culture is also called a *locale category*. In this sense, a locale is composed of several locale categories: the locale category describing the codeset, the locale category describing the formatting of numbers, the locale category containing the translated messages, and so on.

Components of locale outside of message handling are standardized in the ISO C standard and the POSIX:2001 standard (also known as the SUSV3 specification). GNU `libc` fully implements this, and most other modern systems provide a more or less reasonable support for at least some of the missing components.

1.4 Files Conveying Translations

The letters PO in `.po` files means Portable Object, to distinguish it from `.mo` files, where MO stands for Machine Object. This paradigm, as well as the PO file format, is inspired by the NLS standard developed by Uniforum, and first implemented by Sun in their Solaris system.

PO files are meant to be read and edited by humans, and associate each original, translatable string of a given package with its translation in a particular target language. A single PO file is dedicated to a single target language. If a package supports many languages, there is one such PO file per language supported, and each package has its own set of PO files. These PO files are best created by the `xgettext` program, and later updated or refreshed through the `msgmerge` program. Program `xgettext` extracts all marked messages from a set of C files and initializes a PO file with empty translations. Program `msgmerge` takes care of adjusting PO files between releases of the corresponding sources, commenting obsolete entries, initializing new ones, and updating all source line references. Files ending with `.pot` are kind of base translation files found in distributions, in PO file format.

MO files are meant to be read by programs, and are binary in nature. A few systems already offer tools for creating and handling MO files as part of the Native Language Support coming with the system, but the format of these MO files is often different from system to system, and non-portable. The tools already provided with these systems don't support all the features of GNU `gettext`. Therefore GNU `gettext` uses its own format for MO files. Files ending with `.gmo` are really MO files, when it is known that these files use the GNU format.

1.5 Overview of GNU `gettext`

The following diagram summarizes the relation between the files handled by GNU `gettext` and the tools acting on these files. It is followed by somewhat detailed explanations, which you should read while keeping an eye on the diagram. Having a clear understanding of these interrelations will surely help programmers, translators and maintainers.

```
Original C Sources ---> Preparation ---> Marked C Sources ---.
                                                             |
              .---------<--- GNU gettext Library            |
.--- make <---+                                             |
|             '---------<--------------------+--------------'
|                                            |
|    .-----<--- PACKAGE.pot <--- xgettext <---'    .---<--- PO Compendium
|    |                                             |           ^
|    |                                             '---.       |
|    '---.                                              +---> PO editor ---.
|        +----> msgmerge ------> LANG.po ---->--------'                    |
|    .---'                                                                 |
|    |                                                                     |
|    '-------------<--------------.                                        |
|                                 +--- New LANG.po <-----------------------'
|    .--- LANG.gmo <--- msgfmt <---'
|    |
|    '---> install ---> /.../LANG/PACKAGE.mo ---.
|                                               +---> "Hello world!"
'-------> install ---> /.../bin/PROGRAM -------'
```

As a programmer, the first step to bringing GNU gettext into your package is identifying, right in the C sources, those strings which are meant to be translatable, and those which are untranslatable. This tedious job can be done a little more comfortably using emacs PO mode, but you can use any means familiar to you for modifying your C sources. Beside this some other simple, standard changes are needed to properly initialize the translation library. See Chapter 4 [Sources], page 19, for more information about all this.

For newly written software the strings of course can and should be marked while writing it. The gettext approach makes this very easy. Simply put the following lines at the beginning of each file or in a central header file:

```
#define _(String) (String)
#define N_(String) String
#define textdomain(Domain)
#define bindtextdomain(Package, Directory)
```

Doing this allows you to prepare the sources for internationalization. Later when you feel ready for the step to use the gettext library simply replace these definitions by the following:

```
#include <libintl.h>
#define _(String) gettext (String)
#define gettext_noop(String) String
#define N_(String) gettext_noop (String)
```

and link against libintl.a or libintl.so. Note that on GNU systems, you don't need to link with libintl because the gettext library functions are already contained in GNU libc. That is all you have to change.

Once the C sources have been modified, the xgettext program is used to find and extract all translatable strings, and create a PO template file out of all these. This package.pot file contains all original program strings. It has sets of pointers to exactly where in C sources each string is used. All translations are set to empty. The letter t in .pot marks this as a Template PO file, not yet oriented towards any particular language. See Section 5.1 [xgettext Invocation], page 33, for more details about how one calls the xgettext program. If you are *really* lazy, you might be interested at working a lot more right away, and preparing the whole distribution setup (see Chapter 13 [Maintainers], page 140). By doing so, you spare yourself typing the xgettext command, as make should now generate the proper things automatically for you!

The first time through, there is no *lang*.po yet, so the msgmerge step may be skipped and replaced by a mere copy of *package*.pot to *lang*.po, where *lang* represents the target language. See Chapter 6 [Creating], page 42 for details.

Then comes the initial translation of messages. Translation in itself is a whole matter, still exclusively meant for humans, and whose complexity far overwhelms the level of this manual. Nevertheless, a few hints are given in some other chapter of this manual (see Chapter 12 [Translators], page 131). You will also find there indications about how to contact translating teams, or becoming part of them, for sharing your translating concerns with others who target the same native language.

While adding the translated messages into the *lang*.po PO file, if you are not using one of the dedicated PO file editors (see Chapter 8 [Editing], page 52), you are on your own for ensuring that your efforts fully respect the PO file format, and quoting conventions (see Chapter 3 [PO Files], page 13). This is surely not an impossible task, as this is the way many people have handled PO files around 1995. On the other hand, by using a PO file editor, most details of PO file format are taken care of for you, but you have to acquire some familiarity with PO file editor itself.

If some common translations have already been saved into a compendium PO file, translators may use PO mode for initializing untranslated entries from the compendium, and also save selected translations into the compendium, updating it (see Section 8.4 [Compendium], page 67). Compendium files are meant to be exchanged between members of a given translation team.

Programs, or packages of programs, are dynamic in nature: users write bug reports and suggestion for improvements, maintainers react by modifying programs in various ways. The fact that a package has already been internationalized should not make maintainers shy of adding new strings, or modifying strings already translated. They just do their job the best they can. For the Translation Project to work smoothly, it is important that maintainers do not carry translation concerns on their already loaded shoulders, and that translators be kept as free as possible of programming concerns.

The only concern maintainers should have is carefully marking new strings as translatable, when they should be, and do not otherwise worry about them being translated, as this will come in proper time. Consequently, when programs and their strings are adjusted in various ways by maintainers, and for matters usually unrelated to translation, xgettext would construct *package*.pot files which are evolving over time, so the translations carried by *lang*.po are slowly fading out of date.

It is important for translators (and even maintainers) to understand that package translation is a continuous process in the lifetime of a package, and not something which is done once and for all at the start. After an initial burst of translation activity for a given package, interventions are needed once in a while, because here and there, translated entries become obsolete, and new untranslated entries appear, needing translation.

The `msgmerge` program has the purpose of refreshing an already existing `lang.po` file, by comparing it with a newer `package.pot` template file, extracted by `xgettext` out of recent C sources. The refreshing operation adjusts all references to C source locations for strings, since these strings move as programs are modified. Also, `msgmerge` comments out as obsolete, in `lang.po`, those already translated entries which are no longer used in the program sources (see Section 8.3.8 [Obsolete Entries], page 59). It finally discovers new strings and inserts them in the resulting PO file as untranslated entries (see Section 8.3.7 [Untranslated Entries], page 58). See Section 7.1 [msgmerge Invocation], page 48, for more information about what `msgmerge` really does.

Whatever route or means taken, the goal is to obtain an updated `lang.po` file offering translations for all strings.

The temporal mobility, or fluidity of PO files, is an integral part of the translation game, and should be well understood, and accepted. People resisting it will have a hard time participating in the Translation Project, or will give a hard time to other participants! In particular, maintainers should relax and include all available official PO files in their distributions, even if these have not recently been updated, without exerting pressure on the translator teams to get the job done. The pressure should rather come from the community of users speaking a particular language, and maintainers should consider themselves fairly relieved of any concern about the adequacy of translation files. On the other hand, translators should reasonably try updating the PO files they are responsible for, while the package is undergoing pretest, prior to an official distribution.

Once the PO file is complete and dependable, the `msgfmt` program is used for turning the PO file into a machine-oriented format, which may yield efficient retrieval of translations by the programs of the package, whenever needed at runtime (see Section 10.3 [MO Files], page 110). See Section 10.1 [msgfmt Invocation], page 103, for more information about all modes of execution for the `msgfmt` program.

Finally, the modified and marked C sources are compiled and linked with the GNU `gettext` library, usually through the operation of `make`, given a suitable `Makefile` exists for the project, and the resulting executable is installed somewhere users will find it. The MO files themselves should also be properly installed. Given the appropriate environment variables are set (see Section 2.3 [Setting the POSIX Locale], page 10), the program should localize itself automatically, whenever it executes.

The remainder of this manual has the purpose of explaining in depth the various steps outlined above.

2 The User's View

Nowadays, when users log into a computer, they usually find that all their programs show messages in their native language – at least for users of languages with an active free software community, like French or German; to a lesser extent for languages with a smaller participation in free software and the GNU project, like Hindi and Filipino.

How does this work? How can the user influence the language that is used by the programs? This chapter will answer it.

2.1 Operating System Installation

The default language is often already specified during operating system installation. When the operating system is installed, the installer typically asks for the language used for the installation process and, separately, for the language to use in the installed system. Some OS installers only ask for the language once.

This determines the system-wide default language for all users. But the installers often give the possibility to install extra localizations for additional languages. For example, the localizations of KDE (the K Desktop Environment) and OpenOffice.org are often bundled separately, as one installable package per language.

At this point it is good to consider the intended use of the machine: If it is a machine designated for personal use, additional localizations are probably not necessary. If, however, the machine is in use in an organization or company that has international relationships, one can consider the needs of guest users. If you have a guest from abroad, for a week, what could be his preferred locales? It may be worth installing these additional localizations ahead of time, since they cost only a bit of disk space at this point.

The system-wide default language is the locale configuration that is used when a new user account is created. But the user can have his own locale configuration that is different from the one of the other users of the same machine. He can specify it, typically after the first login, as described in the next section.

2.2 Setting the Locale Used by GUI Programs

The immediately available programs in a user's desktop come from a group of programs called a "desktop environment"; it usually includes the window manager, a web browser, a text editor, and more. The most common free desktop environments are KDE, GNOME, and Xfce.

The locale used by GUI programs of the desktop environment can be specified in a configuration screen called "control center", "language settings" or "country settings".

Individual GUI programs that are not part of the desktop environment can have their locale specified either in a settings panel, or through environment variables.

For some programs, it is possible to specify the locale through environment variables, possibly even to a different locale than the desktop's locale. This means, instead of starting a program through a menu or from the file system, you can start it from the command-line, after having set some environment variables. The environment variables can be those specified in the next section (Section 2.3 [Setting the POSIX Locale], page 10); for some versions of KDE, however, the locale is specified through a variable `KDE_LANG`, rather than `LANG` or `LC_ALL`.

2.3 Setting the Locale through Environment Variables

As a user, if your language has been installed for this package, in the simplest case, you only have to set the LANG environment variable to the appropriate '*ll_CC*' combination. For example, let's suppose that you speak German and live in Germany. At the shell prompt, merely execute 'setenv LANG de_DE' (in csh), 'export LANG; LANG=de_DE' (in sh) or 'export LANG=de_DE' (in bash). This can be done from your .login or .profile file, once and for all.

2.3.1 Locale Names

A locale name usually has the form '*ll_CC*'. Here '*ll*' is an ISO 639 two-letter language code, and '*CC*' is an ISO 3166 two-letter country code. For example, for German in Germany, *ll* is de, and *CC* is DE. You find a list of the language codes in appendix Appendix A [Language Codes], page 206 and a list of the country codes in appendix Appendix B [Country Codes], page 214.

You might think that the country code specification is redundant. But in fact, some languages have dialects in different countries. For example, 'de_AT' is used for Austria, and 'pt_BR' for Brazil. The country code serves to distinguish the dialects.

Many locale names have an extended syntax '*ll_CC.encoding*' that also specifies the character encoding. These are in use because between 2000 and 2005, most users have switched to locales in UTF-8 encoding. For example, the German locale on glibc systems is nowadays 'de_DE.UTF-8'. The older name 'de_DE' still refers to the German locale as of 2000 that stores characters in ISO-8859-1 encoding – a text encoding that cannot even accommodate the Euro currency sign.

Some locale names use '*ll_CC.@variant*' instead of '*ll_CC*'. The '*@variant*' can denote any kind of characteristics that is not already implied by the language *ll* and the country *CC*. It can denote a particular monetary unit. For example, on glibc systems, 'de_DE@euro' denotes the locale that uses the Euro currency, in contrast to the older locale 'de_DE' which implies the use of the currency before 2002. It can also denote a dialect of the language, or the script used to write text (for example, 'sr_RS@latin' uses the Latin script, whereas 'sr_RS' uses the Cyrillic script to write Serbian), or the orthography rules, or similar.

On other systems, some variations of this scheme are used, such as '*ll*'. You can get the list of locales supported by your system for your language by running the command 'locale -a | grep '^*ll*''.

There is also a special locale, called 'C'. When it is used, it disables all localization: in this locale, all programs standardized by POSIX use English messages and an unspecified character encoding (often US-ASCII, but sometimes also ISO-8859-1 or UTF-8, depending on the operating system).

2.3.2 Locale Environment Variables

A locale is composed of several *locale categories*, see Section 1.3 [Aspects], page 3. When a program looks up locale dependent values, it does this according to the following environment variables, in priority order:

1. LANGUAGE
2. LC_ALL

3. `LC_xxx`, according to selected locale category: `LC_CTYPE`, `LC_NUMERIC`, `LC_TIME`, `LC_COLLATE`, `LC_MONETARY`, `LC_MESSAGES`, ...

4. `LANG`

Variables whose value is set but is empty are ignored in this lookup.

`LANG` is the normal environment variable for specifying a locale. As a user, you normally set this variable (unless some of the other variables have already been set by the system, in `/etc/profile` or similar initialization files).

`LC_CTYPE`, `LC_NUMERIC`, `LC_TIME`, `LC_COLLATE`, `LC_MONETARY`, `LC_MESSAGES`, and so on, are the environment variables meant to override `LANG` and affecting a single locale category only. For example, assume you are a Swedish user in Spain, and you want your programs to handle numbers and dates according to Spanish conventions, and only the messages should be in Swedish. Then you could create a locale named 'sv_ES' or 'sv_ES.UTF-8' by use of the `localedef` program. But it is simpler, and achieves the same effect, to set the `LANG` variable to `es_ES.UTF-8` and the `LC_MESSAGES` variable to `sv_SE.UTF-8`; these two locales come already preinstalled with the operating system.

`LC_ALL` is an environment variable that overrides all of these. It is typically used in scripts that run particular programs. For example, `configure` scripts generated by GNU autoconf use `LC_ALL` to make sure that the configuration tests don't operate in locale dependent ways.

Some systems, unfortunately, set `LC_ALL` in `/etc/profile` or in similar initialization files. As a user, you therefore have to unset this variable if you want to set `LANG` and optionally some of the other `LC_xxx` variables.

The `LANGUAGE` variable is described in the next subsection.

2.3.3 Specifying a Priority List of Languages

Not all programs have translations for all languages. By default, an English message is shown in place of a nonexistent translation. If you understand other languages, you can set up a priority list of languages. This is done through a different environment variable, called `LANGUAGE`. GNU `gettext` gives preference to `LANGUAGE` over `LC_ALL` and `LANG` for the purpose of message handling, but you still need to have `LANG` (or `LC_ALL`) set to the primary language; this is required by other parts of the system libraries. For example, some Swedish users who would rather read translations in German than English for when Swedish is not available, set `LANGUAGE` to 'sv:de' while leaving `LANG` to 'sv_SE'.

Special advice for Norwegian users: The language code for Norwegian bokmål changed from 'no' to 'nb' recently (in 2003). During the transition period, while some message catalogs for this language are installed under 'nb' and some older ones under 'no', it is recommended for Norwegian users to set `LANGUAGE` to 'nb:no' so that both newer and older translations are used.

In the `LANGUAGE` environment variable, but not in the other environment variables, '`ll_CC`' combinations can be abbreviated as '`ll`' to denote the language's main dialect. For example, 'de' is equivalent to 'de_DE' (German as spoken in Germany), and 'pt' to 'pt_PT' (Portuguese as spoken in Portugal) in this context.

Note: The variable `LANGUAGE` is ignored if the locale is set to 'C'. In other words, you have to first enable localization, by setting `LANG` (or `LC_ALL`) to a value other than 'C', before you can use a language priority list through the `LANGUAGE` variable.

2.4 Installing Translations for Particular Programs

Languages are not equally well supported in all packages using GNU `gettext`, and more translations are added over time. Usually, you use the translations that are shipped with the operating system or with particular packages that you install afterwards. But you can also install newer localizations directly. For doing this, you will need an understanding where each localization file is stored on the file system.

For programs that participate in the Translation Project, you can start looking for translations here: `http://translationproject.org/team/index.html`. A snapshot of this information is also found in the `ABOUT-NLS` file that is shipped with GNU gettext.

For programs that are part of the KDE project, the starting point is: `http://i18n.kde.org/`.

For programs that are part of the GNOME project, the starting point is: `http://www.gnome.org/i18n/`.

For other programs, you may check whether the program's source code package contains some *ll*`.po` files; often they are kept together in a directory called `po/`. Each *ll*`.po` file contains the message translations for the language whose abbreviation of *ll*.

3 The Format of PO Files

The GNU `gettext` toolset helps programmers and translators at producing, updating and using translation files, mainly those PO files which are textual, editable files. This chapter explains the format of PO files.

A PO file is made up of many entries, each entry holding the relation between an original untranslated string and its corresponding translation. All entries in a given PO file usually pertain to a single project, and all translations are expressed in a single target language. One PO file *entry* has the following schematic structure:

```
white-space
#  translator-comments
#. extracted-comments
#: reference...
#, flag...
#| msgid previous-untranslated-string
msgid untranslated-string
msgstr translated-string
```

The general structure of a PO file should be well understood by the translator. When using PO mode, very little has to be known about the format details, as PO mode takes care of them for her.

A simple entry can look like this:

```
#: lib/error.c:116
msgid "Unknown system error"
msgstr "Error desconegut del sistema"
```

Entries begin with some optional white space. Usually, when generated through GNU `gettext` tools, there is exactly one blank line between entries. Then comments follow, on lines all starting with the character `#`. There are two kinds of comments: those which have some white space immediately following the `#` - the *translator comments* -, which comments are created and maintained exclusively by the translator, and those which have some non-white character just after the `#` - the *automatic comments* -, which comments are created and maintained automatically by GNU `gettext` tools. Comment lines starting with `#.` contain comments given by the programmer, directed at the translator; these comments are called *extracted comments* because the `xgettext` program extracts them from the program's source code. Comment lines starting with `#:` contain references to the program's source code. Comment lines starting with `#,` contain flags; more about these below. Comment lines starting with `#|` contain the previous untranslated string for which the translator gave a translation.

All comments, of either kind, are optional.

After white space and comments, entries show two strings, namely first the untranslated string as it appears in the original program sources, and then, the translation of this string. The original string is introduced by the keyword `msgid`, and the translation, by `msgstr`. The two strings, untranslated and translated, are quoted in various ways in the PO file, using " delimiters and \ escapes, but the translator does not really have to pay attention to the precise quoting format, as PO mode fully takes care of quoting for her.

The `msgid` strings, as well as automatic comments, are produced and managed by other GNU `gettext` tools, and PO mode does not provide means for the translator to alter these. The most she can do is merely deleting them, and only by deleting the whole entry. On the other hand, the `msgstr` string, as well as translator comments, are really meant for the translator, and PO mode gives her the full control she needs.

The comment lines beginning with `#,` are special because they are not completely ignored by the programs as comments generally are. The comma separated list of *flags* is used by the `msgfmt` program to give the user some better diagnostic messages. Currently there are two forms of flags defined:

`fuzzy`   This flag can be generated by the `msgmerge` program or it can be inserted by the translator herself. It shows that the `msgstr` string might not be a correct translation (anymore). Only the translator can judge if the translation requires further modification, or is acceptable as is. Once satisfied with the translation, she then removes this `fuzzy` attribute. The `msgmerge` program inserts this when it combined the `msgid` and `msgstr` entries after fuzzy search only. See Section 8.3.6 [Fuzzy Entries], page 57.

`c-format`
`no-c-format`
              These flags should not be added by a human. Instead only the `xgettext` program adds them. In an automated PO file processing system as proposed here, the user's changes would be thrown away again as soon as the `xgettext` program generates a new template file.

              The `c-format` flag indicates that the untranslated string and the translation are supposed to be C format strings. The `no-c-format` flag indicates that they are not C format strings, even though the untranslated string happens to look like a C format string (with '`%`' directives).

              When the `c-format` flag is given for a string the `msgfmt` program does some more tests to check the validity of the translation. See Section 10.1 [msgfmt Invocation], page 103, Section 4.6 [c-format Flag], page 27 and Section 15.3.1 [c-format], page 161.

`objc-format`
`no-objc-format`
              Likewise for Objective C, see Section 15.3.2 [objc-format], page 162.

`sh-format`
`no-sh-format`
              Likewise for Shell, see Section 15.3.3 [sh-format], page 162.

`python-format`
`no-python-format`
              Likewise for Python, see Section 15.3.4 [python-format], page 162.

`python-brace-format`
`no-python-brace-format`
              Likewise for Python brace, see Section 15.3.4 [python-format], page 162.

```
lisp-format
no-lisp-format
```
        Likewise for Lisp, see Section 15.3.5 [lisp-format], page 162.

```
elisp-format
no-elisp-format
```
        Likewise for Emacs Lisp, see Section 15.3.6 [elisp-format], page 162.

```
librep-format
no-librep-format
```
        Likewise for librep, see Section 15.3.7 [librep-format], page 163.

```
scheme-format
no-scheme-format
```
        Likewise for Scheme, see Section 15.3.8 [scheme-format], page 163.

```
smalltalk-format
no-smalltalk-format
```
        Likewise for Smalltalk, see Section 15.3.9 [smalltalk-format], page 163.

```
java-format
no-java-format
```
        Likewise for Java, see Section 15.3.10 [java-format], page 163.

```
csharp-format
no-csharp-format
```
        Likewise for C#, see Section 15.3.11 [csharp-format], page 163.

```
awk-format
no-awk-format
```
        Likewise for awk, see Section 15.3.12 [awk-format], page 163.

```
object-pascal-format
no-object-pascal-format
```
        Likewise for Object Pascal, see Section 15.3.13 [object-pascal-format], page 163.

```
ycp-format
no-ycp-format
```
        Likewise for YCP, see Section 15.3.14 [ycp-format], page 163.

```
tcl-format
no-tcl-format
```
        Likewise for Tcl, see Section 15.3.15 [tcl-format], page 163.

```
perl-format
no-perl-format
```
        Likewise for Perl, see Section 15.3.16 [perl-format], page 164.

```
perl-brace-format
no-perl-brace-format
```
        Likewise for Perl brace, see Section 15.3.16 [perl-format], page 164.

```
php-format
no-php-format
```
        Likewise for PHP, see Section 15.3.17 [php-format], page 164.

`gcc-internal-format`
`no-gcc-internal-format`

> Likewise for the GCC sources, see Section 15.3.18 [gcc-internal-format], page 164.

`gfc-internal-format`
`no-gfc-internal-format`

> Likewise for the GNU Fortran Compiler sources, see Section 15.3.19 [gfc-internal-format], page 164.

`qt-format`
`no-qt-format`

> Likewise for Qt, see Section 15.3.20 [qt-format], page 164.

`qt-plural-format`
`no-qt-plural-format`

> Likewise for Qt plural forms, see Section 15.3.21 [qt-plural-format], page 164.

`kde-format`
`no-kde-format`

> Likewise for KDE, see Section 15.3.22 [kde-format], page 165.

`boost-format`
`no-boost-format`

> Likewise for Boost, see Section 15.3.24 [boost-format], page 165.

`lua-format`
`no-lua-format`

> Likewise for Lua, see Section 15.3.25 [lua-format], page 165.

`javascript-format`
`no-javascript-format`

> Likewise for JavaScript, see Section 15.3.26 [javascript-format], page 165.

It is also possible to have entries with a context specifier. They look like this:

```
white-space
#  translator-comments
#. extracted-comments
#: reference...
#, flag...
#| msgctxt previous-context
#| msgid previous-untranslated-string
msgctxt context
msgid untranslated-string
msgstr translated-string
```

The context serves to disambiguate messages with the same *untranslated-string*. It is possible to have several entries with the same *untranslated-string* in a PO file, provided that they each have a different *context*. Note that an empty *context* string and an absent `msgctxt` line do not mean the same thing.

A different kind of entries is used for translations which involve plural forms.

```
white-space
#  translator-comments
#. extracted-comments
#: reference...
#, flag...
#| msgid previous-untranslated-string-singular
#| msgid_plural previous-untranslated-string-plural
msgid untranslated-string-singular
msgid_plural untranslated-string-plural
msgstr[0] translated-string-case-0
...
msgstr[N] translated-string-case-n
```

Such an entry can look like this:

```
#: src/msgcmp.c:338 src/po-lex.c:699
#, c-format
msgid "found %d fatal error"
msgid_plural "found %d fatal errors"
msgstr[0] "s'ha trobat %d error fatal"
msgstr[1] "s'han trobat %d errors fatals"
```

Here also, a `msgctxt` context can be specified before `msgid`, like above.

Here, additional kinds of flags can be used:

`range:`   This flag is followed by a range of non-negative numbers, using the syntax `range: minimum-value..maximum-value`. It designates the possible values that the numeric parameter of the message can take. In some languages, translators may produce slightly better translations if they know that the value can only take on values between 0 and 10, for example.

The *previous-untranslated-string* is optionally inserted by the `msgmerge` program, at the same time when it marks a message fuzzy. It helps the translator to see which changes were done by the developers on the *untranslated-string*.

It happens that some lines, usually whitespace or comments, follow the very last entry of a PO file. Such lines are not part of any entry, and will be dropped when the PO file is processed by the tools, or may disturb some PO file editors.

The remainder of this section may be safely skipped by those using a PO file editor, yet it may be interesting for everybody to have a better idea of the precise format of a PO file. On the other hand, those wishing to modify PO files by hand should carefully continue reading on.

An empty *untranslated-string* is reserved to contain the header entry with the meta information (see Section 6.2 [Header Entry], page 44). This header entry should be the first entry of the file. The empty *untranslated-string* is reserved for this purpose and must not be used anywhere else.

Each of *untranslated-string* and *translated-string* respects the C syntax for a character string, including the surrounding quotes and embedded backslashed escape sequences. When the time comes to write multi-line strings, one should not use escaped newlines. Instead, a closing quote should follow the last character on the line to be continued, and an opening quote should resume the string at the beginning of the following PO file line. For example:

```
msgid ""
"Here is an example of how one might continue a very long string\n"
"for the common case the string represents multi-line output.\n"
```

In this example, the empty string is used on the first line, to allow better alignment of the H from the word 'Here' over the f from the word 'for'. In this example, the msgid keyword is followed by three strings, which are meant to be concatenated. Concatenating the empty string does not change the resulting overall string, but it is a way for us to comply with the necessity of msgid to be followed by a string on the same line, while keeping the multi-line presentation left-justified, as we find this to be a cleaner disposition. The empty string could have been omitted, but only if the string starting with 'Here' was promoted on the first line, right after msgid.[1] It was not really necessary either to switch between the two last quoted strings immediately after the newline '\n', the switch could have occurred after *any* other character, we just did it this way because it is neater.

One should carefully distinguish between end of lines marked as '\n' *inside* quotes, which are part of the represented string, and end of lines in the PO file itself, outside string quotes, which have no incidence on the represented string.

Outside strings, white lines and comments may be used freely. Comments start at the beginning of a line with '#' and extend until the end of the PO file line. Comments written by translators should have the initial '#' immediately followed by some white space. If the '#' is not immediately followed by white space, this comment is most likely generated and managed by specialized GNU tools, and might disappear or be replaced unexpectedly when the PO file is given to msgmerge.

---

[1] This limitation is not imposed by GNU gettext, but is for compatibility with the msgfmt implementation on Solaris.

4 Preparing Program Sources

For the programmer, changes to the C source code fall into three categories. First, you have to make the localization functions known to all modules needing message translation. Second, you should properly trigger the operation of GNU `gettext` when the program initializes, usually from the `main` function. Last, you should identify, adjust and mark all constant strings in your program needing translation.

4.1 Importing the gettext declaration

Presuming that your set of programs, or package, has been adjusted so all needed GNU `gettext` files are available, and your `Makefile` files are adjusted (see Chapter 13 [Maintainers], page 140), each C module having translated C strings should contain the line:

```
#include <libintl.h>
```

Similarly, each C module containing `printf()/fprintf()/...` calls with a format string that could be a translated C string (even if the C string comes from a different C module) should contain the line:

```
#include <libintl.h>
```

4.2 Triggering gettext Operations

The initialization of locale data should be done with more or less the same code in every program, as demonstrated below:

```
int
main (int argc, char *argv[])
{
  ...
  setlocale (LC_ALL, "");
  bindtextdomain (PACKAGE, LOCALEDIR);
  textdomain (PACKAGE);
  ...
}
```

PACKAGE and *LOCALEDIR* should be provided either by `config.h` or by the Makefile. For now consult the `gettext` or `hello` sources for more information.

The use of `LC_ALL` might not be appropriate for you. `LC_ALL` includes all locale categories and especially `LC_CTYPE`. This latter category is responsible for determining character classes with the `isalnum` etc. functions from `ctype.h` which could especially for programs, which process some kind of input language, be wrong. For example this would mean that a source code using the ç (c-cedilla character) is runnable in France but not in the U.S.

Some systems also have problems with parsing numbers using the `scanf` functions if an other but the `LC_ALL` locale category is used. The standards say that additional formats but the one known in the "C" locale might be recognized. But some systems seem to reject numbers in the "C" locale format. In some situation, it might also be a problem with the notation itself which makes it impossible to recognize whether the number is in the "C" locale or the local format. This can happen if thousands separator characters are used.

Some locales define this character according to the national conventions to '.' which is the same character used in the "C" locale to denote the decimal point.

So it is sometimes necessary to replace the `LC_ALL` line in the code above by a sequence of `setlocale` lines

```
{
  ...
  setlocale (LC_CTYPE, "");
  setlocale (LC_MESSAGES, "");
  ...
}
```

On all POSIX conformant systems the locale categories `LC_CTYPE`, `LC_MESSAGES`, `LC_COLLATE`, `LC_MONETARY`, `LC_NUMERIC`, and `LC_TIME` are available. On some systems which are only ISO C compliant, `LC_MESSAGES` is missing, but a substitute for it is defined in GNU gettext's `<libintl.h>` and in GNU gnulib's `<locale.h>`.

Note that changing the `LC_CTYPE` also affects the functions declared in the `<ctype.h>` standard header and some functions declared in the `<string.h>` and `<stdlib.h>` standard headers. If this is not desirable in your application (for example in a compiler's parser), you can use a set of substitute functions which hardwire the C locale, such as found in the modules 'c-ctype', 'c-strcase', 'c-strcasestr', 'c-strtod', 'c-strtold' in the GNU gnulib source distribution.

It is also possible to switch the locale forth and back between the environment dependent locale and the C locale, but this approach is normally avoided because a `setlocale` call is expensive, because it is tedious to determine the places where a locale switch is needed in a large program's source, and because switching a locale is not multithread-safe.

4.3 Preparing Translatable Strings

Before strings can be marked for translations, they sometimes need to be adjusted. Usually preparing a string for translation is done right before marking it, during the marking phase which is described in the next sections. What you have to keep in mind while doing that is the following.

- Decent English style.
- Entire sentences.
- Split at paragraphs.
- Use format strings instead of string concatenation.
- Avoid unusual markup and unusual control characters.

Let's look at some examples of these guidelines.

Translatable strings should be in good English style. If slang language with abbreviations and shortcuts is used, often translators will not understand the message and will produce very inappropriate translations.

```
"%s: is parameter\n"
```

This is nearly untranslatable: Is the displayed item *a* parameter or *the* parameter?

```
"No match"
```

The ambiguity in this message makes it unintelligible: Is the program attempting to set something on fire? Does it mean "The given object does not match the template"? Does it mean "The template does not fit for any of the objects"?

In both cases, adding more words to the message will help both the translator and the English speaking user.

Translatable strings should be entire sentences. It is often not possible to translate single verbs or adjectives in a substitutable way.

```
printf ("File %s is %s protected", filename, rw ? "write" : "read");
```

Most translators will not look at the source and will thus only see the string "File %s is %s protected", which is unintelligible. Change this to

```
printf (rw ? "File %s is write protected" : "File %s is read protected",
        filename);
```

This way the translator will not only understand the message, she will also be able to find the appropriate grammatical construction. A French translator for example translates "write protected" like "protected against writing".

Entire sentences are also important because in many languages, the declination of some word in a sentence depends on the gender or the number (singular/plural) of another part of the sentence. There are usually more interdependencies between words than in English. The consequence is that asking a translator to translate two half-sentences and then combining these two half-sentences through dumb string concatenation will not work, for many languages, even though it would work for English. That's why translators need to handle entire sentences.

Often sentences don't fit into a single line. If a sentence is output using two subsequent `printf` statements, like this

```
printf ("Locale charset \"%s\" is different from\n", lcharset);
printf ("input file charset \"%s\".\n", fcharset);
```

the translator would have to translate two half sentences, but nothing in the POT file would tell her that the two half sentences belong together. It is necessary to merge the two `printf` statements so that the translator can handle the entire sentence at once and decide at which place to insert a line break in the translation (if at all):

```
printf ("Locale charset \"%s\" is different from\n\
input file charset \"%s\".\n", lcharset, fcharset);
```

You may now ask: how about two or more adjacent sentences? Like in this case:

```
puts ("Apollo 13 scenario: Stack overflow handling failed.");
puts ("On the next stack overflow we will crash!!!");
```

Should these two statements merged into a single one? I would recommend to merge them if the two sentences are related to each other, because then it makes it easier for the translator to understand and translate both. On the other hand, if one of the two messages is a stereotypic one, occurring in other places as well, you will do a favour to the translator by not merging the two. (Identical messages occurring in several places are combined by xgettext, so the translator has to handle them once only.)

Translatable strings should be limited to one paragraph; don't let a single message be longer than ten lines. The reason is that when the translatable string changes, the translator is faced with the task of updating the entire translated string. Maybe only a single word will have changed in the English string, but the translator doesn't see that (with the current translation tools), therefore she has to proofread the entire message.

Many GNU programs have a '--help' output that extends over several screen pages. It is a courtesy towards the translators to split such a message into several ones of five to ten lines each. While doing that, you can also attempt to split the documented options into groups, such as the input options, the output options, and the informative output options. This will help every user to find the option he is looking for.

Hardcoded string concatenation is sometimes used to construct English strings:

```
strcpy (s, "Replace ");
strcat (s, object1);
strcat (s, " with ");
strcat (s, object2);
strcat (s, "?");
```

In order to present to the translator only entire sentences, and also because in some languages the translator might want to swap the order of object1 and object2, it is necessary to change this to use a format string:

```
sprintf (s, "Replace %s with %s?", object1, object2);
```

A similar case is compile time concatenation of strings. The ISO C 99 include file <inttypes.h> contains a macro PRId64 that can be used as a formatting directive for outputting an 'int64_t' integer through printf. It expands to a constant string, usually "d" or "ld" or "lld" or something like this, depending on the platform. Assume you have code like

```
printf ("The amount is %0" PRId64 "\n", number);
```

The gettext tools and library have special support for these <inttypes.h> macros. You can therefore simply write

```
printf (gettext ("The amount is %0" PRId64 "\n"), number);
```

The PO file will contain the string "The amount is %0<PRId64>\n". The translators will provide a translation containing "%0<PRId64>" as well, and at runtime the gettext function's result will contain the appropriate constant string, "d" or "ld" or "lld".

This works only for the predefined <inttypes.h> macros. If you have defined your own similar macros, let's say 'MYPRId64', that are not known to xgettext, the solution for this problem is to change the code like this:

```
char buf1[100];
sprintf (buf1, "%0" MYPRId64, number);
printf (gettext ("The amount is %s\n"), buf1);
```

This means, you put the platform dependent code in one statement, and the internationalization code in a different statement. Note that a buffer length of 100 is safe, because all available hardware integer types are limited to 128 bits, and to print a 128 bit integer one needs at most 54 characters, regardless whether in decimal, octal or hexadecimal.

All this applies to other programming languages as well. For example, in Java and C#, string concatenation is very frequently used, because it is a compiler built-in operator. Like in C, in Java, you would change

```
    System.out.println("Replace "+object1+" with "+object2+"?");
```
into a statement involving a format string:
```
    System.out.println(
        MessageFormat.format("Replace {0} with {1}?",
                              new Object[] { object1, object2 }));
```
Similarly, in C#, you would change
```
    Console.WriteLine("Replace "+object1+" with "+object2+"?");
```
into a statement involving a format string:
```
    Console.WriteLine(
        String.Format("Replace {0} with {1}?", object1, object2));
```
Unusual markup or control characters should not be used in translatable strings. Translators will likely not understand the particular meaning of the markup or control characters.

For example, if you have a convention that '|' delimits the left-hand and right-hand part of some GUI elements, translators will often not understand it without specific comments. It might be better to have the translator translate the left-hand and right-hand part separately.

Another example is the 'argp' convention to use a single '\v' (vertical tab) control character to delimit two sections inside a string. This is flawed. Some translators may convert it to a simple newline, some to blank lines. With some PO file editors it may not be easy to even enter a vertical tab control character. So, you cannot be sure that the translation will contain a '\v' character, at the corresponding position. The solution is, again, to let the translator translate two separate strings and combine at run-time the two translated strings with the '\v' required by the convention.

HTML markup, however, is common enough that it's probably ok to use in translatable strings. But please bear in mind that the GNU gettext tools don't verify that the translations are well-formed HTML.

4.4 How Marks Appear in Sources

All strings requiring translation should be marked in the C sources. Marking is done in such a way that each translatable string appears to be the sole argument of some function or preprocessor macro. There are only a few such possible functions or macros meant for translation, and their names are said to be marking keywords. The marking is attached to strings themselves, rather than to what we do with them. This approach has more uses. A blatant example is an error message produced by formatting. The format string needs translation, as well as some strings inserted through some '%s' specification in the format, while the result from sprintf may have so many different instances that it is impractical to list them all in some 'error_string_out()' routine, say.

This marking operation has two goals. The first goal of marking is for triggering the retrieval of the translation, at run time. The keyword is possibly resolved into a routine able to dynamically return the proper translation, as far as possible or wanted, for the argument string. Most localizable strings are found in executable positions, that is, attached to variables or given as parameters to functions. But this is not universal usage, and some translatable strings appear in structured initializations. See Section 4.7 [Special cases], page 28.

The second goal of the marking operation is to help `xgettext` at properly extracting all translatable strings when it scans a set of program sources and produces PO file templates.

The canonical keyword for marking translatable strings is 'gettext', it gave its name to the whole GNU `gettext` package. For packages making only light use of the 'gettext' keyword, macro or function, it is easily used *as is*. However, for packages using the `gettext` interface more heavily, it is usually more convenient to give the main keyword a shorter, less obtrusive name. Indeed, the keyword might appear on a lot of strings all over the package, and programmers usually do not want nor need their program sources to remind them forcefully, all the time, that they are internationalized. Further, a long keyword has the disadvantage of using more horizontal space, forcing more indentation work on sources for those trying to keep them within 79 or 80 columns.

Many packages use '_' (a simple underline) as a keyword, and write '_("Translatable string")' instead of 'gettext ("Translatable string")'. Further, the coding rule, from GNU standards, wanting that there is a space between the keyword and the opening parenthesis is relaxed, in practice, for this particular usage. So, the textual overhead per translatable string is reduced to only three characters: the underline and the two parentheses. However, even if GNU `gettext` uses this convention internally, it does not offer it officially. The real, genuine keyword is truly 'gettext' indeed. It is fairly easy for those wanting to use '_' instead of 'gettext' to declare:

```
#include <libintl.h>
#define _(String) gettext (String)
```

instead of merely using '#include <libintl.h>'.

The marking keywords 'gettext' and '_' take the translatable string as sole argument. It is also possible to define marking functions that take it at another argument position. It is even possible to make the marked argument position depend on the total number of arguments of the function call; this is useful in C++. All this is achieved using `xgettext`'s '--keyword' option. How to pass such an option to `xgettext`, assuming that `gettextize` is used, is described in Section 13.4.3 [po/Makevars], page 145 and Section 13.5.6 [AM_XGETTEXT_OPTION], page 154.

Note also that long strings can be split across lines, into multiple adjacent string tokens. Automatic string concatenation is performed at compile time according to ISO C and ISO C++; `xgettext` also supports this syntax.

Later on, the maintenance is relatively easy. If, as a programmer, you add or modify a string, you will have to ask yourself if the new or altered string requires translation, and include it within '_()' if you think it should be translated. For example, '"%s"' is an example of string *not* requiring translation. But '"%s: %d"' *does* require translation, because in French, unlike in English, it's customary to put a space before a colon.

4.5 Marking Translatable Strings

In PO mode, one set of features is meant more for the programmer than for the translator, and allows him to interactively mark which strings, in a set of program sources, are translatable, and which are not. Even if it is a fairly easy job for a programmer to find and mark such strings by other means, using any editor of his choice, PO mode makes this work more comfortable. Further, this gives translators who feel a little like programmers, or programmers who feel a little like translators, a tool letting them work at marking translatable strings in the program sources, while simultaneously producing a set of translation in some language, for the package being internationalized.

The set of program sources, targeted by the PO mode commands describe here, should have an Emacs tags table constructed for your project, prior to using these PO file commands. This is easy to do. In any shell window, change the directory to the root of your project, then execute a command resembling:

```
etags src/*.[hc] lib/*.[hc]
```

presuming here you want to process all `.h` and `.c` files from the `src/` and `lib/` directories. This command will explore all said files and create a `TAGS` file in your root directory, somewhat summarizing the contents using a special file format Emacs can understand.

For packages following the GNU coding standards, there is a make goal `tags` or `TAGS` which constructs the tag files in all directories and for all files containing source code.

Once your `TAGS` file is ready, the following commands assist the programmer at marking translatable strings in his set of sources. But these commands are necessarily driven from within a PO file window, and it is likely that you do not even have such a PO file yet. This is not a problem at all, as you may safely open a new, empty PO file, mainly for using these commands. This empty PO file will slowly fill in while you mark strings as translatable in your program sources.

,   Search through program sources for a string which looks like a candidate for translation (`po-tags-search`).

M-,   Mark the last string found with '`_()`' (`po-mark-translatable`).

M-.   Mark the last string found with a keyword taken from a set of possible keywords. This command with a prefix allows some management of these keywords (`po-select-mark-and-mark`).

The `,` (`po-tags-search`) command searches for the next occurrence of a string which looks like a possible candidate for translation, and displays the program source in another Emacs window, positioned in such a way that the string is near the top of this other window. If the string is too big to fit whole in this window, it is positioned so only its end is shown. In any case, the cursor is left in the PO file window. If the shown string would be better presented differently in different native languages, you may mark it using M-, or M-.. Otherwise, you might rather ignore it and skip to the next string by merely repeating the `,` command.

A string is a good candidate for translation if it contains a sequence of three or more letters. A string containing at most two letters in a row will be considered as a candidate if it has more letters than non-letters. The command disregards strings containing no letters, or isolated letters only. It also disregards strings within comments, or strings already marked with some keyword PO mode knows (see below).

If you have never told Emacs about some `TAGS` file to use, the command will request that you specify one from the minibuffer, the first time you use the command. You may later change your `TAGS` file by using the regular Emacs command M-x visit-tags-table, which will ask you to name the precise `TAGS` file you want to use. See Section "Tag Tables" in *The Emacs Editor*.

Each time you use the `,` command, the search resumes from where it was left by the previous search, and goes through all program sources, obeying the `TAGS` file, until all sources have been processed. However, by giving a prefix argument to the command (`C-u ,`), you may request that the search be restarted all over again from the first program source; but in this case, strings that you recently marked as translatable will be automatically skipped.

Using this `,` command does not prevent using of other regular Emacs tags commands. For example, regular `tags-search` or `tags-query-replace` commands may be used without disrupting the independent `,` search sequence. However, as implemented, the *initial* `,` command (or the `,` command is used with a prefix) might also reinitialize the regular Emacs tags searching to the first tags file, this reinitialization might be considered spurious.

The `M-,` (`po-mark-translatable`) command will mark the recently found string with the '`_`' keyword. The `M-.` (`po-select-mark-and-mark`) command will request that you type one keyword from the minibuffer and use that keyword for marking the string. Both commands will automatically create a new PO file untranslated entry for the string being marked, and make it the current entry (making it easy for you to immediately proceed to its translation, if you feel like doing it right away). It is possible that the modifications made to the program source by `M-,` or `M-.` render some source line longer than 80 columns, forcing you to break and re-indent this line differently. You may use the `O` command from PO mode, or any other window changing command from Emacs, to break out into the program source window, and do any needed adjustments. You will have to use some regular Emacs command to return the cursor to the PO file window, if you want command `,` for the next string, say.

The `M-.` command has a few built-in speedups, so you do not have to explicitly type all keywords all the time. The first such speedup is that you are presented with a *preferred* keyword, which you may accept by merely typing `RET` at the prompt. The second speedup is that you may type any non-ambiguous prefix of the keyword you really mean, and the command will complete it automatically for you. This also means that PO mode has to *know* all your possible keywords, and that it will not accept mistyped keywords.

If you reply `?` to the keyword request, the command gives a list of all known keywords, from which you may choose. When the command is prefixed by an argument (`C-u M-.`), it inhibits updating any program source or PO file buffer, and does some simple keyword management instead. In this case, the command asks for a keyword, written in full, which becomes a new allowed keyword for later `M-.` commands. Moreover, this new keyword automatically becomes the *preferred* keyword for later commands. By typing an already known keyword in response to `C-u M-.`, one merely changes the *preferred* keyword and does nothing more.

All keywords known for `M-.` are recognized by the `,` command when scanning for strings, and strings already marked by any of those known keywords are automatically skipped. If many PO files are opened simultaneously, each one has its own independent set of known keywords. There is no provision in PO mode, currently, for deleting a known keyword, you have to quit the file (maybe using `q`) and reopen it afresh. When a PO file is newly brought up in an Emacs window, only '`gettext`' and '`_`' are known as keywords, and '`gettext`' is preferred for the `M-.` command. In fact, this is not useful to prefer '`_`', as this one is already built in the `M-,` command.

4.6 Special Comments preceding Keywords

In C programs strings are often used within calls of functions from the `printf` family. The special thing about these format strings is that they can contain format specifiers introduced with `%`. Assume we have the code

```
printf (gettext ("String '%s' has %d characters\n"), s, strlen (s));
```

A possible German translation for the above string might be:

```
"%d Zeichen lang ist die Zeichenkette '%s'"
```

A C programmer, even if he cannot speak German, will recognize that there is something wrong here. The order of the two format specifiers is changed but of course the arguments in the `printf` don't have. This will most probably lead to problems because now the length of the string is regarded as the address.

To prevent errors at runtime caused by translations, the `msgfmt` tool can check statically whether the arguments in the original and the translation string match in type and number. If this is not the case and the '`-c`' option has been passed to `msgfmt`, `msgfmt` will give an error and refuse to produce a MO file. Thus consistent use of '`msgfmt -c`' will catch the error, so that it cannot cause problems at runtime.

If the word order in the above German translation would be correct one would have to write

```
"%2$d Zeichen lang ist die Zeichenkette '%1$s'"
```

The routines in `msgfmt` know about this special notation.

Because not all strings in a program will be format strings, it is not useful for `msgfmt` to test all the strings in the `.po` file. This might cause problems because the string might contain what looks like a format specifier, but the string is not used in `printf`.

Therefore `xgettext` adds a special tag to those messages it thinks might be a format string. There is no absolute rule for this, only a heuristic. In the `.po` file the entry is marked using the `c-format` flag in the `#,` comment line (see Chapter 3 [PO Files], page 13).

The careful reader now might say that this again can cause problems. The heuristic might guess it wrong. This is true and therefore `xgettext` knows about a special kind of comment which lets the programmer take over the decision. If in the same line as or the immediately preceding line to the `gettext` keyword the `xgettext` program finds a comment containing the words `xgettext:c-format`, it will mark the string in any case with the `c-format` flag. This kind of comment should be used when `xgettext` does not recognize the string as a format string but it really is one and it should be tested. Please note that when the comment is in the same line as the `gettext` keyword, it must be before the string to be translated.

This situation happens quite often. The `printf` function is often called with strings which do not contain a format specifier. Of course one would normally use `fputs` but it does happen. In this case `xgettext` does not recognize this as a format string but what happens if the translation introduces a valid format specifier? The `printf` function will try to access one of the parameters but none exists because the original code does not pass any parameters.

`xgettext` of course could make a wrong decision the other way round, i.e. a string marked as a format string actually is not a format string. In this case the `msgfmt` might give too many warnings and would prevent translating the `.po` file. The method to prevent this wrong decision is similar to the one used above, only the comment to use must contain the string xgettext:no-c-format.

If a string is marked with c-format and this is not correct the user can find out who is responsible for the decision. See Section 5.1 [xgettext Invocation], page 33 to see how the --debug option can be used for solving this problem.

4.7 Special Cases of Translatable Strings

The attentive reader might now point out that it is not always possible to mark translatable string with gettext or something like this. Consider the following case:

```
{
  static const char *messages[] = {
    "some very meaningful message",
    "and another one"
  };
  const char *string;
  ...
  string
    = index > 1 ? "a default message" : messages[index];

  fputs (string);
  ...
}
```

While it is no problem to mark the string "a default message" it is not possible to mark the string initializers for messages. What is to be done? We have to fulfill two tasks. First we have to mark the strings so that the xgettext program (see Section 5.1 [xgettext Invocation], page 33) can find them, and second we have to translate the string at runtime before printing them.

The first task can be fulfilled by creating a new keyword, which names a no-op. For the second we have to mark all access points to a string from the array. So one solution can look like this:

```
#define gettext_noop(String) String

{
  static const char *messages[] = {
    gettext_noop ("some very meaningful message"),
    gettext_noop ("and another one")
  };
  const char *string;
  ...
  string
    = index > 1 ? gettext ("a default message") : gettext (messages[index]);

  fputs (string);
  ...
}
```

Please convince yourself that the string which is written by `fputs` is translated in any case. How to get `xgettext` know the additional keyword `gettext_noop` is explained in Section 5.1 [xgettext Invocation], page 33.

The above is of course not the only solution. You could also come along with the following one:

```
#define gettext_noop(String) String

{
  static const char *messages[] = {
    gettext_noop ("some very meaningful message",
    gettext_noop ("and another one")
  };
  const char *string;
  ...
  string
    = index > 1 ? gettext_noop ("a default message") : messages[index];

  fputs (gettext (string));
  ...
}
```

But this has a drawback. The programmer has to take care that he uses `gettext_noop` for the string `"a default message"`. A use of `gettext` could have in rare cases unpredictable results.

One advantage is that you need not make control flow analysis to make sure the output is really translated in any case. But this analysis is generally not very difficult. If it should be in any situation you can use this second method in this situation.

4.8 Letting Users Report Translation Bugs

Code sometimes has bugs, but translations sometimes have bugs too. The users need to be able to report them. Reporting translation bugs to the programmer or maintainer of a package is not very useful, since the maintainer must never change a translation, except on behalf of the translator. Hence the translation bugs must be reported to the translators.

Here is a way to organize this so that the maintainer does not need to forward translation bug reports, nor even keep a list of the addresses of the translators or their translation teams.

Every program has a place where is shows the bug report address. For GNU programs, it is the code which handles the "–help" option, typically in a function called "usage". In this place, instruct the translator to add her own bug reporting address. For example, if that code has a statement

```
printf (_("Report bugs to <%s>.\n"), PACKAGE_BUGREPORT);
```

you can add some translator instructions like this:

```
/* TRANSLATORS: The placeholder indicates the bug-reporting address
   for this package.  Please add _another line_ saying
   "Report translation bugs to <...>\n" with the address for translation
   bugs (typically your translation team's web or email address).  */
printf (_("Report bugs to <%s>.\n"), PACKAGE_BUGREPORT);
```

These will be extracted by 'xgettext', leading to a .pot file that contains this:

```
#. TRANSLATORS: The placeholder indicates the bug-reporting address
#. for this package.  Please add _another line_ saying
#. "Report translation bugs to <...>\n" with the address for translation
#. bugs (typically your translation team's web or email address).
#: src/hello.c:178
#, c-format
msgid "Report bugs to <%s>.\n"
msgstr ""
```

4.9 Marking Proper Names for Translation

Should names of persons, cities, locations etc. be marked for translation or not? People who only know languages that can be written with Latin letters (English, Spanish, French, German, etc.) are tempted to say "no", because names usually do not change when transported between these languages. However, in general when translating from one script to another, names are translated too, usually phonetically or by transliteration. For example, Russian or Greek names are converted to the Latin alphabet when being translated to English, and English or French names are converted to the Katakana script when being translated to Japanese. This is necessary because the speakers of the target language in general cannot read the script the name is originally written in.

As a programmer, you should therefore make sure that names are marked for translation, with a special comment telling the translators that it is a proper name and how to pronounce it. In its simple form, it looks like this:

```
printf (_("Written by %s.\n"),
        /* TRANSLATORS: This is a proper name.  See the gettext
           manual, section Names.  Note this is actually a non-ASCII
           name: The first name is (with Unicode escapes)
           "Fran\u00e7ois" or (with HTML entities) "Fran&ccedil;ois".
           Pronunciation is like "fraa-swa pee-nar".  */
        _("Francois Pinard"));
```

The GNU gnulib library offers a module 'propername' (http://www.gnu.org/software/gnulib/MODULES.html#module=propername) which takes care to automatically append the original name, in parentheses, to the translated name. For names that cannot be written in ASCII, it also frees the translator from the task of entering the appropriate non-ASCII characters if no script change is needed. In this more comfortable form, it looks like this:

```
printf (_("Written by %s and %s.\n"),
        proper_name ("Ulrich Drepper"),
        /* TRANSLATORS: This is a proper name.  See the gettext
           manual, section Names.  Note this is actually a non-ASCII
           name: The first name is (with Unicode escapes)
           "Fran\u00e7ois" or (with HTML entities) "Fran&ccedil;ois".
           Pronunciation is like "fraa-swa pee-nar".  */
        proper_name_utf8 ("Francois Pinard", "Fran\303\247ois Pinard"));
```

You can also write the original name directly in Unicode (rather than with Unicode escapes or HTML entities) and denote the pronunciation using the International Phonetic Alphabet (see `http://www.wikipedia.org/wiki/International_Phonetic_Alphabet`).

As a translator, you should use some care when translating names, because it is frustrating if people see their names mutilated or distorted.

If your language uses the Latin script, all you need to do is to reproduce the name as perfectly as you can within the usual character set of your language. In this particular case, this means to provide a translation containing the c-cedilla character. If your language uses a different script and the people speaking it don't usually read Latin words, it means transliteration. If the programmer used the simple case, you should still give, in parentheses, the original writing of the name – for the sake of the people that do read the Latin script. If the programmer used the 'propername' module mentioned above, you don't need to give the original writing of the name in parentheses, because the program will already do so. Here is an example, using Greek as the target script:

```
#. This is a proper name.  See the gettext
#. manual, section Names.  Note this is actually a non-ASCII
#. name: The first name is (with Unicode escapes)
#. "Fran\u00e7ois" or (with HTML entities) "Fran&ccedil;ois".
#. Pronunciation is like "fraa-swa pee-nar".
msgid "Francois Pinard"
msgstr "\phi\rho\alpha\sigma\omicron\alpha \pi\iota\nu\alpha\rho"
        " (Francois Pinard)"
```

Because translation of names is such a sensitive domain, it is a good idea to test your translation before submitting it.

4.10 Preparing Library Sources

When you are preparing a library, not a program, for the use of `gettext`, only a few details are different. Here we assume that the library has a translation domain and a POT file of its own. (If it uses the translation domain and POT file of the main program, then the previous sections apply without changes.)

1. The library code doesn't call `setlocale (LC_ALL, "")`. It's the responsibility of the main program to set the locale. The library's documentation should mention this fact, so that developers of programs using the library are aware of it.

2. The library code doesn't call `textdomain (PACKAGE)`, because it would interfere with the text domain set by the main program.

3. The initialization code for a program was

```
setlocale (LC_ALL, "");
bindtextdomain (PACKAGE, LOCALEDIR);
textdomain (PACKAGE);
```

For a library it is reduced to

```
bindtextdomain (PACKAGE, LOCALEDIR);
```

If your library's API doesn't already have an initialization function, you need to create one, containing at least the `bindtextdomain` invocation. However, you usually don't need to export and document this initialization function: It is sufficient that all entry points of the library call the initialization function if it hasn't been called before. The

typical idiom used to achieve this is a static boolean variable that indicates whether
the initialization function has been called. Like this:

```
static bool libfoo_initialized;

static void
libfoo_initialize (void)
{
  bindtextdomain (PACKAGE, LOCALEDIR);
  libfoo_initialized = true;
}

/* This function is part of the exported API.  */
struct foo *
create_foo (...)
{
  /* Must ensure the initialization is performed.  */
  if (!libfoo_initialized)
    libfoo_initialize ();
  ...
}

/* This function is part of the exported API.  The argument must be
   non-NULL and have been created through create_foo().  */
int
foo_refcount (struct foo *argument)
{
  /* No need to invoke the initialization function here, because
     create_foo() must already have been called before.  */
  ...
}
```

4. The usual declaration of the '_' macro in each source file was

```
#include <libintl.h>
#define _(String) gettext (String)
```

for a program. For a library, which has its own translation domain, it reads like this:

```
#include <libintl.h>
#define _(String) dgettext (PACKAGE, String)
```

In other words, **dgettext** is used instead of **gettext**. Similarly, the **dngettext** function
should be used in place of the **ngettext** function.

5 Making the PO Template File

After preparing the sources, the programmer creates a PO template file. This section explains how to use `xgettext` for this purpose.

`xgettext` creates a file named *domainname*`.po`. You should then rename it to *domainname*`.pot`. (Why doesn't `xgettext` create it under the name *domainname*`.pot` right away? The answer is: for historical reasons. When `xgettext` was specified, the distinction between a PO file and PO file template was fuzzy, and the suffix '`.pot`' wasn't in use at that time.)

5.1 Invoking the xgettext Program

        xgettext [*option*] [*inputfile*] ...

The `xgettext` program extracts translatable strings from given input files.

5.1.1 Input file location

'*inputfile* ...'
>   Input files.

'`-f` *file*'
'`--files-from=`*file*'
>   Read the names of the input files from *file* instead of getting them from the
>   command line.

'`-D` *directory*'
'`--directory=`*directory*'
>   Add *directory* to the list of directories. Source files are searched relative to this
>   list of directories. The resulting `.po` file will be written relative to the current
>   directory, though.

If *inputfile* is '`-`', standard input is read.

5.1.2 Output file location

'`-d` *name*'
'`--default-domain=`*name*'
>   Use *name*`.po` for output (instead of `messages.po`).

'`-o` *file*'
'`--output=`*file*'
>   Write output to specified file (instead of *name*`.po` or `messages.po`).

'`-p` *dir*'
'`--output-dir=`*dir*'
>   Output files will be placed in directory *dir*.

If the output *file* is '`-`' or '`/dev/stdout`', the output is written to standard output.

5.1.3 Choice of input file language

'-L *name*'
'--language=*name*'

> Specifies the language of the input files. The supported languages are C,
> C++, ObjectiveC, PO, Shell, Python, Lisp, EmacsLisp, librep, Scheme,
> Smalltalk, Java, JavaProperties, C#, awk, YCP, Tcl, Perl, PHP, GCC-source,
> NXStringTable, RST, Glade, Lua, JavaScript, Vala, GSettings, Desktop.

'-C'
'--c++'   This is a shorthand for --language=C++.

By default the language is guessed depending on the input file name extension.

5.1.4 Input file interpretation

'--from-code=*name*'

> Specifies the encoding of the input files. This option is needed only if some
> untranslated message strings or their corresponding comments contain non-
> ASCII characters. Note that Tcl and Glade input files are always assumed to
> be in UTF-8, regardless of this option.

By default the input files are assumed to be in ASCII.

5.1.5 Operation mode

'-j'
'--join-existing'

> Join messages with existing file.

'-x *file*'
'--exclude-file=*file*'

> Entries from *file* are not extracted. *file* should be a PO or POT file.

'-c[*tag*]'
'--add-comments[=*tag*]'

> Place comment blocks starting with *tag* and preceding keyword lines in the out-
> put file. Without a *tag*, the option means to put *all* comment blocks preceding
> keyword lines in the output file.
>
> Note that comment blocks supposed to be extracted must be adjacent to key-
> word lines. For example, in the following C source code:

```
/* This is the first comment.  */
gettext ("foo");

/* This is the second comment: not extracted  */
gettext (
  "bar");

gettext (
  /* This is the third comment.  */
  "baz");
```

The second comment line will not be extracted, because there is one blank line between the comment line and the keyword.

'--check[=*CHECK*]'

> Perform a syntax check on msgid and msgid_plural. The supported checks are:

> 'ellipsis-unicode'

>> Prefer Unicode ellipsis character over ASCII ...

> 'space-ellipsis'

>> Prohibit whitespace before an ellipsis character

> 'quote-unicode'

>> Prefer Unicode quotation marks over ASCII "'`

> The option has an effect on all input files. To enable or disable checks for a certain string, you can mark it with an xgettext: special comment in the source file. For example, if you specify the --check=space-ellipsis option, but want to suppress the check on a particular string, add the following comment:

```
/* xgettext: no-space-ellipsis-check */
gettext ("We really want a space before ellipsis here ...");
```

> The xgettext: comment can be followed by flags separated with a comma. The possible flags are of the form '[no-]*name*-check', where *name* is the name of a valid syntax check. If a flag is prefixed by no-, the meaning is negated.

> Some tests apply the checks to each sentence within the msgid, rather than the whole string. xgettext detects the end of sentence by performing a pattern match, which usually looks for a period followed by a certain number of spaces. The number is specified with the --sentence-end option.

'--sentence-end[=*TYPE*]'

> The supported values are:

> 'single-space'

>> Expect at least one whitespace after a period

> 'double-space'

>> Expect at least two whitespaces after a period

5.1.6 Language specific options

'-a'
'--extract-all'

> Extract all strings.

> This option has an effect with most languages, namely C, C++, ObjectiveC, Shell, Python, Lisp, EmacsLisp, librep, Java, C#, awk, Tcl, Perl, PHP, GCC-source, Glade, Lua, JavaScript, Vala, GSettings.

'-k[*keywordspec*]'
'--keyword[=*keywordspec*]'

> Specify *keywordspec* as an additional keyword to be looked for. Without a *keywordspec*, the option means to not use default keywords.

If *keywordspec* is a C identifier *id*, xgettext looks for strings in the first argument of each call to the function or macro *id*. If *keywordspec* is of the form '*id*:`argnum`', xgettext looks for strings in the *argnum*th argument of the call. If *keywordspec* is of the form '*id*:`argnum1,argnum2`', xgettext looks for strings in the *argnum1*st argument and in the *argnum2*nd argument of the call, and treats them as singular/plural variants for a message with plural handling. Also, if *keywordspec* is of the form '*id*:`contextargnumc,argnum`' or '*id*:`argnum,contextargnumc`', xgettext treats strings in the *contextargnum*th argument as a context specifier. And, as a special-purpose support for GNOME, if *keywordspec* is of the form '*id*:`argnumg`', xgettext recognizes the *argnum*th argument as a string with context, using the GNOME `glib` syntax '"msgctxt|msgid"'.

Furthermore, if *keywordspec* is of the form '*id*:`...,totalnumargst`', xgettext recognizes this argument specification only if the number of actual arguments is equal to *totalnumargs*. This is useful for disambiguating overloaded function calls in C++.

Finally, if *keywordspec* is of the form '*id*:`argnum...,"xcomment"`', xgettext, when extracting a message from the specified argument strings, adds an extracted comment *xcomment* to the message. Note that when used through a normal shell command line, the double-quotes around the *xcomment* need to be escaped.

This option has an effect with most languages, namely C, C++, ObjectiveC, Shell, Python, Lisp, EmacsLisp, librep, Java, C#, awk, Tcl, Perl, PHP, GCC-source, Glade, Lua, JavaScript, Vala, GSettings, Desktop.

The default keyword specifications, which are always looked for if not explicitly disabled, are language dependent. They are:

- For C, C++, and GCC-source: `gettext`, `dgettext:2`, `dcgettext:2`, `ngettext:1,2`, `dngettext:2,3`, `dcngettext:2,3`, `gettext_noop`, and `pgettext:1c,2`, `dpgettext:2c,3`, `dcpgettext:2c,3`, `npgettext:1c,2,3`, `dnpgettext:2c,3,4`, `dcnpgettext:2c,3,4`.

- For Objective C: Like for C, and also `NSLocalizedString`, `_`, `NSLocalizedStaticString`, `__`.

- For Shell scripts: `gettext`, `ngettext:1,2`, `eval_gettext`, `eval_ngettext:1,2`.

- For Python: `gettext`, `ugettext`, `dgettext:2`, `ngettext:1,2`, `ungettext:1,2`, `dngettext:2,3`, `_`.

- For Lisp: `gettext`, `ngettext:1,2`, `gettext-noop`.

- For EmacsLisp: `_`.

- For librep: `_`.

- For Scheme: `gettext`, `ngettext:1,2`, `gettext-noop`.

- For Java: `GettextResource.gettext:2`, `GettextResource.ngettext:2,3`, `GettextResource.pgettext:2c,3`, `GettextResource.npgettext:2c,3,4`, `gettext`, `ngettext:1,2`, `pgettext:1c,2`, `npgettext:1c,2,3`, `getString`.

- For C#: `GetString`, `GetPluralString:1,2`, `GetParticularString:1c,2`, `GetParticularPluralString:1c,2,3`.

- For awk: `dcgettext`, `dcngettext:1,2`.
- For Tcl: `::msgcat::mc`.
- For Perl: `gettext`, `%gettext`, `$gettext`, `dgettext:2`, `dcgettext:2`, `ngettext:1,2`, `dngettext:2,3`, `dcngettext:2,3`, `gettext_noop`.
- For PHP: `_`, `gettext`, `dgettext:2`, `dcgettext:2`, `ngettext:1,2`, `dngettext:2,3`, `dcngettext:2,3`.
- For Glade 1: `label`, `title`, `text`, `format`, `copyright`, `comments`, `preview_text`, `tooltip`.
- For Lua: `_`, `gettext.gettext`, `gettext.dgettext:2`, `gettext.dcgettext:2`, `gettext.ngettext:1,2`, `gettext.dngettext:2,3`, `gettext.dcngettext:2,3`.
- For JavaScript: `_`, `gettext`, `dgettext:2`, `dcgettext:2`, `ngettext:1,2`, `dngettext:2,3`, `pgettext:1c,2`, `dpgettext:2c,3`.
- For Vala: `_`, `Q_`, `N_`, `NC_`, `dgettext:2`, `dcgettext:2`, `ngettext:1,2`, `dngettext:2,3`, `dpgettext:2c,3`, `dpgettext2:2c,3`.
- For Desktop: `Name`, `GenericName`, `Comment`, `Icon`, `Keywords`.

To disable the default keyword specifications, the option '`-k`' or '`--keyword`' or '`--keyword=`', without a *keywordspec*, can be used.

'`--flag=word:arg:flag`'

Specifies additional flags for strings occurring as part of the *arg*th argument of the function *word*. The possible flags are the possible format string indicators, such as '`c-format`', and their negations, such as '`no-c-format`', possibly prefixed with '`pass-`'.

The meaning of `--flag=function:arg:lang-format` is that in language *lang*, the specified *function* expects as *arg*th argument a format string. (For those of you familiar with GCC function attributes, `--flag=function:arg:c-format` is roughly equivalent to the declaration '`__attribute__ ((__format__ (__printf__, arg, ...)))`' attached to *function* in a C source file.) For example, if you use the '`error`' function from GNU libc, you can specify its behaviour through `--flag=error:3:c-format`. The effect of this specification is that `xgettext` will mark as format strings all `gettext` invocations that occur as *arg*th argument of *function*. This is useful when such strings contain no format string directives: together with the checks done by '`msgfmt -c`' it will ensure that translators cannot accidentally use format string directives that would lead to a crash at runtime.

The meaning of `--flag=function:arg:pass-lang-format` is that in language *lang*, if the *function* call occurs in a position that must yield a format string, then its *arg*th argument must yield a format string of the same type as well. (If you know GCC function attributes, the `--flag=function:arg:pass-c-format` option is roughly equivalent to the declaration '`__attribute__ ((__format_arg__ (arg)))`' attached to *function* in a C source file.) For example, if you use the '`_`' shortcut for the `gettext` function, you should use `--flag=_:1:pass-c-format`. The effect of this specification is that `xgettext` will propagate a format string requirement for a `_("string")` call to its first argument, the literal `"string"`, and thus mark it as a format string. This is useful when such strings contain no format string directives: together with the checks done by 'msgfmt -c' it will ensure that translators cannot accidentally use format string directives that would lead to a crash at runtime.

This option has an effect with most languages, namely C, C++, ObjectiveC, Shell, Python, Lisp, EmacsLisp, librep, Scheme, Java, C#, awk, YCP, Tcl, Perl, PHP, GCC-source, Lua, JavaScript, Vala.

'-T'
'--trigraphs'

>   Understand ANSI C trigraphs for input.
>   This option has an effect only with the languages C, C++, ObjectiveC.

'--qt'   Recognize Qt format strings.
>   This option has an effect only with the language C++.

'--kde'   Recognize KDE 4 format strings.
>   This option has an effect only with the language C++.

'--boost'   Recognize Boost format strings.
>   This option has an effect only with the language C++.

'--debug'   Use the flags c-format and possible-c-format to show who was responsible for marking a message as a format string. The latter form is used if the xgettext program decided, the former form is used if the programmer prescribed it.

>   By default only the c-format form is used. The translator should not have to care about these details.

This implementation of xgettext is able to process a few awkward cases, like strings in preprocessor macros, ANSI concatenation of adjacent strings, and escaped end of lines for continued strings.

5.1.7 Output details

'--color'
'--color=when'

>   Specify whether or when to use colors and other text attributes. See Section 9.11.1 [The –color option], page 95 for details.

'--style=style_file'

>   Specify the CSS style rule file to use for --color. See Section 9.11.3 [The –style option], page 96 for details.

'--force-po'

>   Always write an output file even if no message is defined.

'-i'
'--indent'

>   Write the .po file using indented style.

'--no-location'

>   Do not write '#: filename:line' lines. Note that using this option makes it harder for technically skilled translators to understand each message's context.

'-n'
'--add-location=*type*'

> Generate '#: *filename*:*line*' lines (default).
>
> The optional *type* can be either 'full', 'file', or 'never'. If it is not given or 'full', it generates the lines with both file name and line number. If it is 'file', the line number part is omitted. If it is 'never', it completely suppresses the lines (same as --no-location).

'--strict'

> Write out a strict Uniforum conforming PO file. Note that this Uniforum format should be avoided because it doesn't support the GNU extensions.

'--properties-output'

> Write out a Java ResourceBundle in Java .properties syntax. Note that this file format doesn't support plural forms and silently drops obsolete messages.

'--stringtable-output'

> Write out a NeXTstep/GNUstep localized resource file in .strings syntax. Note that this file format doesn't support plural forms.

'-w *number*'
'--width=*number*'

> Set the output page width. Long strings in the output files will be split across multiple lines in order to ensure that each line's width (= number of screen columns) is less or equal to the given *number*.

'--no-wrap'

> Do not break long message lines. Message lines whose width exceeds the output page width will not be split into several lines. Only file reference lines which are wider than the output page width will be split.

'-s'
'--sort-output'

> Generate sorted output. Note that using this option makes it much harder for the translator to understand each message's context.

'-F'
'--sort-by-file'

> Sort output by file location.

'--omit-header'

> Don't write header with 'msgid ""' entry.
>
> This is useful for testing purposes because it eliminates a source of variance for generated .gmo files. With --omit-header, two invocations of xgettext on the same files with the same options at different times are guaranteed to produce the same results.
>
> Note that using this option will lead to an error if the resulting file would not entirely be in ASCII.

'--copyright-holder=*string*'

> Set the copyright holder in the output. *string* should be the copyright holder of the surrounding package. (Note that the msgstr strings, extracted from the

package's sources, belong to the copyright holder of the package.) Translators are expected to transfer or disclaim the copyright for their translations, so that package maintainers can distribute them without legal risk. If *string* is empty, the output files are marked as being in the public domain; in this case, the translators are expected to disclaim their copyright, again so that package maintainers can distribute them without legal risk.

The default value for *string* is the Free Software Foundation, Inc., simply because `xgettext` was first used in the GNU project.

`'--foreign-user'`

> Omit FSF copyright in output. This option is equivalent to `'--copyright-holder='''`. It can be useful for packages outside the GNU project that want their translations to be in the public domain.

`'--package-name=package'`

> Set the package name in the header of the output.

`'--package-version=version'`

> Set the package version in the header of the output. This option has an effect only if the `'--package-name'` option is also used.

`'--msgid-bugs-address=email@address'`

> Set the reporting address for msgid bugs. This is the email address or URL to which the translators shall report bugs in the untranslated strings:
>
> - Strings which are not entire sentences; see the maintainer guidelines in Section 4.3 [Preparing Strings], page 20.
> - Strings which use unclear terms or require additional context to be understood.
> - Strings which make invalid assumptions about notation of date, time or money.
> - Pluralisation problems.
> - Incorrect English spelling.
> - Incorrect formatting.
>
> It can be your email address, or a mailing list address where translators can write to without being subscribed, or the URL of a web page through which the translators can contact you.
>
> The default value is empty, which means that translators will be clueless! Don't forget to specify this option.

`'-m[string]'`
`'--msgstr-prefix[=string]'`

> Use *string* (or "" if not specified) as prefix for msgstr values.

`'-M[string]'`
`'--msgstr-suffix[=string]'`

> Use *string* (or "" if not specified) as suffix for msgstr values.

5.1.8 Informative output

'-h'
'--help'   Display this help and exit.

'-V'
'--version'
              Output version information and exit.

6 Creating a New PO File

When starting a new translation, the translator creates a file called *LANG*.po, as a copy of the *package*.pot template file with modifications in the initial comments (at the beginning of the file) and in the header entry (the first entry, near the beginning of the file).

The easiest way to do so is by use of the 'msginit' program. For example:

```
$ cd PACKAGE-VERSION
$ cd po
$ msginit
```

The alternative way is to do the copy and modifications by hand. To do so, the translator copies *package*.pot to *LANG*.po. Then she modifies the initial comments and the header entry of this file.

6.1 Invoking the msginit Program

```
msginit [option]
```

The msginit program creates a new PO file, initializing the meta information with values from the user's environment.

Here are more details. The following header fields of a PO file are automatically filled, when possible.

'Project-Id-Version'

> The value is guessed from the **configure** script or any other files in the current directory.

'PO-Revision-Date'

> The value is taken from the **PO-Creation-Data** in the input POT file, or the current date is used.

'Last-Translator'

> The value is taken from user's password file entry and the mailer configuration files.

'Language-Team, Language'

> These values are set according to the current locale and the predefined list of translation teams.

'MIME-Version, Content-Type, Content-Transfer-Encoding'

> These values are set according to the content of the POT file and the current locale. If the POT file contains charset=UTF-8, it means that the POT file contains non-ASCII characters, and we keep the UTF-8 encoding. Otherwise, when the POT file is plain ASCII, we use the locale's encoding.

'Plural-Forms'

> The value is first looked up from the embedded table.
>
> As an experimental feature, you can instruct **msginit** to use the information from Unicode CLDR, by setting the **GETTEXTCLDRDIR** environment variable.

6.1.1 Input file location

'-i *inputfile*'
'--input=*inputfile*'
>   Input POT file.

If no *inputfile* is given, the current directory is searched for the POT file. If it is '-', standard input is read.

6.1.2 Output file location

'-o *file*'
'--output-file=*file*'
>   Write output to specified PO file.

If no output file is given, it depends on the '--locale' option or the user's locale setting. If it is '-', the results are written to standard output.

6.1.3 Input file syntax

'-p'
'--properties-input'
>   Assume the input file is a Java ResourceBundle in Java .properties syntax, not in PO file syntax.

'--stringtable-input'
>   Assume the input file is a NeXTstep/GNUstep localized resource file in .strings syntax, not in PO file syntax.

6.1.4 Output details

'-l *ll_CC*'
'--locale=*ll_CC*'
>   Set target locale. *ll* should be a language code, and *CC* should be a country code. The command 'locale -a' can be used to output a list of all installed locales. The default is the user's locale setting.

'--no-translator'
>   Declares that the PO file will not have a human translator and is instead automatically generated.

'--color'
'--color=*when*'
>   Specify whether or when to use colors and other text attributes. See Section 9.11.1 [The –color option], page 95 for details.

'--style=*style_file*'
>   Specify the CSS style rule file to use for --color. See Section 9.11.3 [The –style option], page 96 for details.

'-p'
'--properties-output'
>   Write out a Java ResourceBundle in Java .properties syntax. Note that this file format doesn't support plural forms and silently drops obsolete messages.

'`--stringtable-output`'

> Write out a NeXTstep/GNUstep localized resource file in `.strings` syntax. Note that this file format doesn't support plural forms.

'`-w number`'
'`--width=number`'

> Set the output page width. Long strings in the output files will be split across multiple lines in order to ensure that each line's width (= number of screen columns) is less or equal to the given *number*.

'`--no-wrap`'

> Do not break long message lines. Message lines whose width exceeds the output page width will not be split into several lines. Only file reference lines which are wider than the output page width will be split.

6.1.5 Informative output

'`-h`'
'`--help`'   Display this help and exit.

'`-V`'
'`--version`'

> Output version information and exit.

6.2 Filling in the Header Entry

The initial comments "SOME DESCRIPTIVE TITLE", "YEAR" and "FIRST AUTHOR <EMAIL@ADDRESS>, YEAR" ought to be replaced by sensible information. This can be done in any text editor; if Emacs is used and it switched to PO mode automatically (because it has recognized the file's suffix), you can disable it by typing *M-x fundamental-mode*.

Modifying the header entry can already be done using PO mode: in Emacs, type *M-x po-mode RET* and then *RET* again to start editing the entry. You should fill in the following fields.

Project-Id-Version

> This is the name and version of the package. Fill it in if it has not already been filled in by `xgettext`.

Report-Msgid-Bugs-To

> This has already been filled in by `xgettext`. It contains an email address or URL where you can report bugs in the untranslated strings:
>
> - Strings which are not entire sentences, see the maintainer guidelines in Section 4.3 [Preparing Strings], page 20.
>
> - Strings which use unclear terms or require additional context to be understood.
>
> - Strings which make invalid assumptions about notation of date, time or money.
>
> - Pluralisation problems.

- Incorrect English spelling.

- Incorrect formatting.

POT-Creation-Date

> This has already been filled in by `xgettext`.

PO-Revision-Date

> You don't need to fill this in. It will be filled by the PO file editor when you save the file.

Last-Translator

> Fill in your name and email address (without double quotes).

Language-Team

> Fill in the English name of the language, and the email address or homepage URL of the language team you are part of.
>
> Before starting a translation, it is a good idea to get in touch with your translation team, not only to make sure you don't do duplicated work, but also to coordinate difficult linguistic issues.
>
> In the Free Translation Project, each translation team has its own mailing list. The up-to-date list of teams can be found at the Free Translation Project's homepage, `http://translationproject.org/`, in the "Teams" area.

Language

Fill in the language code of the language. This can be in one of three forms:

- '`ll`', an ISO 639 two-letter language code (lowercase). See Appendix A [Language Codes], page 206 for the list of codes.

- '`ll_CC`', where '`ll`' is an ISO 639 two-letter language code (lowercase) and '`CC`' is an ISO 3166 two-letter country code (uppercase). The country code specification is not redundant: Some languages have dialects in different countries. For example, '`de_AT`' is used for Austria, and '`pt_BR`' for Brazil. The country code serves to distinguish the dialects. See Appendix A [Language Codes], page 206 and Appendix B [Country Codes], page 214 for the lists of codes.

- '`ll_CC@variant`', where '`ll`' is an ISO 639 two-letter language code (lowercase), '`CC`' is an ISO 3166 two-letter country code (uppercase), and '`variant`' is a variant designator. The variant designator (lowercase) can be a script designator, such as '`latin`' or '`cyrillic`'.

The naming convention '`ll_CC`' is also the way locales are named on systems based on GNU libc. But there are three important differences:

- In this PO file field, but not in locale names, '`ll_CC`' combinations denoting a language's main dialect are abbreviated as '`ll`'. For example, '`de`' is equivalent to '`de_DE`' (German as spoken in Germany), and '`pt`' to '`pt_PT`' (Portuguese as spoken in Portugal) in this context.

- In this PO file field, suffixes like '`.encoding`' are not used.

- In this PO file field, variant designators that are not relevant to message translation, such as '`@euro`', are not used.

So, if your locale name is '`de_DE.UTF-8`', the language specification in PO files is just '`de`'.

Content-Type

Replace 'CHARSET' with the character encoding used for your language, in your locale, or UTF-8. This field is needed for correct operation of the msgmerge and msgfmt programs, as well as for users whose locale's character encoding differs from yours (see Section 11.2.4 [Charset conversion], page 116).

You get the character encoding of your locale by running the shell command 'locale charmap'. If the result is 'C' or 'ANSI_X3.4-1968', which is equivalent to 'ASCII' (= 'US-ASCII'), it means that your locale is not correctly configured. In this case, ask your translation team which charset to use. 'ASCII' is not usable for any language except Latin.

Because the PO files must be portable to operating systems with less advanced internationalization facilities, the character encodings that can be used are limited to those supported by both GNU libc and GNU libiconv. These are: ASCII, ISO-8859-1, ISO-8859-2, ISO-8859-3, ISO-8859-4, ISO-8859-5, ISO-8859-6, ISO-8859-7, ISO-8859-8, ISO-8859-9, ISO-8859-13, ISO-8859-14, ISO-8859-15, KOI8-R, KOI8-U, KOI8-T, CP850, CP866, CP874, CP932, CP949, CP950, CP1250, CP1251, CP1252, CP1253, CP1254, CP1255, CP1256, CP1257, GB2312, EUC-JP, EUC-KR, EUC-TW, BIG5, BIG5-HKSCS, GBK, GB18030, SHIFT_JIS, JOHAB, TIS-620, VISCII, GEORGIAN-PS, UTF-8.

In the GNU system, the following encodings are frequently used for the corresponding languages.

- ISO-8859-1 for Afrikaans, Albanian, Basque, Breton, Catalan, Cornish, Danish, Dutch, English, Estonian, Faroese, Finnish, French, Galician, German, Greenlandic, Icelandic, Indonesian, Irish, Italian, Malay, Manx, Norwegian, Occitan, Portuguese, Spanish, Swedish, Tagalog, Uzbek, Walloon,
- ISO-8859-2 for Bosnian, Croatian, Czech, Hungarian, Polish, Romanian, Serbian, Slovak, Slovenian,
- ISO-8859-3 for Maltese,
- ISO-8859-5 for Macedonian, Serbian,
- ISO-8859-6 for Arabic,
- ISO-8859-7 for Greek,
- ISO-8859-8 for Hebrew,
- ISO-8859-9 for Turkish,
- ISO-8859-13 for Latvian, Lithuanian, Maori,
- ISO-8859-14 for Welsh,
- ISO-8859-15 for Basque, Catalan, Dutch, English, Finnish, French, Galician, German, Irish, Italian, Portuguese, Spanish, Swedish, Walloon,
- KOI8-R for Russian,
- KOI8-U for Ukrainian,
- KOI8-T for Tajik,
- CP1251 for Bulgarian, Belarusian,
- GB2312, GBK, GB18030 for simplified writing of Chinese,
- BIG5, BIG5-HKSCS for traditional writing of Chinese,

- EUC-JP for Japanese,
- EUC-KR for Korean,
- TIS-620 for Thai,
- GEORGIAN-PS for Georgian,
- UTF-8 for any language, including those listed above.

When single quote characters or double quote characters are used in translations for your language, and your locale's encoding is one of the ISO-8859-* charsets, it is best if you create your PO files in UTF-8 encoding, instead of your locale's encoding. This is because in UTF-8 the real quote characters can be represented (single quote characters: U+2018, U+2019, double quote characters: U+201C, U+201D), whereas none of ISO-8859-* charsets has them all. Users in UTF-8 locales will see the real quote characters, whereas users in ISO-8859-* locales will see the vertical apostrophe and the vertical double quote instead (because that's what the character set conversion will transliterate them to).

To enter such quote characters under X11, you can change your keyboard mapping using the xmodmap program. The X11 names of the quote characters are "leftsinglequotemark", "rightsinglequotemark", "leftdoublequotemark", "rightdoublequotemark", "singlelowquotemark", "doublelowquotemark".

Note that only recent versions of GNU Emacs support the UTF-8 encoding: Emacs 20 with Mule-UCS, and Emacs 21. As of January 2001, XEmacs doesn't support the UTF-8 encoding.

The character encoding name can be written in either upper or lower case. Usually upper case is preferred.

Content-Transfer-Encoding

Set this to 8bit.

Plural-Forms

This field is optional. It is only needed if the PO file has plural forms. You can find them by searching for the 'msgid_plural' keyword. The format of the plural forms field is described in Section 11.2.6 [Plural forms], page 119 and Section 12.6 [Translating plural forms], page 136.

7 Updating Existing PO Files

7.1 Invoking the `msgmerge` Program

```
msgmerge [option] def.po ref.pot
```

The `msgmerge` program merges two Uniforum style .po files together. The *def*.po file is an existing PO file with translations which will be taken over to the newly created file as long as they still match; comments will be preserved, but extracted comments and file positions will be discarded. The *ref*.pot file is the last created PO file with up-to-date source references but old translations, or a PO Template file (generally created by `xgettext`); any translations or comments in the file will be discarded, however dot comments and file positions will be preserved. Where an exact match cannot be found, fuzzy matching is used to produce better results.

7.1.1 Input file location

'`def.po`'   Translations referring to old sources.

'`ref.pot`'   References to the new sources.

'`-D directory`'
'`--directory=directory`'

> Add *directory* to the list of directories. Source files are searched relative to this list of directories. The resulting `.po` file will be written relative to the current directory, though.

'`-C file`'
'`--compendium=file`'

> Specify an additional library of message translations. See Section 8.4 [Compendium], page 67. This option may be specified more than once.

7.1.2 Operation mode

'`-U`'
'`--update`'

> Update *def*.po. Do nothing if *def*.po is already up to date.

7.1.3 Output file location

'`-o file`'
'`--output-file=file`'

> Write output to specified file.

The results are written to standard output if no output file is specified or if it is '`-`'.

7.1.4 Output file location in update mode

The result is written back to *def*.po.

'`--backup=control`'

> Make a backup of *def*.po

'`--suffix=suffix`'

> Override the usual backup suffix.

The version control method may be selected via the `--backup` option or through the `VERSION_CONTROL` environment variable. Here are the values:

'`none`'
'`off`'   Never make backups (even if `--backup` is given).

'`numbered`'
'`t`'   Make numbered backups.

'`existing`'
'`nil`'   Make numbered backups if numbered backups for this file already exist, otherwise make simple backups.

'`simple`'
'`never`'   Always make simple backups.

The backup suffix is '`~`', unless set with `--suffix` or the `SIMPLE_BACKUP_SUFFIX` environment variable.

7.1.5 Operation modifiers

'`-m`'
'`--multi-domain`'

> Apply *ref*.pot to each of the domains in *def*.po.

'`-N`'
'`--no-fuzzy-matching`'

> Do not use fuzzy matching when an exact match is not found. This may speed up the operation considerably.

'`--previous`'

> Keep the previous msgids of translated messages, marked with '`#|`', when adding the fuzzy marker to such messages.

7.1.6 Input file syntax

'`-P`'
'`--properties-input`'

> Assume the input files are Java ResourceBundles in Java `.properties` syntax, not in PO file syntax.

'`--stringtable-input`'

> Assume the input files are NeXTstep/GNUstep localized resource files in `.strings` syntax, not in PO file syntax.

7.1.7 Output details

'`--lang=catalogname`'

> Specify the '`Language`' field to be used in the header entry. See Section 6.2 [Header Entry], page 44 for the meaning of this field. Note: The '`Language-Team`' and '`Plural-Forms`' fields are left unchanged. If this option

is not specified, the 'Language' field is inferred, as best as possible, from the 'Language-Team' field.

'--color'

'--color=*when*'

> Specify whether or when to use colors and other text attributes. See Section 9.11.1 [The –color option], page 95 for details.

'--style=*style_file*'

> Specify the CSS style rule file to use for --color. See Section 9.11.3 [The –style option], page 96 for details.

'--force-po'

> Always write an output file even if it contains no message.

'-i'

'--indent'

> Write the .po file using indented style.

'--no-location'

> Do not write '#: *filename*:*line*' lines.

'-n'

'--add-location=*type*'

> Generate '#: *filename*:*line*' lines (default).
>
> The optional *type* can be either 'full', 'file', or 'never'. If it is not given or 'full', it generates the lines with both file name and line number. If it is 'file', the line number part is omitted. If it is 'never', it completely suppresses the lines (same as --no-location).

'--strict'

> Write out a strict Uniforum conforming PO file. Note that this Uniforum format should be avoided because it doesn't support the GNU extensions.

'-p'

'--properties-output'

> Write out a Java ResourceBundle in Java .properties syntax. Note that this file format doesn't support plural forms and silently drops obsolete messages.

'--stringtable-output'

> Write out a NeXTstep/GNUstep localized resource file in .strings syntax. Note that this file format doesn't support plural forms.

'-w *number*'

'--width=*number*'

> Set the output page width. Long strings in the output files will be split across multiple lines in order to ensure that each line's width (= number of screen columns) is less or equal to the given *number*.

'--no-wrap'

> Do not break long message lines. Message lines whose width exceeds the output page width will not be split into several lines. Only file reference lines which are wider than the output page width will be split.

'`-s`'
'`--sort-output`'
> Generate sorted output. Note that using this option makes it much harder for the translator to understand each message's context.

'`-F`'
'`--sort-by-file`'
> Sort output by file location.

7.1.8 Informative output

'`-h`'
'`--help`'   Display this help and exit.

'`-V`'
'`--version`'
> Output version information and exit.

'`-v`'
'`--verbose`'
> Increase verbosity level.

'`-q`'
'`--quiet`'
'`--silent`'
> Suppress progress indicators.

8 Editing PO Files

8.1 KDE's PO File Editor

8.2 GNOME's PO File Editor

8.3 Emacs's PO File Editor

For those of you being the lucky users of Emacs, PO mode has been specifically created for providing a cozy environment for editing or modifying PO files. While editing a PO file, PO mode allows for the easy browsing of auxiliary and compendium PO files, as well as for following references into the set of C program sources from which PO files have been derived. It has a few special features, among which are the interactive marking of program strings as translatable, and the validation of PO files with easy repositioning to PO file lines showing errors.

For the beginning, besides main PO mode commands (see Section 8.3.2 [Main PO Commands], page 53), you should know how to move between entries (see Section 8.3.3 [Entry Positioning], page 54), and how to handle untranslated entries (see Section 8.3.7 [Untranslated Entries], page 58).

8.3.1 Completing GNU gettext Installation

Once you have received, unpacked, configured and compiled the GNU gettext distribution, the 'make install' command puts in place the programs xgettext, msgfmt, gettext, and msgmerge, as well as their available message catalogs. To top off a comfortable installation, you might also want to make the PO mode available to your Emacs users.

During the installation of the PO mode, you might want to modify your file .emacs, once and for all, so it contains a few lines looking like:

```
(setq auto-mode-alist
      (cons '("\\.po\\'\\|\\.po\\." . po-mode) auto-mode-alist))
(autoload 'po-mode "po-mode" "Major mode for translators to edit PO files" t)
```

Later, whenever you edit some .po file, or any file having the string '.po.' within its name, Emacs loads po-mode.elc (or po-mode.el) as needed, and automatically activates PO mode commands for the associated buffer. The string *PO* appears in the mode line for any buffer for which PO mode is active. Many PO files may be active at once in a single Emacs session.

If you are using Emacs version 20 or newer, and have already installed the appropriate international fonts on your system, you may also tell Emacs how to determine automatically the coding system of every PO file. This will often (but not always) cause the necessary fonts to be loaded and used for displaying the translations on your Emacs screen. For this to happen, add the lines:

```
(modify-coding-system-alist 'file "\\.po\\'\\|\\.po\\."
                            'po-find-file-coding-system)
(autoload 'po-find-file-coding-system "po-mode")
```

to your .emacs file. If, with this, you still see boxes instead of international characters, try a different font set (via Shift Mouse button 1).

8.3.2 Main PO mode Commands

After setting up Emacs with something similar to the lines in Section 8.3.1 [Installation], page 52, PO mode is activated for a window when Emacs finds a PO file in that window. This puts the window read-only and establishes a po-mode-map, which is a genuine Emacs mode, in a way that is not derived from text mode in any way. Functions found on `po-mode-hook`, if any, will be executed.

When PO mode is active in a window, the letters 'PO' appear in the mode line for that window. The mode line also displays how many entries of each kind are held in the PO file. For example, the string '132t+3f+10u+2o' would tell the translator that the PO mode contains 132 translated entries (see Section 8.3.5 [Translated Entries], page 57, 3 fuzzy entries (see Section 8.3.6 [Fuzzy Entries], page 57), 10 untranslated entries (see Section 8.3.7 [Untranslated Entries], page 58) and 2 obsolete entries (see Section 8.3.8 [Obsolete Entries], page 59). Zero-coefficients items are not shown. So, in this example, if the fuzzy entries were unfuzzied, the untranslated entries were translated and the obsolete entries were deleted, the mode line would merely display '145t' for the counters.

The main PO commands are those which do not fit into the other categories of subsequent sections. These allow for quitting PO mode or for managing windows in special ways.

`_`   Undo last modification to the PO file (`po-undo`).

`Q`   Quit processing and save the PO file (`po-quit`).

`q`   Quit processing, possibly after confirmation (`po-confirm-and-quit`).

`O`   Temporary leave the PO file window (`po-other-window`).

`?`
`h`   Show help about PO mode (`po-help`).

`=`   Give some PO file statistics (`po-statistics`).

`V`   Batch validate the format of the whole PO file (`po-validate`).

The command `_` (`po-undo`) interfaces to the Emacs *undo* facility. See Section "Undoing Changes" in *The Emacs Editor*. Each time `_` is typed, modifications which the translator did to the PO file are undone a little more. For the purpose of undoing, each PO mode command is atomic. This is especially true for the `RET` command: the whole edition made by using a single use of this command is undone at once, even if the edition itself implied several actions. However, while in the editing window, one can undo the edition work quite parsimoniously.

The commands `Q` (`po-quit`) and `q` (`po-confirm-and-quit`) are used when the translator is done with the PO file. The former is a bit less verbose than the latter. If the file has been modified, it is saved to disk first. In both cases, and prior to all this, the commands check if any untranslated messages remain in the PO file and, if so, the translator is asked if she really wants to leave off working with this PO file. This is the preferred way of getting rid of an Emacs PO file buffer. Merely killing it through the usual command `C-x k` (`kill-buffer`) is not the tidiest way to proceed.

The command `O` (`po-other-window`) is another, softer way, to leave PO mode, temporarily. It just moves the cursor to some other Emacs window, and pops one if necessary. For example, if the translator just got PO mode to show some source context in some other, she might discover some apparent bug in the program source that needs correction. This command allows the translator to change sex, become a programmer, and have the cursor right into the window containing the program she (or rather *he*) wants to modify. By later getting the cursor back in the PO file window, or by asking Emacs to edit this file once again, PO mode is then recovered.

The command `h` (`po-help`) displays a summary of all available PO mode commands. The translator should then type any character to resume normal PO mode operations. The command `?` has the same effect as `h`.

The command `=` (`po-statistics`) computes the total number of entries in the PO file, the ordinal of the current entry (counted from 1), the number of untranslated entries, the number of obsolete entries, and displays all these numbers.

The command `V` (`po-validate`) launches `msgfmt` in checking and verbose mode over the current PO file. This command first offers to save the current PO file on disk. The `msgfmt` tool, from GNU `gettext`, has the purpose of creating a MO file out of a PO file, and PO mode uses the features of this program for checking the overall format of a PO file, as well as all individual entries.

The program `msgfmt` runs asynchronously with Emacs, so the translator regains control immediately while her PO file is being studied. Error output is collected in the Emacs '`*compilation*`' buffer, displayed in another window. The regular Emacs command `C-x`' (`next-error`), as well as other usual compile commands, allow the translator to reposition quickly to the offending parts of the PO file. Once the cursor is on the line in error, the translator may decide on any PO mode action which would help correcting the error.

8.3.3 Entry Positioning

The cursor in a PO file window is almost always part of an entry. The only exceptions are the special case when the cursor is after the last entry in the file, or when the PO file is empty. The entry where the cursor is found to be is said to be the current entry. Many PO mode commands operate on the current entry, so moving the cursor does more than allowing the translator to browse the PO file, this also selects on which entry commands operate.

Some PO mode commands alter the position of the cursor in a specialized way. A few of those special purpose positioning are described here, the others are described in following sections (for a complete list try `C-h m`):

.	Redisplay the current entry (`po-current-entry`).
n	Select the entry after the current one (`po-next-entry`).
p	Select the entry before the current one (`po-previous-entry`).
<	Select the first entry in the PO file (`po-first-entry`).
>	Select the last entry in the PO file (`po-last-entry`).
m	Record the location of the current entry for later use (`po-push-location`).
r	Return to a previously saved entry location (`po-pop-location`).
x	Exchange the current entry location with the previously saved one (`po-exchange-location`).

Any Emacs command able to reposition the cursor may be used to select the current entry in PO mode, including commands which move by characters, lines, paragraphs, screens or pages, and search commands. However, there is a kind of standard way to display the current entry in PO mode, which usual Emacs commands moving the cursor do not especially try to enforce. The command . (`po-current-entry`) has the sole purpose of redisplaying the current entry properly, after the current entry has been changed by means external to PO mode, or the Emacs screen otherwise altered.

It is yet to be decided if PO mode helps the translator, or otherwise irritates her, by forcing a rigid window disposition while she is doing her work. We originally had quite precise ideas about how windows should behave, but on the other hand, anyone used to Emacs is often happy to keep full control. Maybe a fixed window disposition might be offered as a PO mode option that the translator might activate or deactivate at will, so it could be offered on an experimental basis. If nobody feels a real need for using it, or a compulsion for writing it, we should drop this whole idea. The incentive for doing it should come from translators rather than programmers, as opinions from an experienced translator are surely more worth to me than opinions from programmers *thinking* about how *others* should do translation.

The commands `n` (`po-next-entry`) and `p` (`po-previous-entry`) move the cursor the entry following, or preceding, the current one. If `n` is given while the cursor is on the last entry of the PO file, or if `p` is given while the cursor is on the first entry, no move is done.

The commands `<` (`po-first-entry`) and `>` (`po-last-entry`) move the cursor to the first entry, or last entry, of the PO file. When the cursor is located past the last entry in a PO file, most PO mode commands will return an error saying 'After last entry'. Moreover, the commands `<` and `>` have the special property of being able to work even when the cursor is not into some PO file entry, and one may use them for nicely correcting this situation. But even these commands will fail on a truly empty PO file. There are development plans for the PO mode for it to interactively fill an empty PO file from sources. See Section 4.5 [Marking], page 24.

The translator may decide, before working at the translation of a particular entry, that she needs to browse the remainder of the PO file, maybe for finding the terminology or phraseology used in related entries. She can of course use the standard Emacs idioms for saving the current cursor location in some register, and use that register for getting back, or else, use the location ring.

PO mode offers another approach, by which cursor locations may be saved onto a special stack. The command `m` (`po-push-location`) merely adds the location of current entry to the stack, pushing the already saved locations under the new one. The command `r` (`po-pop-location`) consumes the top stack element and repositions the cursor to the entry associated with that top element. This position is then lost, for the next `r` will move the cursor to the previously saved location, and so on until no locations remain on the stack.

If the translator wants the position to be kept on the location stack, maybe for taking a look at the entry associated with the top element, then go elsewhere with the intent of getting back later, she ought to use `m` immediately after `r`.

The command `x` (`po-exchange-location`) simultaneously repositions the cursor to the entry associated with the top element of the stack of saved locations, and replaces that top element with the location of the current entry before the move. Consequently, repeating the *x* command toggles alternatively between two entries. For achieving this, the translator will position the cursor on the first entry, use *m*, then position to the second entry, and merely use *x* for making the switch.

8.3.4 Normalizing Strings in Entries

There are many different ways for encoding a particular string into a PO file entry, because there are so many different ways to split and quote multi-line strings, and even, to represent special characters by backslashed escaped sequences. Some features of PO mode rely on the ability for PO mode to scan an already existing PO file for a particular string encoded into the `msgid` field of some entry. Even if PO mode has internally all the built-in machinery for implementing this recognition easily, doing it fast is technically difficult. To facilitate a solution to this efficiency problem, we decided on a canonical representation for strings.

A conventional representation of strings in a PO file is currently under discussion, and PO mode experiments with a canonical representation. Having both `xgettext` and PO mode converging towards a uniform way of representing equivalent strings would be useful, as the internal normalization needed by PO mode could be automatically satisfied when using `xgettext` from GNU `gettext`. An explicit PO mode normalization should then be only necessary for PO files imported from elsewhere, or for when the convention itself evolves.

So, for achieving normalization of at least the strings of a given PO file needing a canonical representation, the following PO mode command is available:

`M-x po-normalize`
> Tidy the whole PO file by making entries more uniform.

The special command `M-x po-normalize`, which has no associated keys, revises all entries, ensuring that strings of both original and translated entries use uniform internal quoting in the PO file. It also removes any crumb after the last entry. This command may be useful for PO files freshly imported from elsewhere, or if we ever improve on the canonical quoting format we use. This canonical format is not only meant for getting cleaner PO files, but also for greatly speeding up `msgid` string lookup for some other PO mode commands.

`M-x po-normalize` presently makes three passes over the entries. The first implements heuristics for converting PO files for GNU `gettext` 0.6 and earlier, in which `msgid` and `msgstr` fields were using K&R style C string syntax for multi-line strings. These heuristics may fail for comments not related to obsolete entries and ending with a backslash; they also depend on subsequent passes for finalizing the proper commenting of continued lines for obsolete entries. This first pass might disappear once all oldish PO files would have been adjusted. The second and third pass normalize all `msgid` and `msgstr` strings respectively. They also clean out those trailing backslashes used by XView's `msgfmt` for continued lines.

Having such an explicit normalizing command allows for importing PO files from other sources, but also eases the evolution of the current convention, evolution driven mostly by aesthetic concerns, as of now. It is easy to make suggested adjustments at a later time, as the normalizing command and eventually, other GNU `gettext` tools should greatly automate conformance. A description of the canonical string format is given below, for the particular benefit of those not having Emacs handy, and who would nevertheless want to handcraft their PO files in nice ways.

Right now, in PO mode, strings are single line or multi-line. A string goes multi-line if and only if it has *embedded* newlines, that is, if it matches '[^\n]\n+[^\n]'. So, we would have:

```
msgstr "\n\nHello, world!\n\n\n"
```

but, replacing the space by a newline, this becomes:

```
msgstr ""
"\n"
"\n"
"Hello,\n"
"world!\n"
"\n"
"\n"
```

We are deliberately using a caricatural example, here, to make the point clearer. Usually, multi-lines are not that bad looking. It is probable that we will implement the following suggestion. We might lump together all initial newlines into the empty string, and also all newlines introducing empty lines (that is, for $n > 1$, the n-1'th last newlines would go together on a separate string), so making the previous example appear:

```
msgstr "\n\n"
"Hello,\n"
"world!\n"
"\n\n"
```

There are a few yet undecided little points about string normalization, to be documented in this manual, once these questions settle.

8.3.5 Translated Entries

Each PO file entry for which the `msgstr` field has been filled with a translation, and which is not marked as fuzzy (see Section 8.3.6 [Fuzzy Entries], page 57), is said to be a *translated* entry. Only translated entries will later be compiled by GNU `msgfmt` and become usable in programs. Other entry types will be excluded; translation will not occur for them.

Some commands are more specifically related to translated entry processing.

t   Find the next translated entry (`po-next-translated-entry`).

T   Find the previous translated entry (`po-previous-translated-entry`).

The commands *t* (`po-next-translated-entry`) and *T* (`po-previous-translated-entry`) move forwards or backwards, chasing for an translated entry. If none is found, the search is extended and wraps around in the PO file buffer.

Translated entries usually result from the translator having edited in a translation for them, Section 8.3.9 [Modifying Translations], page 60. However, if the variable `po-auto-fuzzy-on-edit` is not `nil`, the entry having received a new translation first becomes a fuzzy entry, which ought to be later unfuzzied before becoming an official, genuine translated entry. See Section 8.3.6 [Fuzzy Entries], page 57.

8.3.6 Fuzzy Entries

Each PO file entry may have a set of *attributes*, which are qualities given a name and explicitly associated with the translation, using a special system comment. One of these attributes has the name `fuzzy`, and entries having this attribute are said to have a fuzzy translation. They are called fuzzy entries, for short.

Fuzzy entries, even if they account for translated entries for most other purposes, usually call for revision by the translator. Those may be produced by applying the program `msgmerge` to update an older translated PO files according to a new PO template file, when this tool hypothesises that some new `msgid` has been modified only slightly out of an older one, and chooses to pair what it thinks to be the old translation for the new modified entry. The slight alteration in the original string (the `msgid` string) should often be reflected in the translated string, and this requires the intervention of the translator. For this reason, `msgmerge` might mark some entries as being fuzzy.

Also, the translator may decide herself to mark an entry as fuzzy for her own convenience, when she wants to remember that the entry has to be later revisited. So, some commands are more specifically related to fuzzy entry processing.

`f`   Find the next fuzzy entry (`po-next-fuzzy-entry`).

`F`   Find the previous fuzzy entry (`po-previous-fuzzy-entry`).

`TAB`   Remove the fuzzy attribute of the current entry (`po-unfuzzy`).

The commands `f` (`po-next-fuzzy-entry`) and `F` (`po-previous-fuzzy-entry`) move forwards or backwards, chasing for a fuzzy entry. If none is found, the search is extended and wraps around in the PO file buffer.

The command `TAB` (`po-unfuzzy`) removes the fuzzy attribute associated with an entry, usually leaving it translated. Further, if the variable `po-auto-select-on-unfuzzy` has not the `nil` value, the `TAB` command will automatically chase for another interesting entry to work on. The initial value of `po-auto-select-on-unfuzzy` is `nil`.

The initial value of `po-auto-fuzzy-on-edit` is `nil`. However, if the variable `po-auto-fuzzy-on-edit` is set to `t`, any entry edited through the `RET` command is marked fuzzy, as a way to ensure some kind of double check, later. In this case, the usual paradigm is that an entry becomes fuzzy (if not already) whenever the translator modifies it. If she is satisfied with the translation, she then uses `TAB` to pick another entry to work on, clearing the fuzzy attribute on the same blow. If she is not satisfied yet, she merely uses `SPC` to chase another entry, leaving the entry fuzzy.

The translator may also use the `DEL` command (`po-fade-out-entry`) over any translated entry to mark it as being fuzzy, when she wants to easily leave a trace she wants to later return working at this entry.

Also, when time comes to quit working on a PO file buffer with the `q` command, the translator is asked for confirmation, if fuzzy string still exists.

8.3.7 Untranslated Entries

When `xgettext` originally creates a PO file, unless told otherwise, it initializes the `msgid` field with the untranslated string, and leaves the `msgstr` string to be empty. Such entries, having an empty translation, are said to be *untranslated* entries. Later, when the programmer slightly modifies some string right in the program, this change is later reflected in the PO file by the appearance of a new untranslated entry for the modified string.

The usual commands moving from entry to entry consider untranslated entries on the same level as active entries. Untranslated entries are easily recognizable by the fact they end with 'msgstr ""'.

The work of the translator might be (quite naively) seen as the process of seeking for an untranslated entry, editing a translation for it, and repeating these actions until no untranslated entries remain. Some commands are more specifically related to untranslated entry processing.

u   Find the next untranslated entry (po-next-untranslated-entry).

U   Find the previous untranslated entry (po-previous-untransted-entry).

k   Turn the current entry into an untranslated one (po-kill-msgstr).

The commands u (po-next-untranslated-entry) and U (po-previous-untransted-entry) move forwards or backwards, chasing for an untranslated entry. If none is found, the search is extended and wraps around in the PO file buffer.

An entry can be turned back into an untranslated entry by merely emptying its translation, using the command k (po-kill-msgstr). See Section 8.3.9 [Modifying Translations], page 60.

Also, when time comes to quit working on a PO file buffer with the q command, the translator is asked for confirmation, if some untranslated string still exists.

8.3.8 Obsolete Entries

By *obsolete* PO file entries, we mean those entries which are commented out, usually by msgmerge when it found that the translation is not needed anymore by the package being localized.

The usual commands moving from entry to entry consider obsolete entries on the same level as active entries. Obsolete entries are easily recognizable by the fact that all their lines start with #, even those lines containing msgid or msgstr.

Commands exist for emptying the translation or reinitializing it to the original untranslated string. Commands interfacing with the kill ring may force some previously saved text into the translation. The user may interactively edit the translation. All these commands may apply to obsolete entries, carefully leaving the entry obsolete after the fact.

Moreover, some commands are more specifically related to obsolete entry processing.

o   Find the next obsolete entry (po-next-obsolete-entry).

O   Find the previous obsolete entry (po-previous-obsolete-entry).

DEL   Make an active entry obsolete, or zap out an obsolete entry (po-fade-out-entry).

The commands o (po-next-obsolete-entry) and O (po-previous-obsolete-entry) move forwards or backwards, chasing for an obsolete entry. If none is found, the search is extended and wraps around in the PO file buffer.

PO mode does not provide ways for un-commenting an obsolete entry and making it active, because this would reintroduce an original untranslated string which does not correspond to any marked string in the program sources. This goes with the philosophy of never introducing useless msgid values.

However, it is possible to comment out an active entry, so making it obsolete. GNU `gettext` utilities will later react to the disappearance of a translation by using the untranslated string. The command `DEL` (`po-fade-out-entry`) pushes the current entry a little further towards annihilation. If the entry is active (it is a translated entry), then it is first made fuzzy. If it is already fuzzy, then the entry is merely commented out, with confirmation. If the entry is already obsolete, then it is completely deleted from the PO file. It is easy to recycle the translation so deleted into some other PO file entry, usually one which is untranslated. See Section 8.3.9 [Modifying Translations], page 60.

Here is a quite interesting problem to solve for later development of PO mode, for those nights you are not sleepy. The idea would be that PO mode might become bright enough, one of these days, to make good guesses at retrieving the most probable candidate, among all obsolete entries, for initializing the translation of a newly appeared string. I think it might be a quite hard problem to do this algorithmically, as we have to develop good and efficient measures of string similarity. Right now, PO mode completely lets the decision to the translator, when the time comes to find the adequate obsolete translation, it merely tries to provide handy tools for helping her to do so.

8.3.9 Modifying Translations

PO mode prevents direct modification of the PO file, by the usual means Emacs gives for altering a buffer's contents. By doing so, it pretends helping the translator to avoid little clerical errors about the overall file format, or the proper quoting of strings, as those errors would be easily made. Other kinds of errors are still possible, but some may be caught and diagnosed by the batch validation process, which the translator may always trigger by the `V` command. For all other errors, the translator has to rely on her own judgment, and also on the linguistic reports submitted to her by the users of the translated package, having the same mother tongue.

When the time comes to create a translation, correct an error diagnosed mechanically or reported by a user, the translators have to resort to using the following commands for modifying the translations.

RET   Interactively edit the translation (`po-edit-msgstr`).

LFD
C-j   Reinitialize the translation with the original, untranslated string (`po-msgid-to-msgstr`).

k   Save the translation on the kill ring, and delete it (`po-kill-msgstr`).

w   Save the translation on the kill ring, without deleting it (`po-kill-ring-save-msgstr`).

y   Replace the translation, taking the new from the kill ring (`po-yank-msgstr`).

The command RET (`po-edit-msgstr`) opens a new Emacs window meant to edit in a new translation, or to modify an already existing translation. The new window contains a copy of the translation taken from the current PO file entry, all ready for edition, expunged of all quoting marks, fully modifiable and with the complete extent of Emacs modifying commands. When the translator is done with her modifications, she may use `C-c C-c` to close the subedit window with the automatically requoted results, or `C-c C-k` to abort her modifications. See Section 8.3.11 [Subedit], page 63, for more information.

The command `LFD` (`po-msgid-to-msgstr`) initializes, or reinitializes the translation with the original string. This command is normally used when the translator wants to redo a fresh translation of the original string, disregarding any previous work.

It is possible to arrange so, whenever editing an untranslated entry, the `LFD` command be automatically executed. If you set `po-auto-edit-with-msgid` to `t`, the translation gets initialised with the original string, in case none exists already. The default value for `po-auto-edit-with-msgid` is `nil`.

In fact, whether it is best to start a translation with an empty string, or rather with a copy of the original string, is a matter of taste or habit. Sometimes, the source language and the target language are so different that is simply best to start writing on an empty page. At other times, the source and target languages are so close that it would be a waste to retype a number of words already being written in the original string. A translator may also like having the original string right under her eyes, as she will progressively overwrite the original text with the translation, even if this requires some extra editing work to get rid of the original.

The command `k` (`po-kill-msgstr`) merely empties the translation string, so turning the entry into an untranslated one. But while doing so, its previous contents is put apart in a special place, known as the kill ring. The command `w` (`po-kill-ring-save-msgstr`) has also the effect of taking a copy of the translation onto the kill ring, but it otherwise leaves the entry alone, and does *not* remove the translation from the entry. Both commands use exactly the Emacs kill ring, which is shared between buffers, and which is well known already to Emacs lovers.

The translator may use `k` or `w` many times in the course of her work, as the kill ring may hold several saved translations. From the kill ring, strings may later be reinserted in various Emacs buffers. In particular, the kill ring may be used for moving translation strings between different entries of a single PO file buffer, or if the translator is handling many such buffers at once, even between PO files.

To facilitate exchanges with buffers which are not in PO mode, the translation string put on the kill ring by the `k` command is fully unquoted before being saved: external quotes are removed, multi-line strings are concatenated, and backslash escaped sequences are turned into their corresponding characters. In the special case of obsolete entries, the translation is also uncommented prior to saving.

The command `y` (`po-yank-msgstr`) completely replaces the translation of the current entry by a string taken from the kill ring. Following Emacs terminology, we then say that the replacement string is *yanked* into the PO file buffer. See Section "Yanking" in *The Emacs Editor*. The first time `y` is used, the translation receives the value of the most recent addition to the kill ring. If `y` is typed once again, immediately, without intervening keystrokes, the translation just inserted is taken away and replaced by the second most recent addition to the kill ring. By repeating `y` many times in a row, the translator may travel along the kill ring for saved strings, until she finds the string she really wanted.

When a string is yanked into a PO file entry, it is fully and automatically requoted for complying with the format PO files should have. Further, if the entry is obsolete, PO mode then appropriately push the inserted string inside comments. Once again, translators should not burden themselves with quoting considerations besides, of course, the necessity of the translated string itself respective to the program using it.

Note that *k* or *w* are not the only commands pushing strings on the kill ring, as almost any PO mode command replacing translation strings (or the translator comments) automatically saves the old string on the kill ring. The main exceptions to this general rule are the yanking commands themselves.

To better illustrate the operation of killing and yanking, let's use an actual example, taken from a common situation. When the programmer slightly modifies some string right in the program, his change is later reflected in the PO file by the appearance of a new untranslated entry for the modified string, and the fact that the entry translating the original or unmodified string becomes obsolete. In many cases, the translator might spare herself some work by retrieving the unmodified translation from the obsolete entry, then initializing the untranslated entry `msgstr` field with this retrieved translation. Once this done, the obsolete entry is not wanted anymore, and may be safely deleted.

When the translator finds an untranslated entry and suspects that a slight variant of the translation exists, she immediately uses *m* to mark the current entry location, then starts chasing obsolete entries with *o*, hoping to find some translation corresponding to the unmodified string. Once found, she uses the `DEL` command for deleting the obsolete entry, knowing that `DEL` also *kills* the translation, that is, pushes the translation on the kill ring. Then, *r* returns to the initial untranslated entry, and *y* then *yanks* the saved translation right into the `msgstr` field. The translator is then free to use `RET` for fine tuning the translation contents, and maybe to later use *u*, then *m* again, for going on with the next untranslated string.

When some sequence of keys has to be typed over and over again, the translator may find it useful to become better acquainted with the Emacs capability of learning these sequences and playing them back under request. See Section "Keyboard Macros" in *The Emacs Editor*.

8.3.10 Modifying Comments

Any translation work done seriously will raise many linguistic difficulties, for which decisions have to be made, and the choices further documented. These documents may be saved within the PO file in form of translator comments, which the translator is free to create, delete, or modify at will. These comments may be useful to herself when she returns to this PO file after a while.

Comments not having whitespace after the initial '#', for example, those beginning with '#.' or '#:', are *not* translator comments, they are exclusively created by other `gettext` tools. So, the commands below will never alter such system added comments, they are not meant for the translator to modify. See Chapter 3 [PO Files], page 13.

The following commands are somewhat similar to those modifying translations, so the general indications given for those apply here. See Section 8.3.9 [Modifying Translations], page 60.

#	Interactively edit the translator comments (`po-edit-comment`).
K	Save the translator comments on the kill ring, and delete it (`po-kill-comment`).
W	Save the translator comments on the kill ring, without deleting it (`po-kill-ring-save-comment`).

Y   Replace the translator comments, taking the new from the kill ring (po-yank-
             comment).

These commands parallel PO mode commands for modifying the translation strings, and
behave much the same way as they do, except that they handle this part of PO file comments
meant for translator usage, rather than the translation strings. So, if the descriptions given
below are slightly succinct, it is because the full details have already been given. See
Section 8.3.9 [Modifying Translations], page 60.

The command # (po-edit-comment) opens a new Emacs window containing a copy of
the translator comments on the current PO file entry. If there are no such comments,
PO mode understands that the translator wants to add a comment to the entry, and she
is presented with an empty screen. Comment marks (#) and the space following them
are automatically removed before edition, and reinstated after. For translator comments
pertaining to obsolete entries, the uncommenting and recommenting operations are done
twice. Once in the editing window, the keys C-c C-c allow the translator to tell she is
finished with editing the comment. See Section 8.3.11 [Subedit], page 63, for further details.

Functions found on po-subedit-mode-hook, if any, are executed after the string has
been inserted in the edit buffer.

The command K (po-kill-comment) gets rid of all translator comments, while saving
those comments on the kill ring. The command W (po-kill-ring-save-comment) takes a
copy of the translator comments on the kill ring, but leaves them undisturbed in the current
entry. The command Y (po-yank-comment) completely replaces the translator comments
by a string taken at the front of the kill ring. When this command is immediately repeated,
the comments just inserted are withdrawn, and replaced by other strings taken along the
kill ring.

On the kill ring, all strings have the same nature. There is no distinction between
translation strings and *translator comments* strings. So, for example, let's presume the
translator has just finished editing a translation, and wants to create a new translator
comment to document why the previous translation was not good, just to remember what
was the problem. Foreseeing that she will do that in her documentation, the translator
may want to quote the previous translation in her translator comments. To do so, she may
initialize the translator comments with the previous translation, still at the head of the kill
ring. Because editing already pushed the previous translation on the kill ring, she merely
has to type M-w prior to #, and the previous translation will be right there, all ready for
being introduced by some explanatory text.

On the other hand, presume there are some translator comments already and that the
translator wants to add to those comments, instead of wholly replacing them. Then, she
should edit the comment right away with #. Once inside the editing window, she can use the
regular Emacs commands C-y (yank) and M-y (yank-pop) to get the previous translation
where she likes.

8.3.11 Details of Sub Edition

The PO subedit minor mode has a few peculiarities worth being described in fuller detail.
It installs a few commands over the usual editing set of Emacs, which are described below.

C-c C-c   Complete edition (po-subedit-exit).

C-c C-k   Abort edition (`po-subedit-abort`).

C-c C-a   Consult auxiliary PO files (`po-subedit-cycle-auxiliary`).

The window's contents represents a translation for a given message, or a translator comment. The translator may modify this window to her heart's content. Once this is done, the command *C-c C-c* (`po-subedit-exit`) may be used to return the edited translation into the PO file, replacing the original translation, even if it moved out of sight or if buffers were switched.

If the translator becomes unsatisfied with her translation or comment, to the extent she prefers keeping what was existent prior to the RET or # command, she may use the command *C-c C-k* (`po-subedit-abort`) to merely get rid of edition, while preserving the original translation or comment. Another way would be for her to exit normally with *C-c C-c*, then type U once for undoing the whole effect of last edition.

The command *C-c C-a* (`po-subedit-cycle-auxiliary`) allows for glancing through translations already achieved in other languages, directly while editing the current translation. This may be quite convenient when the translator is fluent at many languages, but of course, only makes sense when such completed auxiliary PO files are already available to her (see Section 8.3.13 [Auxiliary], page 66).

Functions found on `po-subedit-mode-hook`, if any, are executed after the string has been inserted in the edit buffer.

While editing her translation, the translator should pay attention to not inserting unwanted RET (newline) characters at the end of the translated string if those are not meant to be there, or to removing such characters when they are required. Since these characters are not visible in the editing buffer, they are easily introduced by mistake. To help her, RET automatically puts the character < at the end of the string being edited, but this < is not really part of the string. On exiting the editing window with *C-c C-c*, PO mode automatically removes such < and all whitespace added after it. If the translator adds characters after the terminating <, it looses its delimiting property and integrally becomes part of the string. If she removes the delimiting <, then the edited string is taken *as is*, with all trailing newlines, even if invisible. Also, if the translated string ought to end itself with a genuine <, then the delimiting < may not be removed; so the string should appear, in the editing window, as ending with two < in a row.

When a translation (or a comment) is being edited, the translator may move the cursor back into the PO file buffer and freely move to other entries, browsing at will. If, with an edition pending, the translator wanders in the PO file buffer, she may decide to start modifying another entry. Each entry being edited has its own subedit buffer. It is possible to simultaneously edit the translation *and* the comment of a single entry, or to edit entries in different PO files, all at once. Typing RET on a field already being edited merely resumes that particular edit. Yet, the translator should better be comfortable at handling many Emacs windows!

Pending subedits may be completed or aborted in any order, regardless of how or when they were started. When many subedits are pending and the translator asks for quitting the PO file (with the q command), subedits are automatically resumed one at a time, so she may decide for each of them.

8.3.12 C Sources Context

PO mode is particularly powerful when used with PO files created through GNU `gettext` utilities, as those utilities insert special comments in the PO files they generate. Some of these special comments relate the PO file entry to exactly where the untranslated string appears in the program sources.

When the translator gets to an untranslated entry, she is fairly often faced with an original string which is not as informative as it normally should be, being succinct, cryptic, or otherwise ambiguous. Before choosing how to translate the string, she needs to understand better what the string really means and how tight the translation has to be. Most of the time, when problems arise, the only way left to make her judgment is looking at the true program sources from where this string originated, searching for surrounding comments the programmer might have put in there, and looking around for helping clues of *any* kind.

Surely, when looking at program sources, the translator will receive more help if she is a fluent programmer. However, even if she is not versed in programming and feels a little lost in C code, the translator should not be shy at taking a look, once in a while. It is most probable that she will still be able to find some of the hints she needs. She will learn quickly to not feel uncomfortable in program code, paying more attention to programmer's comments, variable and function names (if he dared choosing them well), and overall organization, than to the program code itself.

The following commands are meant to help the translator at getting program source context for a PO file entry.

s   Resume the display of a program source context, or cycle through them (`po-cycle-source-reference`).

M-s   Display of a program source context selected by menu (`po-select-source-reference`).

S   Add a directory to the search path for source files (`po-consider-source-path`).

M-S   Delete a directory from the search path for source files (`po-ignore-source-path`).

The commands *s* (`po-cycle-source-reference`) and *M-s* (`po-select-source-reference`) both open another window displaying some source program file, and already positioned in such a way that it shows an actual use of the string to be translated. By doing so, the command gives source program context for the string. But if the entry has no source context references, or if all references are unresolved along the search path for program sources, then the command diagnoses this as an error.

Even if *s* (or *M-s*) opens a new window, the cursor stays in the PO file window. If the translator really wants to get into the program source window, she ought to do it explicitly, maybe by using command *O*.

When *s* is typed for the first time, or for a PO file entry which is different of the last one used for getting source context, then the command reacts by giving the first context available for this entry, if any. If some context has already been recently displayed for the current PO file entry, and the translator wandered off to do other things, typing *s* again will merely resume, in another window, the context last displayed. In particular, if the translator moved the cursor away from the context in the source file, the command will bring the cursor back to the context. By using *s* many times in a row, with no other commands intervening, PO mode will cycle to the next available contexts for this particular entry, getting back to the first context once the last has been shown.

The command *M-s* behaves differently. Instead of cycling through references, it lets the translator choose a particular reference among many, and displays that reference. It is best used with completion, if the translator types TAB immediately after *M-s*, in response to the question, she will be offered a menu of all possible references, as a reminder of which are the acceptable answers. This command is useful only where there are really many contexts available for a single string to translate.

Program source files are usually found relative to where the PO file stands. As a special provision, when this fails, the file is also looked for, but relative to the directory immediately above it. Those two cases take proper care of most PO files. However, it might happen that a PO file has been moved, or is edited in a different place than its normal location. When this happens, the translator should tell PO mode in which directory normally sits the genuine PO file. Many such directories may be specified, and all together, they constitute what is called the *search path* for program sources. The command *S* (po-consider-source-path) is used to interactively enter a new directory at the front of the search path, and the command *M-S* (po-ignore-source-path) is used to select, with completion, one of the directories she does not want anymore on the search path.

8.3.13 Consulting Auxiliary PO Files

PO mode is able to help the knowledgeable translator, being fluent in many languages, at taking advantage of translations already achieved in other languages she just happens to know. It provides these other language translations as additional context for her own work. Moreover, it has features to ease the production of translations for many languages at once, for translators preferring to work in this way.

An *auxiliary* PO file is an existing PO file meant for the same package the translator is working on, but targeted to a different mother tongue language. Commands exist for declaring and handling auxiliary PO files, and also for showing contexts for the entry under work.

Here are the auxiliary file commands available in PO mode.

a   Seek auxiliary files for another translation for the same entry (po-cycle-auxiliary).

C-c C-a   Switch to a particular auxiliary file (po-select-auxiliary).

A   Declare this PO file as an auxiliary file (po-consider-as-auxiliary).

M-A   Remove this PO file from the list of auxiliary files (po-ignore-as-auxiliary).

Command *A* (po-consider-as-auxiliary) adds the current PO file to the list of auxiliary files, while command *M-A* (po-ignore-as-auxiliary just removes it.

The command a (po-cycle-auxiliary) seeks all auxiliary PO files, round-robin, searching for a translated entry in some other language having an msgid field identical as the one for the current entry. The found PO file, if any, takes the place of the current PO file in the display (its window gets on top). Before doing so, the current PO file is also made into an auxiliary file, if not already. So, a in this newly displayed PO file will seek another PO file, and so on, so repeating a will eventually yield back the original PO file.

The command *C-c C-a* (po-select-auxiliary) asks the translator for her choice of a particular auxiliary file, with completion, and then switches to that selected PO file. The command also checks if the selected file has an msgid field identical as the one for the current entry, and if yes, this entry becomes current. Otherwise, the cursor of the selected file is left undisturbed.

For all this to work fully, auxiliary PO files will have to be normalized, in that way that msgid fields should be written *exactly* the same way. It is possible to write msgid fields in various ways for representing the same string, different writing would break the proper behaviour of the auxiliary file commands of PO mode. This is not expected to be much a problem in practice, as most existing PO files have their msgid entries written by the same GNU gettext tools.

However, PO files initially created by PO mode itself, while marking strings in source files, are normalised differently. So are PO files resulting of the 'M-x normalize' command. Until these discrepancies between PO mode and other GNU gettext tools get fully resolved, the translator should stay aware of normalisation issues.

8.4 Using Translation Compendia

A *compendium* is a special PO file containing a set of translations recurring in many different packages. The translator can use gettext tools to build a new compendium, to add entries to her compendium, and to initialize untranslated entries, or to update already translated entries, from translations kept in the compendium.

8.4.1 Creating Compendia

Basically every PO file consisting of translated entries only can be declared as a valid compendium. Often the translator wants to have special compendia; let's consider two cases: *concatenating PO files* and *extracting a message subset from a PO file*.

8.4.1.1 Concatenate PO Files

To concatenate several valid PO files into one compendium file you can use 'msgcomm' or 'msgcat' (the latter preferred):

```
msgcat -o compendium.po file1.po file2.po
```

By default, msgcat will accumulate divergent translations for the same string. Those occurrences will be marked as fuzzy and highly visible decorated; calling msgcat on file1.po:

```
#: src/hello.c:200
#, c-format
msgid "Report bugs to <%s>.\n"
msgstr "Comunicar 'bugs' a <%s>.\n"
```

and file2.po:

```
#: src/bye.c:100
#, c-format
msgid "Report bugs to <%s>.\n"
msgstr "Comunicar \"bugs\" a <%s>.\n"
```

will result in:

```
#: src/hello.c:200 src/bye.c:100
#, fuzzy, c-format
msgid "Report bugs to <%s>.\n"
msgstr ""
"#-#-#-#-#  file1.po  #-#-#-#-#\n"
"Comunicar 'bugs' a <%s>.\n"
"#-#-#-#-#  file2.po  #-#-#-#-#\n"
"Comunicar \"bugs\" a <%s>.\n"
```

The translator will have to resolve this "conflict" manually; she has to decide whether the first or the second version is appropriate (or provide a new translation), to delete the "marker lines", and finally to remove the fuzzy mark.

If the translator knows in advance the first found translation of a message is always the best translation she can make use to the '--use-first' switch:

```
msgcat --use-first -o compendium.po file1.po file2.po
```

A good compendium file must not contain fuzzy or untranslated entries. If input files are "dirty" you must preprocess the input files or postprocess the result using 'msgattrib --translated --no-fuzzy'.

8.4.1.2 Extract a Message Subset from a PO File

Nobody wants to translate the same messages again and again; thus you may wish to have a compendium file containing getopt.c messages.

To extract a message subset (e.g., all getopt.c messages) from an existing PO file into one compendium file you can use 'msggrep':

```
msggrep --location src/getopt.c -o compendium.po file.po
```

8.4.2 Using Compendia

You can use a compendium file to initialize a translation from scratch or to update an already existing translation.

8.4.2.1 Initialize a New Translation File

Since a PO file with translations does not exist the translator can merely use /dev/null to fake the "old" translation file.

```
msgmerge --compendium compendium.po -o file.po /dev/null file.pot
```

8.4.2.2 Update an Existing Translation File

Concatenate the compendium file(s) and the existing PO, merge the result with the POT file and remove the obsolete entries (optional, here done using 'msgattrib'):

```
msgcat --use-first -o update.po compendium1.po compendium2.po file.po
msgmerge update.po file.pot | msgattrib --no-obsolete > file.po
```

9 Manipulating PO Files

Sometimes it is necessary to manipulate PO files in a way that is better performed automatically than by hand. GNU `gettext` includes a complete set of tools for this purpose.

When merging two packages into a single package, the resulting POT file will be the concatenation of the two packages' POT files. Thus the maintainer must concatenate the two existing package translations into a single translation catalog, for each language. This is best performed using '`msgcat`'. It is then the translators' duty to deal with any possible conflicts that arose during the merge.

When a translator takes over the translation job from another translator, but she uses a different character encoding in her locale, she will convert the catalog to her character encoding. This is best done through the '`msgconv`' program.

When a maintainer takes a source file with tagged messages from another package, he should also take the existing translations for this source file (and not let the translators do the same job twice). One way to do this is through '`msggrep`', another is to create a POT file for that source file and use '`msgmerge`'.

When a translator wants to adjust some translation catalog for a special dialect or orthography — for example, German as written in Switzerland versus German as written in Germany — she needs to apply some text processing to every message in the catalog. The tool for doing this is '`msgfilter`'.

Another use of `msgfilter` is to produce approximately the POT file for which a given PO file was made. This can be done through a filter command like '`msgfilter sed -e d | sed -e '/^# /d'`'. Note that the original POT file may have had different comments and different plural message counts, that's why it's better to use the original POT file if available.

When a translator wants to check her translations, for example according to orthography rules or using a non-interactive spell checker, she can do so using the '`msgexec`' program.

When third party tools create PO or POT files, sometimes duplicates cannot be avoided. But the GNU `gettext` tools give an error when they encounter duplicate msgids in the same file and in the same domain. To merge duplicates, the '`msguniq`' program can be used.

'`msgcomm`' is a more general tool for keeping or throwing away duplicates, occurring in different files.

'`msgcmp`' can be used to check whether a translation catalog is completely translated.

'`msgattrib`' can be used to select and extract only the fuzzy or untranslated messages of a translation catalog.

'`msgen`' is useful as a first step for preparing English translation catalogs. It copies each message's msgid to its msgstr.

Finally, for those applications where all these various programs are not sufficient, a library '`libgettextpo`' is provided that can be used to write other specialized programs that process PO files.

9.1 Invoking the `msgcat` Program

        `msgcat [option] [inputfile]...`

The `msgcat` program concatenates and merges the specified PO files. It finds messages which are common to two or more of the specified PO files. By using the `--more-than` option, greater commonality may be requested before messages are printed. Conversely, the `--less-than` option may be used to specify less commonality before messages are printed (i.e. '`--less-than=2`' will only print the unique messages). Translations, comments, extracted comments, and file positions will be cumulated, except that if `--use-first` is specified, they will be taken from the first PO file to define them.

9.1.1 Input file location

'`inputfile ...`'

        Input files.

'`-f file`'
'`--files-from=file`'

        Read the names of the input files from *file* instead of getting them from the command line.

'`-D directory`'
'`--directory=directory`'

        Add *directory* to the list of directories. Source files are searched relative to this list of directories. The resulting `.po` file will be written relative to the current directory, though.

   If *inputfile* is '`-`', standard input is read.

9.1.2 Output file location

'`-o file`'
'`--output-file=file`'

        Write output to specified file.

The results are written to standard output if no output file is specified or if it is '`-`'.

9.1.3 Message selection

'`-< number`'
'`--less-than=number`'

        Print messages with less than *number* definitions, defaults to infinite if not set.

'`-> number`'
'`--more-than=number`'

        Print messages with more than *number* definitions, defaults to 0 if not set.

'`-u`'
'`--unique`'

        Shorthand for '`--less-than=2`'. Requests that only unique messages be printed.

9.1.4 Input file syntax

'-p'
'--properties-input'
> Assume the input files are Java ResourceBundles in Java `.properties` syntax, not in PO file syntax.

'--stringtable-input'
> Assume the input files are NeXTstep/GNUstep localized resource files in `.strings` syntax, not in PO file syntax.

9.1.5 Output details

'-t'
'--to-code=*name*'
> Specify encoding for output.

'--use-first'
> Use first available translation for each message. Don't merge several translations into one.

'--lang=*catalogname*'
> Specify the 'Language' field to be used in the header entry. See Section 6.2 [Header Entry], page 44 for the meaning of this field. Note: The 'Language-Team' and 'Plural-Forms' fields are left unchanged.

'--color'
'--color=*when*'
> Specify whether or when to use colors and other text attributes. See Section 9.11.1 [The –color option], page 95 for details.

'--style=*style_file*'
> Specify the CSS style rule file to use for `--color`. See Section 9.11.3 [The –style option], page 96 for details.

'--force-po'
> Always write an output file even if it contains no message.

'-i'
'--indent'
> Write the .po file using indented style.

'--no-location'
> Do not write '#: *filename*:*line*' lines.

'-n'
'--add-location=*type*'
> Generate '#: *filename*:*line*' lines (default).
>
> The optional *type* can be either 'full', 'file', or 'never'. If it is not given or 'full', it generates the lines with both file name and line number. If it is 'file', the line number part is omitted. If it is 'never', it completely suppresses the lines (same as `--no-location`).

'--strict'
> Write out a strict Uniforum conforming PO file. Note that this Uniforum format should be avoided because it doesn't support the GNU extensions.

'-p'
'--properties-output'
> Write out a Java ResourceBundle in Java `.properties` syntax. Note that this file format doesn't support plural forms and silently drops obsolete messages.

'--stringtable-output'
> Write out a NeXTstep/GNUstep localized resource file in `.strings` syntax. Note that this file format doesn't support plural forms.

'-w *number*'
'--width=*number*'
> Set the output page width. Long strings in the output files will be split across multiple lines in order to ensure that each line's width (= number of screen columns) is less or equal to the given *number*.

'--no-wrap'
> Do not break long message lines. Message lines whose width exceeds the output page width will not be split into several lines. Only file reference lines which are wider than the output page width will be split.

'-s'
'--sort-output'
> Generate sorted output. Note that using this option makes it much harder for the translator to understand each message's context.

'-F'
'--sort-by-file'
> Sort output by file location.

9.1.6 Informative output

'-h'
'--help'   Display this help and exit.

'-V'
'--version'
> Output version information and exit.

9.2 Invoking the `msgconv` Program

> `msgconv [option] [inputfile]`

The `msgconv` program converts a translation catalog to a different character encoding.

9.2.1 Input file location

'*inputfile*'
> Input PO file.

'-D *directory*'
'--directory=*directory*'

> Add *directory* to the list of directories. Source files are searched relative to this list of directories. The resulting .po file will be written relative to the current directory, though.

If no *inputfile* is given or if it is '-', standard input is read.

9.2.2 Output file location

'-o *file*'
'--output-file=*file*'

> Write output to specified file.

The results are written to standard output if no output file is specified or if it is '-'.

9.2.3 Conversion target

'-t'
'--to-code=*name*'

> Specify encoding for output.

The default encoding is the current locale's encoding.

9.2.4 Input file syntax

'-P'
'--properties-input'

> Assume the input file is a Java ResourceBundle in Java .properties syntax, not in PO file syntax.

'--stringtable-input'

> Assume the input file is a NeXTstep/GNUstep localized resource file in .strings syntax, not in PO file syntax.

9.2.5 Output details

'--color'
'--color=*when*'

> Specify whether or when to use colors and other text attributes. See Section 9.11.1 [The –color option], page 95 for details.

'--style=*style_file*'

> Specify the CSS style rule file to use for --color. See Section 9.11.3 [The –style option], page 96 for details.

'--force-po'

> Always write an output file even if it contains no message.

'-i'
'--indent'

> Write the .po file using indented style.

'--no-location'

> Do not write '#: *filename*:*line*' lines.

'-n'
'--add-location=*type*'
> Generate '#: *filename*:*line*' lines (default).
>
> The optional *type* can be either 'full', 'file', or 'never'. If it is not given or 'full', it generates the lines with both file name and line number. If it is 'file', the line number part is omitted. If it is 'never', it completely suppresses the lines (same as --no-location).

'--strict'
> Write out a strict Uniforum conforming PO file. Note that this Uniforum format should be avoided because it doesn't support the GNU extensions.

'-p'
'--properties-output'
> Write out a Java ResourceBundle in Java .properties syntax. Note that this file format doesn't support plural forms and silently drops obsolete messages.

'--stringtable-output'
> Write out a NeXTstep/GNUstep localized resource file in .strings syntax. Note that this file format doesn't support plural forms.

'-w *number*'
'--width=*number*'
> Set the output page width. Long strings in the output files will be split across multiple lines in order to ensure that each line's width (= number of screen columns) is less or equal to the given *number*.

'--no-wrap'
> Do not break long message lines. Message lines whose width exceeds the output page width will not be split into several lines. Only file reference lines which are wider than the output page width will be split.

'-s'
'--sort-output'
> Generate sorted output. Note that using this option makes it much harder for the translator to understand each message's context.

'-F'
'--sort-by-file'
> Sort output by file location.

9.2.6 Informative output

'-h'
'--help'   Display this help and exit.

'-V'
'--version'
> Output version information and exit.

9.3 Invoking the `msggrep` Program

> `msggrep [option] [inputfile]`

The `msggrep` program extracts all messages of a translation catalog that match a given pattern or belong to some given source files.

9.3.1 Input file location

`'inputfile'`

> Input PO file.

`'-D directory'`
`'--directory=directory'`

> Add *directory* to the list of directories. Source files are searched relative to this list of directories. The resulting `.po` file will be written relative to the current directory, though.

If no *inputfile* is given or if it is '-', standard input is read.

9.3.2 Output file location

`'-o file'`
`'--output-file=file'`

> Write output to specified file.

The results are written to standard output if no output file is specified or if it is '-'.

9.3.3 Message selection

> `[-N sourcefile]... [-M domainname]...`
> `[-J msgctxt-pattern] [-K msgid-pattern] [-T msgstr-pattern]`
> `[-C comment-pattern]`

A message is selected if

- it comes from one of the specified source files,
- or if it comes from one of the specified domains,
- or if '-J' is given and its context (msgctxt) matches *msgctxt-pattern*,
- or if '-K' is given and its key (msgid or msgid_plural) matches *msgid-pattern*,
- or if '-T' is given and its translation (msgstr) matches *msgstr-pattern*,
- or if '-C' is given and the translator's comment matches *comment-pattern*.

When more than one selection criterion is specified, the set of selected messages is the union of the selected messages of each criterion.

msgctxt-pattern or *msgid-pattern* or *msgstr-pattern* syntax:

> `[-E | -F] [-e pattern | -f file]...`

patterns are basic regular expressions by default, or extended regular expressions if -E is given, or fixed strings if -F is given.

`'-N sourcefile'`
`'--location=sourcefile'`

> Select messages extracted from *sourcefile*. *sourcefile* can be either a literal file name or a wildcard pattern.

'-M *domainname*'
'--domain=*domainname*'
>   Select messages belonging to domain *domainname*.

'-J'
'--msgctxt'
>   Start of patterns for the msgctxt.

'-K'
'--msgid'   Start of patterns for the msgid.

'-T'
'--msgstr'
>   Start of patterns for the msgstr.

'-C'
'--comment'
>   Start of patterns for the translator's comment.

'-X'
'--extracted-comment'
>   Start of patterns for the extracted comments.

'-E'
'--extended-regexp'
>   Specify that *pattern* is an extended regular expression.

'-F'
'--fixed-strings'
>   Specify that *pattern* is a set of newline-separated strings.

'-e *pattern*'
'--regexp=*pattern*'
>   Use *pattern* as a regular expression.

'-f *file*'
'--file=*file*'
>   Obtain *pattern* from *file*.

'-i'
'--ignore-case'
>   Ignore case distinctions.

'-v'
'--invert-match'
>   Output only the messages that do not match any selection criterion, instead of
>   the messages that match a selection criterion.

9.3.4 Input file syntax

'-P'
'--properties-input'
>   Assume the input file is a Java ResourceBundle in Java .properties syntax,
>   not in PO file syntax.

'--stringtable-input'

> Assume the input file is a NeXTstep/GNUstep localized resource file in .strings syntax, not in PO file syntax.

9.3.5 Output details

'--color'
'--color=*when*'

> Specify whether or when to use colors and other text attributes. See Section 9.11.1 [The –color option], page 95 for details.

'--style=*style_file*'

> Specify the CSS style rule file to use for --color. See Section 9.11.3 [The –style option], page 96 for details.

'--force-po'

> Always write an output file even if it contains no message.

'--indent'

> Write the .po file using indented style.

'--no-location'

> Do not write '#: *filename*:*line*' lines.

'-n'
'--add-location=*type*'

> Generate '#: *filename*:*line*' lines (default).
>
> The optional *type* can be either 'full', 'file', or 'never'. If it is not given or 'full', it generates the lines with both file name and line number. If it is 'file', the line number part is omitted. If it is 'never', it completely suppresses the lines (same as --no-location).

'--strict'

> Write out a strict Uniforum conforming PO file. Note that this Uniforum format should be avoided because it doesn't support the GNU extensions.

'-p'
'--properties-output'

> Write out a Java ResourceBundle in Java .properties syntax. Note that this file format doesn't support plural forms and silently drops obsolete messages.

'--stringtable-output'

> Write out a NeXTstep/GNUstep localized resource file in .strings syntax. Note that this file format doesn't support plural forms.

'-w *number*'
'--width=*number*'

> Set the output page width. Long strings in the output files will be split across multiple lines in order to ensure that each line's width (= number of screen columns) is less or equal to the given *number*.

'--no-wrap'

> Do not break long message lines. Message lines whose width exceeds the output page width will not be split into several lines. Only file reference lines which are wider than the output page width will be split.

'--sort-output'

> Generate sorted output. Note that using this option makes it much harder for the translator to understand each message's context.

'--sort-by-file'

> Sort output by file location.

9.3.6 Informative output

'-h'

'--help'   Display this help and exit.

'-V'

'--version'

> Output version information and exit.

9.3.7 Examples

To extract the messages that come from the source files `gnulib-lib/error.c` and `gnulib-lib/getopt.c`:

```
msggrep -N gnulib-lib/error.c -N gnulib-lib/getopt.c input.po
```

To extract the messages that contain the string "Please specify" in the original string:

```
msggrep --msgid -F -e 'Please specify' input.po
```

To extract the messages that have a context specifier of either "Menu>File" or "Menu>Edit" or a submenu of them:

```
msggrep --msgctxt -E -e '^Menu>(File|Edit)' input.po
```

To extract the messages whose translation contains one of the strings in the file `wordlist.txt`:

```
msggrep --msgstr -F -f wordlist.txt input.po
```

9.4 Invoking the `msgfilter` Program

> `msgfilter [`*option*`]` *filter* `[`*filter-option*`]`

The `msgfilter` program applies a filter to all translations of a translation catalog.

During each *filter* invocation, the environment variable `MSGFILTER_MSGID` is bound to the message's msgid, and the environment variable `MSGFILTER_LOCATION` is bound to the location in the PO file of the message. If the message has a context, the environment variable `MSGFILTER_MSGCTXT` is bound to the message's msgctxt, otherwise it is unbound. If the message has a plural form, environment variable `MSGFILTER_MSGID_PLURAL` is bound to the message's msgid_plural and `MSGFILTER_PLURAL_FORM` is bound to the order number of the plural actually processed (starting with 0), otherwise both are unbound. If the message has a previous msgid (added by `msgmerge`), environment variable `MSGFILTER_PREV_MSGCTXT` is bound to the message's previous msgctxt, `MSGFILTER_PREV_MSGID` is bound to the previous msgid, and `MSGFILTER_PREV_MSGID_PLURAL` is bound to the previous msgid_plural.

9.4.1 Input file location

'-i *inputfile*'
'--input=*inputfile*'
>   Input PO file.

'-D *directory*'
'--directory=*directory*'
>   Add *directory* to the list of directories. Source files are searched relative to this
>   list of directories. The resulting .po file will be written relative to the current
>   directory, though.

If no *inputfile* is given or if it is '-', standard input is read.

9.4.2 Output file location

'-o *file*'
'--output-file=*file*'
>   Write output to specified file.

The results are written to standard output if no output file is specified or if it is '-'.

9.4.3 The filter

The *filter* can be any program that reads a translation from standard input and writes a
modified translation to standard output. A frequently used filter is 'sed'. A few particular
built-in filters are also recognized.

'--newline'
>   Add newline at the end of each input line and also strip the ending newline
>   from the output line.

Note: If the filter is not a built-in filter, you have to care about encodings: It is your
responsibility to ensure that the *filter* can cope with input encoded in the translation catalog's encoding. If the *filter* wants input in a particular encoding, you can in a first step
convert the translation catalog to that encoding using the 'msgconv' program, before invoking 'msgfilter'. If the *filter* wants input in the locale's encoding, but you want to avoid
the locale's encoding, then you can first convert the translation catalog to UTF-8 using
the 'msgconv' program and then make 'msgfilter' work in an UTF-8 locale, by using the
LC_ALL environment variable.

Note: Most translations in a translation catalog don't end with a newline character. For
this reason, unless the --newline option is used, it is important that the *filter* recognizes
its last input line even if it ends without a newline, and that it doesn't add an undesired
trailing newline at the end. The 'sed' program on some platforms is known to ignore the
last line of input if it is not terminated with a newline. You can use GNU sed instead; it
does not have this limitation.

9.4.4 Useful *filter-options* when the *filter* is 'sed'

'-e *script*'
'--expression=*script*'
>   Add *script* to the commands to be executed.

'-f *scriptfile*'
'--file=*scriptfile*'
>   Add the contents of *scriptfile* to the commands to be executed.

'-n'
'--quiet'
'--silent'
>   Suppress automatic printing of pattern space.

9.4.5 Built-in *filters*

The filter 'recode-sr-latin' is recognized as a built-in filter. The command 'recode-sr-latin' converts Serbian text, written in the Cyrillic script, to the Latin script. The command 'msgfilter recode-sr-latin' applies this conversion to the translations of a PO file. Thus, it can be used to convert an sr.po file to an sr@latin.po file.

The filter 'quot' is recognized as a built-in filter. The command 'msgfilter quot' converts any quotations surrounded by a pair of '"', ''', and ''.

The filter 'boldquot' is recognized as a built-in filter. The command 'msgfilter boldquot' converts any quotations surrounded by a pair of '"', ''', and '', also adding the VT100 escape sequences to the text to decorate it as bold.

The use of built-in filters is not sensitive to the current locale's encoding. Moreover, when used with a built-in filter, 'msgfilter' can automatically convert the message catalog to the UTF-8 encoding when needed.

9.4.6 Input file syntax

'-P'
'--properties-input'
>   Assume the input file is a Java ResourceBundle in Java .properties syntax, not in PO file syntax.

'--stringtable-input'
>   Assume the input file is a NeXTstep/GNUstep localized resource file in .strings syntax, not in PO file syntax.

9.4.7 Output details

'--color'
'--color=*when*'
>   Specify whether or when to use colors and other text attributes. See Section 9.11.1 [The –color option], page 95 for details.

'--style=*style_file*'
>   Specify the CSS style rule file to use for --color. See Section 9.11.3 [The –style option], page 96 for details.

'--force-po'
>   Always write an output file even if it contains no message.

'--indent'
>   Write the .po file using indented style.

'`--keep-header`'

> Keep the header entry, i.e. the message with '`msgid ""`', unmodified, instead of filtering it. By default, the header entry is subject to filtering like any other message.

'`--no-location`'

> Do not write '`#: filename:line`' lines.

'`-n`'
'`--add-location=type`'

> Generate '`#: filename:line`' lines (default).
>
> The optional *type* can be either '`full`', '`file`', or '`never`'. If it is not given or '`full`', it generates the lines with both file name and line number. If it is '`file`', the line number part is omitted. If it is '`never`', it completely suppresses the lines (same as `--no-location`).

'`--strict`'

> Write out a strict Uniforum conforming PO file. Note that this Uniforum format should be avoided because it doesn't support the GNU extensions.

'`-p`'
'`--properties-output`'

> Write out a Java ResourceBundle in Java `.properties` syntax. Note that this file format doesn't support plural forms and silently drops obsolete messages.

'`--stringtable-output`'

> Write out a NeXTstep/GNUstep localized resource file in `.strings` syntax. Note that this file format doesn't support plural forms.

'`-w number`'
'`--width=number`'

> Set the output page width. Long strings in the output files will be split across multiple lines in order to ensure that each line's width (= number of screen columns) is less or equal to the given *number*.

'`--no-wrap`'

> Do not break long message lines. Message lines whose width exceeds the output page width will not be split into several lines. Only file reference lines which are wider than the output page width will be split.

'`-s`'
'`--sort-output`'

> Generate sorted output. Note that using this option makes it much harder for the translator to understand each message's context.

'`-F`'
'`--sort-by-file`'

> Sort output by file location.

9.4.8 Informative output

'`-h`'
'`--help`'   Display this help and exit.

'`-V`'
'`--version`'
>   Output version information and exit.

9.4.9 Examples

To convert German translations to Swiss orthography (in an UTF-8 locale):

```
msgconv -t UTF-8 de.po | msgfilter sed -e 's/ß/ss/g'
```

To convert Serbian translations in Cyrillic script to Latin script:

```
msgfilter recode-sr-latin < sr.po
```

9.5 Invoking the `msguniq` Program

```
msguniq [option] [inputfile]
```

The `msguniq` program unifies duplicate translations in a translation catalog. It finds duplicate translations of the same message ID. Such duplicates are invalid input for other programs like `msgfmt`, `msgmerge` or `msgcat`. By default, duplicates are merged together. When using the '`--repeated`' option, only duplicates are output, and all other messages are discarded. Comments and extracted comments will be cumulated, except that if '`--use-first`' is specified, they will be taken from the first translation. File positions will be cumulated. When using the '`--unique`' option, duplicates are discarded.

9.5.1 Input file location

'`inputfile`'
>   Input PO file.

'`-D directory`'
'`--directory=directory`'
>   Add *directory* to the list of directories. Source files are searched relative to this list of directories. The resulting `.po` file will be written relative to the current directory, though.

If no *inputfile* is given or if it is '`-`', standard input is read.

9.5.2 Output file location

'`-o file`'
'`--output-file=file`'
>   Write output to specified file.

The results are written to standard output if no output file is specified or if it is '`-`'.

9.5.3 Message selection

'`-d`'
'`--repeated`'
>   Print only duplicates.

'`-u`'
'`--unique`'
>   Print only unique messages, discard duplicates.

9.5.4 Input file syntax

'-P'
'--properties-input'

> Assume the input file is a Java ResourceBundle in Java `.properties` syntax, not in PO file syntax.

'--stringtable-input'

> Assume the input file is a NeXTstep/GNUstep localized resource file in `.strings` syntax, not in PO file syntax.

9.5.5 Output details

'-t'
'--to-code=*name*'

> Specify encoding for output.

'--use-first'

> Use first available translation for each message. Don't merge several translations into one.

'--color'
'--color=*when*'

> Specify whether or when to use colors and other text attributes. See Section 9.11.1 [The –color option], page 95 for details.

'--style=*style_file*'

> Specify the CSS style rule file to use for `--color`. See Section 9.11.3 [The –style option], page 96 for details.

'--force-po'

> Always write an output file even if it contains no message.

'-i'
'--indent'

> Write the .po file using indented style.

'--no-location'

> Do not write '#: *filename*:*line*' lines.

'-n'
'--add-location=*type*'

> Generate '#: *filename*:*line*' lines (default).
>
> The optional *type* can be either 'full', 'file', or 'never'. If it is not given or 'full', it generates the lines with both file name and line number. If it is 'file', the line number part is omitted. If it is 'never', it completely suppresses the lines (same as `--no-location`).

'--strict'

> Write out a strict Uniforum conforming PO file. Note that this Uniforum format should be avoided because it doesn't support the GNU extensions.

'-p'
'--properties-output'

Write out a Java ResourceBundle in Java .properties syntax. Note that this
file format doesn't support plural forms and silently drops obsolete messages.

'--stringtable-output'

Write out a NeXTstep/GNUstep localized resource file in .strings syntax.
Note that this file format doesn't support plural forms.

'-w number'
'--width=number'

Set the output page width. Long strings in the output files will be split across
multiple lines in order to ensure that each line's width (= number of screen
columns) is less or equal to the given number.

'--no-wrap'

Do not break long message lines. Message lines whose width exceeds the output
page width will not be split into several lines. Only file reference lines which
are wider than the output page width will be split.

'-s'
'--sort-output'

Generate sorted output. Note that using this option makes it much harder for
the translator to understand each message's context.

'-F'
'--sort-by-file'

Sort output by file location.

9.5.6 Informative output

'-h'
'--help'   Display this help and exit.

'-V'
'--version'

Output version information and exit.

9.6 Invoking the msgcomm Program

msgcomm [option] [inputfile]...

The msgcomm program finds messages which are common to two or more of the specified
PO files. By using the --more-than option, greater commonality may be requested before
messages are printed. Conversely, the --less-than option may be used to specify less
commonality before messages are printed (i.e. '--less-than=2' will only print the unique
messages). Translations, comments and extracted comments will be preserved, but only
from the first PO file to define them. File positions from all PO files will be cumulated.

9.6.1 Input file location

'inputfile ...'

Input files.

'-f *file*'
'--files-from=*file*'
> Read the names of the input files from *file* instead of getting them from the command line.

'-D *directory*'
'--directory=*directory*'
> Add *directory* to the list of directories. Source files are searched relative to this list of directories. The resulting .po file will be written relative to the current directory, though.

If *inputfile* is '-', standard input is read.

9.6.2 Output file location

'-o *file*'
'--output-file=*file*'
> Write output to specified file.

The results are written to standard output if no output file is specified or if it is '-'.

9.6.3 Message selection

'-< *number*'
'--less-than=*number*'
> Print messages with less than *number* definitions, defaults to infinite if not set.

'-> *number*'
'--more-than=*number*'
> Print messages with more than *number* definitions, defaults to 1 if not set.

'-u'
'--unique'
> Shorthand for '--less-than=2'. Requests that only unique messages be printed.

9.6.4 Input file syntax

'-p'
'--properties-input'
> Assume the input files are Java ResourceBundles in Java .properties syntax, not in PO file syntax.

'--stringtable-input'
> Assume the input files are NeXTstep/GNUstep localized resource files in .strings syntax, not in PO file syntax.

9.6.5 Output details

'--color'
'--color=*when*'
> Specify whether or when to use colors and other text attributes. See Section 9.11.1 [The –color option], page 95 for details.

'--style=*style_file*'

> Specify the CSS style rule file to use for --color. See Section 9.11.3 [The –style option], page 96 for details.

'--force-po'

> Always write an output file even if it contains no message.

'-i'

'--indent'

> Write the .po file using indented style.

'--no-location'

> Do not write '#: *filename:line*' lines.

'-n'

'--add-location=*type*'

> Generate '#: *filename:line*' lines (default).
>
> The optional *type* can be either 'full', 'file', or 'never'. If it is not given or 'full', it generates the lines with both file name and line number. If it is 'file', the line number part is omitted. If it is 'never', it completely suppresses the lines (same as --no-location).

'--strict'

> Write out a strict Uniforum conforming PO file. Note that this Uniforum format should be avoided because it doesn't support the GNU extensions.

'-p'

'--properties-output'

> Write out a Java ResourceBundle in Java .properties syntax. Note that this file format doesn't support plural forms and silently drops obsolete messages.

'--stringtable-output'

> Write out a NeXTstep/GNUstep localized resource file in .strings syntax. Note that this file format doesn't support plural forms.

'-w *number*'

'--width=*number*'

> Set the output page width. Long strings in the output files will be split across multiple lines in order to ensure that each line's width (= number of screen columns) is less or equal to the given *number*.

'--no-wrap'

> Do not break long message lines. Message lines whose width exceeds the output page width will not be split into several lines. Only file reference lines which are wider than the output page width will be split.

'-s'

'--sort-output'

> Generate sorted output. Note that using this option makes it much harder for the translator to understand each message's context.

'-F'

'--sort-by-file'

> Sort output by file location.

'--omit-header'
> Don't write header with 'msgid ""' entry.

9.6.6 Informative output

'-h'
'--help'   Display this help and exit.

'-V'
'--version'
> Output version information and exit.

9.7 Invoking the msgcmp Program

> msgcmp [option] def.po ref.pot

The msgcmp program compares two Uniforum style .po files to check that both contain the same set of msgid strings. The def.po file is an existing PO file with the translations. The ref.pot file is the last created PO file, or a PO Template file (generally created by xgettext). This is useful for checking that you have translated each and every message in your program. Where an exact match cannot be found, fuzzy matching is used to produce better diagnostics.

9.7.1 Input file location

'def.po'   Translations.

'ref.pot'   References to the sources.

'-D directory'
'--directory=directory'
> Add directory to the list of directories. Source files are searched relative to this list of directories.

9.7.2 Operation modifiers

'-m'
'--multi-domain'
> Apply ref.pot to each of the domains in def.po.

'-N'
'--no-fuzzy-matching'
> Do not use fuzzy matching when an exact match is not found. This may speed up the operation considerably.

'--use-fuzzy'
> Consider fuzzy messages in the def.po file like translated messages. Note that using this option is usually wrong, because fuzzy messages are exactly those which have not been validated by a human translator.

'--use-untranslated'
> Consider untranslated messages in the def.po file like translated messages. Note that using this option is usually wrong.

9.7.3 Input file syntax

'-P'

'--properties-input'

> Assume the input files are Java ResourceBundles in Java `.properties` syntax, not in PO file syntax.

'--stringtable-input'

> Assume the input files are NeXTstep/GNUstep localized resource files in `.strings` syntax, not in PO file syntax.

9.7.4 Informative output

'-h'

'--help'   Display this help and exit.

'-V'

'--version'

> Output version information and exit.

9.8 Invoking the `msgattrib` Program

> `msgattrib [option] [inputfile]`

The `msgattrib` program filters the messages of a translation catalog according to their attributes, and manipulates the attributes.

9.8.1 Input file location

'`inputfile`'

> Input PO file.

'-D `directory`'

'--directory=`directory`'

> Add `directory` to the list of directories. Source files are searched relative to this list of directories. The resulting `.po` file will be written relative to the current directory, though.

If no *inputfile* is given or if it is '-', standard input is read.

9.8.2 Output file location

'-o `file`'

'--output-file=`file`'

> Write output to specified file.

The results are written to standard output if no output file is specified or if it is '-'.

9.8.3 Message selection

'--translated'

> Keep translated messages, remove untranslated messages.

'--untranslated'

> Keep untranslated messages, remove translated messages.

'--no-fuzzy'
> Remove 'fuzzy' marked messages.

'--only-fuzzy'
> Keep 'fuzzy' marked messages, remove all other messages.

'--no-obsolete'
> Remove obsolete #~ messages.

'--only-obsolete'
> Keep obsolete #~ messages, remove all other messages.

9.8.4 Attribute manipulation

Attributes are modified after the message selection/removal has been performed. If the '--only-file' or '--ignore-file' option is specified, the attribute modification is applied only to those messages that are listed in the *only-file* and not listed in the *ignore-file*.

'--set-fuzzy'
> Set all messages 'fuzzy'.

'--clear-fuzzy'
> Set all messages non-'fuzzy'.

'--set-obsolete'
> Set all messages obsolete.

'--clear-obsolete'
> Set all messages non-obsolete.

'--previous'
> When setting 'fuzzy' mark, keep "previous msgid" of translated messages.

'--clear-previous'
> Remove the "previous msgid" ('#|') comments from all messages.

'--empty'   When removing 'fuzzy' mark, also set msgstr empty.

'--only-file=*file*'
> Limit the attribute changes to entries that are listed in *file*. *file* should be a PO or POT file.

'--ignore-file=*file*'
> Limit the attribute changes to entries that are not listed in *file*. *file* should be a PO or POT file.

'--fuzzy'   Synonym for '--only-fuzzy --clear-fuzzy': It keeps only the fuzzy messages and removes their 'fuzzy' mark.

'--obsolete'
> Synonym for '--only-obsolete --clear-obsolete': It keeps only the obsolete messages and makes them non-obsolete.

9.8.5 Input file syntax

'-P'

'--properties-input'

>   Assume the input file is a Java ResourceBundle in Java .properties syntax, not in PO file syntax.

'--stringtable-input'

>   Assume the input file is a NeXTstep/GNUstep localized resource file in .strings syntax, not in PO file syntax.

9.8.6 Output details

'--color'

'--color=*when*'

>   Specify whether or when to use colors and other text attributes. See Section 9.11.1 [The –color option], page 95 for details.

'--style=*style_file*'

>   Specify the CSS style rule file to use for --color. See Section 9.11.3 [The –style option], page 96 for details.

'--force-po'

>   Always write an output file even if it contains no message.

'-i'

'--indent'

>   Write the .po file using indented style.

'--no-location'

>   Do not write '#: *filename*:*line*' lines.

'-n'

'--add-location=*type*'

>   Generate '#: *filename*:*line*' lines (default).

>   The optional *type* can be either 'full', 'file', or 'never'. If it is not given or 'full', it generates the lines with both file name and line number. If it is 'file', the line number part is omitted. If it is 'never', it completely suppresses the lines (same as --no-location).

'--strict'

>   Write out a strict Uniforum conforming PO file. Note that this Uniforum format should be avoided because it doesn't support the GNU extensions.

'-p'

'--properties-output'

>   Write out a Java ResourceBundle in Java .properties syntax. Note that this file format doesn't support plural forms and silently drops obsolete messages.

'--stringtable-output'

>   Write out a NeXTstep/GNUstep localized resource file in .strings syntax. Note that this file format doesn't support plural forms.

'`-w number`'
'`--width=number`'

> Set the output page width. Long strings in the output files will be split across multiple lines in order to ensure that each line's width (= number of screen columns) is less or equal to the given *number*.

'`--no-wrap`'

> Do not break long message lines. Message lines whose width exceeds the output page width will not be split into several lines. Only file reference lines which are wider than the output page width will be split.

'`-s`'
'`--sort-output`'

> Generate sorted output. Note that using this option makes it much harder for the translator to understand each message's context.

'`-F`'
'`--sort-by-file`'

> Sort output by file location.

9.8.7 Informative output

'`-h`'
'`--help`'   Display this help and exit.

'`-V`'
'`--version`'

> Output version information and exit.

9.9 Invoking the `msgen` Program

> `msgen [option] inputfile`

The `msgen` program creates an English translation catalog. The input file is the last created English PO file, or a PO Template file (generally created by xgettext). Untranslated entries are assigned a translation that is identical to the msgid.

Note: '`msginit --no-translator --locale=en`' performs a very similar task. The main difference is that `msginit` cares specially about the header entry, whereas `msgen` doesn't.

9.9.1 Input file location

'`inputfile`'

> Input PO or POT file.

'`-D directory`'
'`--directory=directory`'

> Add *directory* to the list of directories. Source files are searched relative to this list of directories. The resulting `.po` file will be written relative to the current directory, though.

If *inputfile* is '`-`', standard input is read.

9.9.2 Output file location

'-o *file*'
'--output-file=*file*'
> Write output to specified file.

The results are written to standard output if no output file is specified or if it is '-'.

9.9.3 Input file syntax

'-p'
'--properties-input'
> Assume the input file is a Java ResourceBundle in Java `.properties` syntax, not in PO file syntax.

'--stringtable-input'
> Assume the input file is a NeXTstep/GNUstep localized resource file in `.strings` syntax, not in PO file syntax.

9.9.4 Output details

'--lang=*catalogname*'
> Specify the 'Language' field to be used in the header entry. See Section 6.2 [Header Entry], page 44 for the meaning of this field. Note: The 'Language-Team' and 'Plural-Forms' fields are not set by this option.

'--color'
'--color=*when*'
> Specify whether or when to use colors and other text attributes. See Section 9.11.1 [The –color option], page 95 for details.

'--style=*style_file*'
> Specify the CSS style rule file to use for `--color`. See Section 9.11.3 [The –style option], page 96 for details.

'--force-po'
> Always write an output file even if it contains no message.

'-i'
'--indent'
> Write the .po file using indented style.

'--no-location'
> Do not write '#: *filename*:*line*' lines.

'-n'
'--add-location=*type*'
> Generate '#: *filename*:*line*' lines (default).
>
> The optional *type* can be either 'full', 'file', or 'never'. If it is not given or 'full', it generates the lines with both file name and line number. If it is 'file', the line number part is omitted. If it is 'never', it completely suppresses the lines (same as `--no-location`).

'--strict'

> Write out a strict Uniforum conforming PO file. Note that this Uniforum format should be avoided because it doesn't support the GNU extensions.

'-p'
'--properties-output'

> Write out a Java ResourceBundle in Java `.properties` syntax. Note that this file format doesn't support plural forms and silently drops obsolete messages.

'--stringtable-output'

> Write out a NeXTstep/GNUstep localized resource file in `.strings` syntax. Note that this file format doesn't support plural forms.

'-w *number*'
'--width=*number*'

> Set the output page width. Long strings in the output files will be split across multiple lines in order to ensure that each line's width (= number of screen columns) is less or equal to the given *number*.

'--no-wrap'

> Do not break long message lines. Message lines whose width exceeds the output page width will not be split into several lines. Only file reference lines which are wider than the output page width will be split.

'-s'
'--sort-output'

> Generate sorted output. Note that using this option makes it much harder for the translator to understand each message's context.

'-F'
'--sort-by-file'

> Sort output by file location.

9.9.5 Informative output

'-h'
'--help'   Display this help and exit.

'-V'
'--version'

> Output version information and exit.

9.10 Invoking the `msgexec` Program

> `msgexec [option] command [command-option]`

The `msgexec` program applies a command to all translations of a translation catalog. The *command* can be any program that reads a translation from standard input. It is invoked once for each translation. Its output becomes msgexec's output. `msgexec`'s return code is the maximum return code across all invocations.

A special builtin command called '0' outputs the translation, followed by a null byte. The output of '`msgexec 0`' is suitable as input for '`xargs -0`'.

'--newline'
>   Add newline at the end of each input line.

During each *command* invocation, the environment variable MSGEXEC_MSGID is bound to the message's msgid, and the environment variable MSGEXEC_LOCATION is bound to the location in the PO file of the message. If the message has a context, the environment variable MSGEXEC_MSGCTXT is bound to the message's msgctxt, otherwise it is unbound. If the message has a plural form, environment variable MSGEXEC_MSGID_PLURAL is bound to the message's msgid_plural and MSGEXEC_PLURAL_FORM is bound to the order number of the plural actually processed (starting with 0), otherwise both are unbound. If the message has a previous msgid (added by **msgmerge**), environment variable MSGEXEC_PREV_MSGCTXT is bound to the message's previous msgctxt, MSGEXEC_PREV_MSGID is bound to the previous msgid, and MSGEXEC_PREV_MSGID_PLURAL is bound to the previous msgid_plural.

Note: It is your responsibility to ensure that the *command* can cope with input encoded in the translation catalog's encoding. If the *command* wants input in a particular encoding, you can in a first step convert the translation catalog to that encoding using the '**msgconv**' program, before invoking '**msgexec**'. If the *command* wants input in the locale's encoding, but you want to avoid the locale's encoding, then you can first convert the translation catalog to UTF-8 using the '**msgconv**' program and then make '**msgexec**' work in an UTF-8 locale, by using the LC_ALL environment variable.

9.10.1 Input file location

'-i *inputfile*'
'--input=*inputfile*'
>   Input PO file.

'-D *directory*'
'--directory=*directory*'
>   Add *directory* to the list of directories. Source files are searched relative to this list of directories. The resulting .po file will be written relative to the current directory, though.

If no *inputfile* is given or if it is '-', standard input is read.

9.10.2 Input file syntax

'-p'
'--properties-input'
>   Assume the input file is a Java ResourceBundle in Java .properties syntax, not in PO file syntax.

'--stringtable-input'
>   Assume the input file is a NeXTstep/GNUstep localized resource file in .strings syntax, not in PO file syntax.

9.10.3 Informative output

'-h'
'--help'   Display this help and exit.

'`-V`'
'`--version`'
> Output version information and exit.

9.11 Highlighting parts of PO files

Translators are usually only interested in seeing the untranslated and fuzzy messages of a PO file. Also, when a message is set fuzzy because the msgid changed, they want to see the differences between the previous msgid and the current one (especially if the msgid is long and only few words in it have changed). Finally, it's always welcome to highlight the different sections of a message in a PO file (comments, msgid, msgstr, etc.).

Such highlighting is possible through the `msgcat` options '`--color`' and '`--style`'.

9.11.1 The `--color` option

The '`--color=`*when*' option specifies under which conditions colorized output should be generated. The *when* part can be one of the following:

`always`
`yes`   The output will be colorized.

`never`
`no`   The output will not be colorized.

`auto`
`tty`   The output will be colorized if the output device is a tty, i.e. when the output goes directly to a text screen or terminal emulator window.

`html`   The output will be colorized and be in HTML format.

'`--color`' is equivalent to '`--color=yes`'. The default is '`--color=auto`'.

Thus, a command like '`msgcat vi.po`' will produce colorized output when called by itself in a command window. Whereas in a pipe, such as '`msgcat vi.po | less -R`', it will not produce colorized output. To get colorized output in this situation nevertheless, use the command '`msgcat --color vi.po | less -R`'.

The '`--color=html`' option will produce output that can be viewed in a browser. This can be useful, for example, for Indic languages, because the renderic of Indic scripts in browser is usually better than in terminal emulators.

Note that the output produced with the `--color` option is *not* a valid PO file in itself. It contains additional terminal-specific escape sequences or HTML tags. A PO file reader will give a syntax error when confronted with such content. Except for the '`--color=html`' case, you therefore normally don't need to save output produced with the `--color` option in a file.

9.11.2 The environment variable `TERM`

The environment variable `TERM` contains a identifier for the text window's capabilities. You can get a detailed list of these cababilities by using the '`infocmp`' command, using '`man 5 terminfo`' as a reference.

When producing text with embedded color directives, `msgcat` looks at the `TERM` variable. Text windows today typically support at least 8 colors. Often, however, the text window supports 16 or more colors, even though the `TERM` variable is set to a identifier denoting only 8 supported colors. It can be worth setting the `TERM` variable to a different value in these cases:

xterm   `xterm` is in most cases built with support for 16 colors. It can also be built with support for 88 or 256 colors (but not both). You can try to set `TERM` to either `xterm-16color`, `xterm-88color`, or `xterm-256color`.

rxvt   `rxvt` is often built with support for 16 colors. You can try to set `TERM` to `rxvt-16color`.

konsole   `konsole` too is often built with support for 16 colors. You can try to set `TERM` to `konsole-16color` or `xterm-16color`.

After setting `TERM`, you can verify it by invoking 'msgcat --color=test' and seeing whether the output looks like a reasonable color map.

9.11.3 The --style option

The '`--style=style_file`' option specifies the style file to use when colorizing. It has an effect only when the `--color` option is effective.

If the `--style` option is not specified, the environment variable `PO_STYLE` is considered. It is meant to point to the user's preferred style for PO files.

The default style file is `$prefix/share/gettext/styles/po-default.css`, where `$prefix` is the installation location.

A few style files are predefined:

po-vim.css
        This style imitates the look used by vim 7.

po-emacs-x.css
        This style imitates the look used by GNU Emacs 21 and 22 in an X11 window.

po-emacs-xterm.css
po-emacs-xterm16.css
po-emacs-xterm256.css
        This style imitates the look used by GNU Emacs 22 in a terminal of type 'xterm' (8 colors) or 'xterm-16color' (16 colors) or 'xterm-256color' (256 colors), respectively.

You can use these styles without specifying a directory. They are actually located in `$prefix/share/gettext/styles/`, where `$prefix` is the installation location.

You can also design your own styles. This is described in the next section.

9.11.4 Style rules for PO files

The same style file can be used for styling of a PO file, for terminal output and for HTML output. It is written in CSS (Cascading Style Sheet) syntax. See `http://www.w3.org/TR/css2/cover.html` for a formal definition of CSS. Many HTML authoring tutorials also contain explanations of CSS.

In the case of HTML output, the style file is embedded in the HTML output. In the case of text output, the style file is interpreted by the `msgcat` program. This means, in particular, that when `@import` is used with relative file names, the file names are

— relative to the resulting HTML file, in the case of HTML output,

— relative to the style sheet containing the `@import`, in the case of text output. (Actually, `@import`s are not yet supported in this case, due to a limitation in `libcroco`.)

CSS rules are built up from selectors and declarations. The declarations specify graphical properties; the selectors specify specify when they apply.

In PO files, the following simple selectors (based on "CSS classes", see the CSS2 spec, section 5.8.3) are supported.

- Selectors that apply to entire messages:

  `.header`   This matches the header entry of a PO file.

  `.translated`
  > This matches a translated message.

  `.untranslated`
  > This matches an untranslated message (i.e. a message with empty translation).

  `.fuzzy`   This matches a fuzzy message (i.e. a message which has a translation that needs review by the translator).

  `.obsolete`
  > This matches an obsolete message (i.e. a message that was translated but is not needed by the current POT file any more).

- Selectors that apply to parts of a message in PO syntax. Recall the general structure of a message in PO syntax:

  ```
  white-space
  #  translator-comments
  #. extracted-comments
  #: reference...
  #, flag...
  #| msgid previous-untranslated-string
  msgid untranslated-string
  msgstr translated-string
  ```

  `.comment`   This matches all comments (translator comments, extracted comments, source file reference comments, flag comments, previous message comments, as well as the entire obsolete messages).

  `.translator-comment`
  > This matches the translator comments.

  `.extracted-comment`
  > This matches the extracted comments, i.e. the comments placed by the programmer at the attention of the translator.

  `.reference-comment`
  > This matches the source file reference comments (entire lines).

  `.reference`
  > This matches the individual source file references inside the source file reference comment lines.

`.flag-comment`
> This matches the flag comment lines (entire lines).

`.flag`   This matches the individual flags inside flag comment lines.

`.fuzzy-flag`
> This matches the 'fuzzy' flag inside flag comment lines.

`.previous-comment`
> This matches the comments containing the previous untranslated string (entire lines).

`.previous`
> This matches the previous untranslated string including the string delimiters, the associated keywords (`msgid` etc.) and the spaces between them.

`.msgid`   This matches the untranslated string including the string delimiters, the associated keywords (`msgid` etc.) and the spaces between them.

`.msgstr`   This matches the translated string including the string delimiters, the associated keywords (`msgstr` etc.) and the spaces between them.

`.keyword`   This matches the keywords (`msgid`, `msgstr`, etc.).

`.string`   This matches strings, including the string delimiters (double quotes).

- Selectors that apply to parts of strings:

  `.text`   This matches the entire contents of a string (excluding the string delimiters, i.e. the double quotes).

  `.escape-sequence`
  > This matches an escape sequence (starting with a backslash).

  `.format-directive`
  > This matches a format string directive (starting with a '%' sign in the case of most programming languages, with a '{' in the case of `java-format` and `csharp-format`, with a '~' in the case of `lisp-format` and `scheme-format`, or with '$' in the case of `sh-format`).

  `.invalid-format-directive`
  > This matches an invalid format string directive.

  `.added`   In an untranslated string, this matches a part of the string that was not present in the previous untranslated string. (Not yet implemented in this release.)

  `.changed`   In an untranslated string or in a previous untranslated string, this matches a part of the string that is changed or replaced. (Not yet implemented in this release.)

  `.removed`   In a previous untranslated string, this matches a part of the string that is not present in the current untranslated string. (Not yet implemented in this release.)

These selectors can be combined to hierarchical selectors. For example,

```
.msgstr .invalid-format-directive { color: red; }
```

will highlight the invalid format directives in the translated strings.

In text mode, pseudo-classes (CSS2 spec, section 5.11) and pseudo-elements (CSS2 spec, section 5.12) are not supported.

The declarations in HTML mode are not limited; any graphical attribute supported by the browsers can be used.

The declarations in text mode are limited to the following properties. Other properties will be silently ignored.

`color` (CSS2 spec, section 14.1)

`background-color` (CSS2 spec, section 14.2.1)

> These properties is supported. Colors will be adjusted to match the terminal's capabilities. Note that many terminals support only 8 colors.

`font-weight` (CSS2 spec, section 15.2.3)

> This property is supported, but most terminals can only render two different weights: `normal` and `bold`. Values >= 600 are rendered as `bold`.

`font-style` (CSS2 spec, section 15.2.3)

> This property is supported. The values `italic` and `oblique` are rendered the same way.

`text-decoration` (CSS2 spec, section 16.3.1)

> This property is supported, limited to the values `none` and `underline`.

9.11.5 Customizing `less` for viewing PO files

The '`less`' program is a popular text file browser for use in a text screen or terminal emulator. It also supports text with embedded escape sequences for colors and text decorations.

You can use `less` to view a PO file like this (assuming an UTF-8 environment):

```
msgcat --to-code=UTF-8 --color xyz.po | less -R
```

You can simplify this to this simple command:

```
less xyz.po
```

after these three preparations:

1. Add the options '`-R`' and '`-f`' to the `LESS` environment variable. In sh shells:

   ```
   $ LESS="$LESS -R -f"
   $ export LESS
   ```

2. If your system does not already have the `lessopen.sh` and `lessclose.sh` scripts, create them and set the `LESSOPEN` and `LESSCLOSE` environment variables, as indicated in the manual page ('`man less`').

3. Add to `lessopen.sh` a piece of script that recognizes PO files through their file extension and invokes `msgcat` on them, producing a temporary file. Like this:

   ```
   case "$1" in
     *.po)
       tmpfile=`mktemp "${TMPDIR-/tmp}/less.XXXXXX"`
       msgcat --to-code=UTF-8 --color "$1" > "$tmpfile"
       echo "$tmpfile"
       exit 0
       ;;
   esac
   ```

9.12 Writing your own programs that process PO files

For the tasks for which a combination of 'msgattrib', 'msgcat' etc. is not sufficient, a set of C functions is provided in a library, to make it possible to process PO files in your own programs. When you use this library, you don't need to write routines to parse the PO file; instead, you retrieve a pointer in memory to each of messages contained in the PO file. Functions for writing PO files are not provided at this time.

The functions are declared in the header file '<gettext-po.h>', and are defined in a library called 'libgettextpo'.

po_file_t   [Data Type]
> This is a pointer type that refers to the contents of a PO file, after it has been read into memory.

po_message_iterator_t   [Data Type]
> This is a pointer type that refers to an iterator that produces a sequence of messages.

po_message_t   [Data Type]
> This is a pointer type that refers to a message of a PO file, including its translation.

po_file_t po_file_read (*const char *filename*)   [Function]
> The **po_file_read** function reads a PO file into memory. The file name is given as argument. The return value is a handle to the PO file's contents, valid until **po_file_free** is called on it. In case of error, the return value is NULL, and **errno** is set.

void po_file_free (*po_file_t file*)   [Function]
> The **po_file_free** function frees a PO file's contents from memory, including all messages that are only implicitly accessible through iterators.

const char * const * po_file_domains (*po_file_t file*)   [Function]
> The **po_file_domains** function returns the domains for which the given PO file has messages. The return value is a NULL terminated array which is valid as long as the *file* handle is valid. For PO files which contain no 'domain' directive, the return value contains only one domain, namely the default domain "messages".

po_message_iterator_t po_message_iterator (*po_file_t file,*   [Function]
>   *const char *domain*)
> The **po_message_iterator** returns an iterator that will produce the messages of *file* that belong to the given *domain*. If *domain* is NULL, the default domain is used instead. To list the messages, use the function **po_next_message** repeatedly.

void po_message_iterator_free (*po_message_iterator_t iterator*)   [Function]
> The **po_message_iterator_free** function frees an iterator previously allocated through the **po_message_iterator** function.

po_message_t po_next_message (*po_message_iterator_t iterator*)   [Function]
> The **po_next_message** function returns the next message from *iterator* and advances the iterator. It returns NULL when the iterator has reached the end of its message list.

The following functions returns details of a `po_message_t`. Recall that the results are
valid as long as the *file* handle is valid.

const char * po_message_msgid (*po_message_t message*)   [Function]
    The `po_message_msgid` function returns the `msgid` (untranslated English string) of
    a message. This is guaranteed to be non-NULL.

const char * po_message_msgid_plural (*po_message_t message*)   [Function]
    The `po_message_msgid_plural` function returns the `msgid_plural` (untranslated
    English plural string) of a message with plurals, or NULL for a message without plural.

const char * po_message_msgstr (*po_message_t message*)   [Function]
    The `po_message_msgstr` function returns the `msgstr` (translation) of a message. For
    an untranslated message, the return value is an empty string.

const char * po_message_msgstr_plural (*po_message_t message*,   [Function]
        int index)
    The `po_message_msgstr_plural` function returns the `msgstr[index]` of a message
    with plurals, or NULL when the *index* is out of range or for a message without plural.

Here is an example code how these functions can be used.

```
const char *filename = ...;
po_file_t file = po_file_read (filename);

if (file == NULL)
  error (EXIT_FAILURE, errno, "couldn't open the PO file %s", filename);
{
  const char * const *domains = po_file_domains (file);
  const char * const *domainp;

  for (domainp = domains; *domainp; domainp++)
    {
      const char *domain = *domainp;
      po_message_iterator_t iterator = po_message_iterator (file, domain);

      for (;;)
        {
          po_message_t *message = po_next_message (iterator);

          if (message == NULL)
            break;
          {
            const char *msgid = po_message_msgid (message);
            const char *msgstr = po_message_msgstr (message);


            ...

          }
        }
```

```
        po_message_iterator_free (iterator);
      }
  }
po_file_free (file);
```

10 Producing Binary MO Files

10.1 Invoking the `msgfmt` Program

```
msgfmt [option] filename.po ...
```
The `msgfmt` programs generates a binary message catalog from a textual translation description.

10.1.1 Input file location

'`filename.po ...`'
'`-D directory`'
'`--directory=directory`'

> Add *directory* to the list of directories. Source files are searched relative to this list of directories. The resulting binary file will be written relative to the current directory, though.

If an input file is '`-`', standard input is read.

10.1.2 Operation mode

'`-j`'
'`--java`' Java mode: generate a Java `ResourceBundle` class.

'`--java2`' Like –java, and assume Java2 (JDK 1.2 or higher).

'`--csharp`'
> C# mode: generate a .NET .dll file containing a subclass of `GettextResourceSet`.

'`--csharp-resources`'
> C# resources mode: generate a .NET `.resources` file.

'`--tcl`' Tcl mode: generate a tcl/msgcat `.msg` file.

'`--qt`' Qt mode: generate a Qt `.qm` file.

'`--desktop`'
> Desktop Entry mode: generate a `.desktop` file.

10.1.3 Output file location

'`-o file`'
'`--output-file=file`'
> Write output to specified file.

'`--strict`'
> Direct the program to work strictly following the Uniforum/Sun implementation. Currently this only affects the naming of the output file. If this option is not given the name of the output file is the same as the domain name. If the strict Uniforum mode is enabled the suffix `.mo` is added to the file name if it is not already present.

> We find this behaviour of Sun's implementation rather silly and so by default this mode is *not* selected.

If the output *file* is '-', output is written to standard output.

10.1.4 Output file location in Java mode

'-r *resource*'
'--resource=*resource*'
>   Specify the resource name.

'-l *locale*'
'--locale=*locale*'
>   Specify the locale name, either a language specification of the form *ll* or a
>   combined language and country specification of the form *ll_CC*.

'-d *directory*'
>   Specify the base directory of classes directory hierarchy.

'--source'
>   Produce a .java source file, instead of a compiled .class file.

The class name is determined by appending the locale name to the resource name, separated with an underscore. The '-d' option is mandatory. The class is written under the specified directory.

10.1.5 Output file location in C# mode

'-r *resource*'
'--resource=*resource*'
>   Specify the resource name.

'-l *locale*'
'--locale=*locale*'
>   Specify the locale name, either a language specification of the form *ll* or a
>   combined language and country specification of the form *ll_CC*.

'-d *directory*'
>   Specify the base directory for locale dependent .dll files.

The '-l' and '-d' options are mandatory. The .dll file is written in a subdirectory of the specified directory whose name depends on the locale.

10.1.6 Output file location in Tcl mode

'-l *locale*'
'--locale=*locale*'
>   Specify the locale name, either a language specification of the form *ll* or a
>   combined language and country specification of the form *ll_CC*.

'-d *directory*'
>   Specify the base directory of .msg message catalogs.

The '-l' and '-d' options are mandatory. The .msg file is written in the specified directory.

10.1.7 Desktop Entry mode operations

'--template=*template*'

> Specify a .desktop file used as a template.

'-k[*keywordspec*]'
'--keyword[=*keywordspec*]'

> Specify *keywordspec* as an additional keyword to be looked for. Without a *keywordspec*, the option means to not use default keywords.

'-l *locale*'
'--locale=*locale*'

> Specify the locale name, either a language specification of the form *ll* or a combined language and country specification of the form *ll_CC*.

'-d *directory*'

> Specify the base directory of .msg message catalogs.

To generate a '.desktop' file for a single locale, you can use it as follows.

```
msgfmt --desktop --template=template --locale=locale \
   -o file filename.po ...
```

On the other hand, when using msgfmt from a Makefile, it is cumbersome to loop over all locales under a particular directory. msgfmt provides a special operation mode for this use-case. To generate a '.desktop' file from multiple '.po' files under a directory, specify the directory with the '-d' option.

```
msgfmt --desktop --template=template -d directory -o file
```

msgfmt first reads the 'LINGUAS' file under *directory*, and then processes all '.po' files listed there. You can also limit the locales to a subset, through the 'LINGUAS' environment variable.

For either operation modes, the '-o' and '--template' options are mandatory.

10.1.8 Input file syntax

'-P'
'--properties-input'

> Assume the input files are Java ResourceBundles in Java .properties syntax, not in PO file syntax.

'--stringtable-input'

> Assume the input files are NeXTstep/GNUstep localized resource files in .strings syntax, not in PO file syntax.

10.1.9 Input file interpretation

'-c'
'--check'   Perform all the checks implied by --check-format, --check-header, --check-domain.

'--check-format'

> Check language dependent format strings.

If the string represents a format string used in a `printf`-like function both strings should have the same number of '%' format specifiers, with matching types. If the flag `c-format` or `possible-c-format` appears in the special comment `#,` for this entry a check is performed. For example, the check will diagnose using '%.*s' against '%s', or '%d' against '%s', or '%d' against '%x'. It can even handle positional parameters.

Normally the `xgettext` program automatically decides whether a string is a format string or not. This algorithm is not perfect, though. It might regard a string as a format string though it is not used in a `printf`-like function and so `msgfmt` might report errors where there are none.

To solve this problem the programmer can dictate the decision to the `xgettext` program (see Section 15.3.1 [c-format], page 161). The translator should not consider removing the flag from the `#,` line. This "fix" would be reversed again as soon as `msgmerge` is called the next time.

'`--check-header`'

> Verify presence and contents of the header entry. See Section 6.2 [Header Entry], page 44, for a description of the various fields in the header entry.

'`--check-domain`'

> Check for conflicts between domain directives and the `--output-file` option

'`-C`'
'`--check-compatibility`'

> Check that GNU msgfmt behaves like X/Open msgfmt. This will give an error when attempting to use the GNU extensions.

'`--check-accelerators[=char]`'

> Check presence of keyboard accelerators for menu items. This is based on the convention used in some GUIs that a keyboard accelerator in a menu item string is designated by an immediately preceding '&' character. Sometimes a keyboard accelerator is also called "keyboard mnemonic". This check verifies that if the untranslated string has exactly one '&' character, the translated string has exactly one '&' as well. If this option is given with a *char* argument, this *char* should be a non-alphanumeric character and is used as keyboard accelerator mark instead of '&'.

'`-f`'
'`--use-fuzzy`'

> Use fuzzy entries in output. Note that using this option is usually wrong, because fuzzy messages are exactly those which have not been validated by a human translator.

10.1.10 Output details

'`-a number`'
'`--alignment=number`'

> Align strings to *number* bytes (default: 1).

'--endianness=*byteorder*'

>Write out 32-bit numbers in the given byte order. The possible values are `big` and `little`. The default depends on the platform, namely on the endianness of the CPU.

>MO files of any endianness can be used on any platform. When a MO file has an endianness other than the platform's one, the 32-bit numbers from the MO file are swapped at runtime. The performance impact is negligible.

>This option can be useful to produce MO files that are independent of the platform.

'--no-hash'

>Don't include a hash table in the binary file. Lookup will be more expensive at run time (binary search instead of hash table lookup).

10.1.11 Informative output

'-h'
'--help'   Display this help and exit.

'-V'
'--version'

>Output version information and exit.

'--statistics'

>Print statistics about translations. When the option --verbose is used in combination with --statistics, the input file name is printed in front of the statistics line.

'-v'
'--verbose'

>Increase verbosity level.

10.2 Invoking the `msgunfmt` Program

>msgunfmt [*option*] [*file*]...

The `msgunfmt` program converts a binary message catalog to a Uniforum style .po file.

10.2.1 Operation mode

'-j'
'--java'   Java mode: input is a Java `ResourceBundle` class.

'--csharp'

>C# mode: input is a .NET .dll file containing a subclass of `GettextResourceSet`.

'--csharp-resources'

>C# resources mode: input is a .NET `.resources` file.

'--tcl'   Tcl mode: input is a tcl/msgcat `.msg` file.

10.2.2 Input file location

'`file ...`' Input .mo files.

If no input *file* is given or if it is '`-`', standard input is read.

10.2.3 Input file location in Java mode

'`-r `*resource*'
'`--resource=`*resource*'
> Specify the resource name.

'`-l `*locale*'
'`--locale=`*locale*'
> Specify the locale name, either a language specification of the form *ll* or a combined language and country specification of the form *ll_CC*.

The class name is determined by appending the locale name to the resource name, separated with an underscore. The class is located using the `CLASSPATH`.

10.2.4 Input file location in C# mode

'`-r `*resource*'
'`--resource=`*resource*'
> Specify the resource name.

'`-l `*locale*'
'`--locale=`*locale*'
> Specify the locale name, either a language specification of the form *ll* or a combined language and country specification of the form *ll_CC*.

'`-d `*directory*'
> Specify the base directory for locale dependent `.dll` files.

The '`-l`' and '`-d`' options are mandatory. The `.msg` file is located in a subdirectory of the specified directory whose name depends on the locale.

10.2.5 Input file location in Tcl mode

'`-l `*locale*'
'`--locale=`*locale*'
> Specify the locale name, either a language specification of the form *ll* or a combined language and country specification of the form *ll_CC*.

'`-d `*directory*'
> Specify the base directory of `.msg` message catalogs.

The '`-l`' and '`-d`' options are mandatory. The `.msg` file is located in the specified directory.

10.2.6 Output file location

'`-o `*file*'
'`--output-file=`*file*'
> Write output to specified file.

The results are written to standard output if no output file is specified or if it is '`-`'.

10.2.7 Output details

'`--color`'
'`--color=when`'

> Specify whether or when to use colors and other text attributes. See Section 9.11.1 [The –color option], page 95 for details.

'`--style=style_file`'

> Specify the CSS style rule file to use for `--color`. See Section 9.11.3 [The –style option], page 96 for details.

'`--force-po`'

> Always write an output file even if it contains no message.

'`-i`'
'`--indent`'

> Write the .po file using indented style.

'`--strict`'

> Write out a strict Uniforum conforming PO file. Note that this Uniforum format should be avoided because it doesn't support the GNU extensions.

'`-p`'
'`--properties-output`'

> Write out a Java ResourceBundle in Java `.properties` syntax. Note that this file format doesn't support plural forms and silently drops obsolete messages.

'`--stringtable-output`'

> Write out a NeXTstep/GNUstep localized resource file in `.strings` syntax. Note that this file format doesn't support plural forms.

'`-w number`'
'`--width=number`'

> Set the output page width. Long strings in the output files will be split across multiple lines in order to ensure that each line's width (= number of screen columns) is less or equal to the given *number*.

'`--no-wrap`'

> Do not break long message lines. Message lines whose width exceeds the output page width will not be split into several lines. Only file reference lines which are wider than the output page width will be split.

'`-s`'
'`--sort-output`'

> Generate sorted output. Note that using this option makes it much harder for the translator to understand each message's context.

10.2.8 Informative output

'`-h`'
'`--help`'   Display this help and exit.

'`-V`'
'`--version`'

> Output version information and exit.

'`-v`'
'`--verbose`'
> Increase verbosity level.

10.3 The Format of GNU MO Files

The format of the generated MO files is best described by a picture, which appears below.

The first two words serve the identification of the file. The magic number will always signal GNU MO files. The number is stored in the byte order of the generating machine, so the magic number really is two numbers: `0x950412de` and `0xde120495`.

The second word describes the current revision of the file format, composed of a major and a minor revision number. The revision numbers ensure that the readers of MO files can distinguish new formats from old ones and handle their contents, as far as possible. For now the major revision is 0 or 1, and the minor revision is also 0 or 1. More revisions might be added in the future. A program seeing an unexpected major revision number should stop reading the MO file entirely; whereas an unexpected minor revision number means that the file can be read but will not reveal its full contents, when parsed by a program that supports only smaller minor revision numbers.

The version is kept separate from the magic number, instead of using different magic numbers for different formats, mainly because `/etc/magic` is not updated often.

Follow a number of pointers to later tables in the file, allowing for the extension of the prefix part of MO files without having to recompile programs reading them. This might become useful for later inserting a few flag bits, indication about the charset used, new tables, or other things.

Then, at offset O and offset T in the picture, two tables of string descriptors can be found. In both tables, each string descriptor uses two 32 bits integers, one for the string length, another for the offset of the string in the MO file, counting in bytes from the start of the file. The first table contains descriptors for the original strings, and is sorted so the original strings are in increasing lexicographical order. The second table contains descriptors for the translated strings, and is parallel to the first table: to find the corresponding translation one has to access the array slot in the second array with the same index.

Having the original strings sorted enables the use of simple binary search, for when the MO file does not contain an hashing table, or for when it is not practical to use the hashing table provided in the MO file. This also has another advantage, as the empty string in a PO file GNU `gettext` is usually *translated* into some system information attached to that particular MO file, and the empty string necessarily becomes the first in both the original and translated tables, making the system information very easy to find.

The size S of the hash table can be zero. In this case, the hash table itself is not contained in the MO file. Some people might prefer this because a precomputed hashing table takes disk space, and does not win *that* much speed. The hash table contains indices to the sorted array of strings in the MO file. Conflict resolution is done by double hashing. The precise hashing algorithm used is fairly dependent on GNU `gettext` code, and is not documented here.

As for the strings themselves, they follow the hash file, and each is terminated with a `NUL`, and this `NUL` is not counted in the length which appears in the string descriptor. The `msgfmt` program has an option selecting the alignment for MO file strings. With this option, each string is separately aligned so it starts at an offset which is a multiple of the alignment value. On some RISC machines, a correct alignment will speed things up.

Contexts are stored by storing the concatenation of the context, a `EOT` byte, and the original string, instead of the original string.

Plural forms are stored by letting the plural of the original string follow the singular of the original string, separated through a `NUL` byte. The length which appears in the string descriptor includes both. However, only the singular of the original string takes part in the hash table lookup. The plural variants of the translation are all stored consecutively, separated through a `NUL` byte. Here also, the length in the string descriptor includes all of them.

Nothing prevents a MO file from having embedded `NUL`s in strings. However, the program interface currently used already presumes that strings are `NUL` terminated, so embedded `NUL`s are somewhat useless. But the MO file format is general enough so other interfaces would be later possible, if for example, we ever want to implement wide characters right in MO files, where `NUL` bytes may accidentally appear. (No, we don't want to have wide characters in MO files. They would make the file unnecessarily large, and the '`wchar_t`' type being platform dependent, MO files would be platform dependent as well.)

This particular issue has been strongly debated in the GNU `gettext` development forum, and it is expectable that MO file format will evolve or change over time. It is even possible that many formats may later be supported concurrently. But surely, we have to start somewhere, and the MO file format described here is a good start. Nothing is cast in concrete, and the format may later evolve fairly easily, so we should feel comfortable with the current approach.

```
          byte
                +------------------------------------------+
         0  | magic number = 0x950412de                |
            |                                          |
         4  | file format revision = 0                 |
            |                                          |
         8  | number of strings                        | == N
            |                                          |
        12  | offset of table with original strings    | == O
            |                                          |
        16  | offset of table with translation strings | == T
            |                                          |
        20  | size of hashing table                    | == S
            |                                          |
        24  | offset of hashing table                  | == H
            |                                          |
            .                                          .
            .     (possibly more entries later)        .
            .                                          .
            |                                          |
         O  | length & offset 0th string  ----------------.
       O + 8  | length & offset 1st string  ------------------.
            ...                               ...    | |
O + ((N-1)*8)| length & offset (N-1)th string    |   | |
            |                                   |   | |
         T  | length & offset 0th translation  ---------------.
       T + 8  | length & offset 1st translation  -----------------.
            ...                               ...    | | | |
T + ((N-1)*8)| length & offset (N-1)th translation |   | | | |
            |                                   |   | | | |
         H  | start hash table                 |   | | | |
            ...                               ...    | | | |
    H + S * 4  | end hash table                  |   | | | |
            |                                   |   | | | |
            | NUL terminated 0th string  <-----------------' | | |
            |                                   |   | | |
            | NUL terminated 1st string  <-------------------' | |
            |                                   |     | |
            ...                               ...      | |
            |                                   |     | |
            | NUL terminated 0th translation  <---------------' |
            |                                   |       |
            | NUL terminated 1st translation  <-----------------'
            |                                   |
            ...                               ...
            |                                   |
            +------------------------------------------+
```

11 The Programmer's View

One aim of the current message catalog implementation provided by GNU `gettext` was to use the system's message catalog handling, if the installer wishes to do so. So we perhaps should first take a look at the solutions we know about. The people in the POSIX committee did not manage to agree on one of the semi-official standards which we'll describe below. In fact they couldn't agree on anything, so they decided only to include an example of an interface. The major Unix vendors are split in the usage of the two most important specifications: X/Open's catgets vs. Uniforum's gettext interface. We'll describe them both and later explain our solution of this dilemma.

11.1 About `catgets`

The `catgets` implementation is defined in the X/Open Portability Guide, Volume 3, XSI Supplementary Definitions, Chapter 5. But the process of creating this standard seemed to be too slow for some of the Unix vendors so they created their implementations on preliminary versions of the standard. Of course this leads again to problems while writing platform independent programs: even the usage of `catgets` does not guarantee a unique interface.

Another, personal comment on this that only a bunch of committee members could have made this interface. They never really tried to program using this interface. It is a fast, memory-saving implementation, an user can happily live with it. But programmers hate it (at least I and some others do...)

But we must not forget one point: after all the trouble with transferring the rights on Unix(tm) they at last came to X/Open, the very same who published this specification. This leads me to making the prediction that this interface will be in future Unix standards (e.g. Spec1170) and therefore part of all Unix implementation (implementations, which are *allowed* to wear this name).

11.1.1 The Interface

The interface to the `catgets` implementation consists of three functions which correspond to those used in file access: `catopen` to open the catalog for using, `catgets` for accessing the message tables, and `catclose` for closing after work is done. Prototypes for the functions and the needed definitions are in the `<nl_types.h>` header file.

`catopen` is used like in this:

```
nl_catd catd = catopen ("catalog_name", 0);
```

The function takes as the argument the name of the catalog. This usual refers to the name of the program or the package. The second parameter is not further specified in the standard. I don't even know whether it is implemented consistently among various systems. So the common advice is to use 0 as the value. The return value is a handle to the message catalog, equivalent to handles to file returned by `open`.

This handle is of course used in the `catgets` function which can be used like this:

```
char *translation = catgets (catd, set_no, msg_id, "original string");
```

The first parameter is this catalog descriptor. The second parameter specifies the set of messages in this catalog, in which the message described by `msg_id` is obtained. `catgets` therefore uses a three-stage addressing:

catalog name ⇒ set number ⇒ message ID ⇒ translation

The fourth argument is not used to address the translation. It is given as a default value in case when one of the addressing stages fail. One important thing to remember is that although the return type of catgets is `char *` the resulting string *must not* be changed. It should better be `const char *`, but the standard is published in 1988, one year before ANSI C.

The last of these functions is used and behaves as expected:

```
catclose (catd);
```

After this no `catgets` call using the descriptor is legal anymore.

11.1.2 Problems with the `catgets` Interface?!

Now that this description seemed to be really easy — where are the problems we speak of? In fact the interface could be used in a reasonable way, but constructing the message catalogs is a pain. The reason for this lies in the third argument of `catgets`: the unique message ID. This has to be a numeric value for all messages in a single set. Perhaps you could imagine the problems keeping such a list while changing the source code. Add a new message here, remove one there. Of course there have been developed a lot of tools helping to organize this chaos but one as the other fails in one aspect or the other. We don't want to say that the other approach has no problems but they are far more easy to manage.

11.2 About `gettext`

The definition of the `gettext` interface comes from a Uniforum proposal. It was submitted there by Sun, who had implemented the `gettext` function in SunOS 4, around 1990. Nowadays, the `gettext` interface is specified by the OpenI18N standard.

The main point about this solution is that it does not follow the method of normal file handling (open-use-close) and that it does not burden the programmer with so many tasks, especially the unique key handling. Of course here also a unique key is needed, but this key is the message itself (how long or short it is). See Section 11.3 [Comparison], page 126 for a more detailed comparison of the two methods.

The following section contains a rather detailed description of the interface. We make it that detailed because this is the interface we chose for the GNU `gettext` Library. Programmers interested in using this library will be interested in this description.

11.2.1 The Interface

The minimal functionality an interface must have is a) to select a domain the strings are coming from (a single domain for all programs is not reasonable because its construction and maintenance is difficult, perhaps impossible) and b) to access a string in a selected domain.

This is principally the description of the `gettext` interface. It has a global domain which unqualified usages reference. Of course this domain is selectable by the user.

```
char *textdomain (const char *domain_name);
```

This provides the possibility to change or query the current status of the current global domain of the `LC_MESSAGE` category. The argument is a null-terminated string, whose characters must be legal in the use in filenames. If the *domain_name* argument is `NULL`, the function returns the current value. If no value has been set before, the name of the default domain is returned: *messages*. Please note that although the return value of `textdomain` is of type `char *` no changing is allowed. It is also important to know that no checks of the availability are made. If the name is not available you will see this by the fact that no translations are provided.

To use a domain set by `textdomain` the function

```
char *gettext (const char *msgid);
```

is to be used. This is the simplest reasonable form one can imagine. The translation of the string *msgid* is returned if it is available in the current domain. If it is not available, the argument itself is returned. If the argument is `NULL` the result is undefined.

One thing which should come into mind is that no explicit dependency to the used domain is given. The current value of the domain is used. If this changes between two executions of the same `gettext` call in the program, both calls reference a different message catalog.

For the easiest case, which is normally used in internationalized packages, once at the beginning of execution a call to `textdomain` is issued, setting the domain to a unique name, normally the package name. In the following code all strings which have to be translated are filtered through the gettext function. That's all, the package speaks your language.

11.2.2 Solving Ambiguities

While this single name domain works well for most applications there might be the need to get translations from more than one domain. Of course one could switch between different domains with calls to `textdomain`, but this is really not convenient nor is it fast. A possible situation could be one case subject to discussion during this writing: all error messages of functions in the set of common used functions should go into a separate domain `error`. By this mean we would only need to translate them once. Another case are messages from a library, as these *have* to be independent of the current domain set by the application.

For this reasons there are two more functions to retrieve strings:

```
char *dgettext (const char *domain_name, const char *msgid);
char *dcgettext (const char *domain_name, const char *msgid,
                 int category);
```

Both take an additional argument at the first place, which corresponds to the argument of `textdomain`. The third argument of `dcgettext` allows to use another locale category but `LC_MESSAGES`. But I really don't know where this can be useful. If the *domain_name* is `NULL` or *category* has an value beside the known ones, the result is undefined. It should also be noted that this function is not part of the second known implementation of this function family, the one found in Solaris.

A second ambiguity can arise by the fact, that perhaps more than one domain has the same name. This can be solved by specifying where the needed message catalog files can be found.

```
char *bindtextdomain (const char *domain_name,
                      const char *dir_name);
```

Calling this function binds the given domain to a file in the specified directory (how this file is determined follows below). Especially a file in the systems default place is not favored against the specified file anymore (as it would be by solely using `textdomain`). A `NULL` pointer for the *dir_name* parameter returns the binding associated with *domain_name*. If *domain_name* itself is `NULL` nothing happens and a `NULL` pointer is returned. Here again as for all the other functions is true that none of the return value must be changed!

It is important to remember that relative path names for the *dir_name* parameter can be trouble. Since the path is always computed relative to the current directory different results will be achieved when the program executes a `chdir` command. Relative paths should always be avoided to avoid dependencies and unreliabilities.

11.2.3 Locating Message Catalog Files

Because many different languages for many different packages have to be stored we need some way to add these information to file message catalog files. The way usually used in Unix environments is have this encoding in the file name. This is also done here. The directory name given in `bindtextdomains` second argument (or the default directory), followed by the name of the locale, the locale category, and the domain name are concatenated:

> *dir_name*/*locale*/LC_*category*/*domain_name*.mo

The default value for *dir_name* is system specific. For the GNU library, and for packages adhering to its conventions, it's:

> /usr/local/share/locale

locale is the name of the locale category which is designated by LC_*category*. For `gettext` and `dgettext` this LC_*category* is always LC_MESSAGES.[1] The name of the locale category is determined through `setlocale (LC_category, NULL)`.[2] When using the function `dcgettext`, you can specify the locale category through the third argument.

11.2.4 How to specify the output character set `gettext` uses

`gettext` not only looks up a translation in a message catalog. It also converts the translation on the fly to the desired output character set. This is useful if the user is working in a different character set than the translator who created the message catalog, because it avoids distributing variants of message catalogs which differ only in the character set.

The output character set is, by default, the value of `nl_langinfo (CODESET)`, which depends on the `LC_CTYPE` part of the current locale. But programs which store strings in a locale independent way (e.g. UTF-8) can request that `gettext` and related functions return the translations in that encoding, by use of the `bind_textdomain_codeset` function.

Note that the *msgid* argument to `gettext` is not subject to character set conversion. Also, when `gettext` does not find a translation for *msgid*, it returns *msgid* unchanged – independently of the current output character set. It is therefore recommended that all *msgids* be US-ASCII strings.

---

[1] Some system, e.g. mingw, don't have `LC_MESSAGES`. Here we use a more or less arbitrary value for it, namely 1729, the smallest positive integer which can be represented in two different ways as the sum of two cubes.

[2] When the system does not support `setlocale` its behavior in setting the locale values is simulated by looking at the environment variables.

char * bind_textdomain_codeset (*const char *domainname, const*   [Function]
    *char *codeset*)

> The `bind_textdomain_codeset` function can be used to specify the output character
> set for message catalogs for domain *domainname*. The *codeset* argument must be a
> valid codeset name which can be used for the `iconv_open` function, or a null pointer.

> If the *codeset* parameter is the null pointer, `bind_textdomain_codeset` returns the
> currently selected codeset for the domain with the name *domainname*. It returns
> `NULL` if no codeset has yet been selected.

> The `bind_textdomain_codeset` function can be used several times. If used multiple
> times with the same *domainname* argument, the later call overrides the settings made
> by the earlier one.

> The `bind_textdomain_codeset` function returns a pointer to a string containing the
> name of the selected codeset. The string is allocated internally in the function and
> must not be changed by the user. If the system went out of core during the execution
> of `bind_textdomain_codeset`, the return value is `NULL` and the global variable *errno*
> is set accordingly.

11.2.5 Using contexts for solving ambiguities

One place where the `gettext` functions, if used normally, have big problems is within
programs with graphical user interfaces (GUIs). The problem is that many of the strings
which have to be translated are very short. They have to appear in pull-down menus
which restricts the length. But strings which are not containing entire sentences or at least
large fragments of a sentence may appear in more than one situation in the program but
might have different translations. This is especially true for the one-word strings which are
frequently used in GUI programs.

As a consequence many people say that the `gettext` approach is wrong and instead
`catgets` should be used which indeed does not have this problem. But there is a very
simple and powerful method to handle this kind of problems with the `gettext` functions.

Contexts can be added to strings to be translated. A context dependent translation
lookup is when a translation for a given string is searched, that is limited to a given context.
The translation for the same string in a different context can be different. The different
translations of the same string in different contexts can be stored in the in the same MO
file, and can be edited by the translator in the same PO file.

The `gettext.h` include file contains the lookup macros for strings with contexts. They
are implemented as thin macros and inline functions over the functions from `<libintl.h>`.

```
const char *pgettext (const char *msgctxt, const char *msgid);
```

In a call of this macro, *msgctxt* and *msgid* must be string literals. The macro returns
the translation of *msgid*, restricted to the context given by *msgctxt*.

The *msgctxt* string is visible in the PO file to the translator. You should try to make
it somehow canonical and never changing. Because every time you change an *msgctxt*, the
translator will have to review the translation of *msgid*.

Finding a canonical *msgctxt* string that doesn't change over time can be hard. But you
shouldn't use the file name or class name containing the `pgettext` call – because it is a
common development task to rename a file or a class, and it shouldn't cause translator

work. Also you shouldn't use a comment in the form of a complete English sentence as *msgctxt* – because orthography or grammar changes are often applied to such sentences, and again, it shouldn't force the translator to do a review.

The 'p' in 'pgettext' stands for "particular": pgettext fetches a particular translation of the *msgid*.

```
const char *dpgettext (const char *domain_name,
                       const char *msgctxt, const char *msgid);
const char *dcpgettext (const char *domain_name,
                        const char *msgctxt, const char *msgid,
                        int category);
```

These are generalizations of pgettext. They behave similarly to dgettext and dcgettext, respectively. The *domain_name* argument defines the translation domain. The *category* argument allows to use another locale category than LC_MESSAGES.

As as example consider the following fictional situation. A GUI program has a menu bar with the following entries:

```
+------------+------------+--------------------------------------+
| File       | Printer    |                                      |
+------------+------------+--------------------------------------+
| Open       | | Select   |
| New        | | Open     |
+----------+ | Connect  |
             +----------+
```

To have the strings File, Printer, Open, New, Select, and Connect translated there has to be at some point in the code a call to a function of the gettext family. But in two places the string passed into the function would be Open. The translations might not be the same and therefore we are in the dilemma described above.

What distinguishes the two places is the menu path from the menu root to the particular menu entries:

```
Menu|File
Menu|Printer
Menu|File|Open
Menu|File|New
Menu|Printer|Select
Menu|Printer|Open
Menu|Printer|Connect
```

The context is thus the menu path without its last part. So, the calls look like this:

```
pgettext ("Menu|", "File")
pgettext ("Menu|", "Printer")
pgettext ("Menu|File|", "Open")
pgettext ("Menu|File|", "New")
pgettext ("Menu|Printer|", "Select")
pgettext ("Menu|Printer|", "Open")
pgettext ("Menu|Printer|", "Connect")
```

Whether or not to use the '|' character at the end of the context is a matter of style.

For more complex cases, where the *msgctxt* or *msgid* are not string literals, more general macros are available:

```
const char *pgettext_expr (const char *msgctxt, const char *msgid);
const char *dpgettext_expr (const char *domain_name,
```

```
                                    const char *msgctxt, const char *msgid);
    const char *dcpgettext_expr (const char *domain_name,
                                    const char *msgctxt, const char *msgid,
                                    int category);
```

Here *msgctxt* and *msgid* can be arbitrary string-valued expressions. These macros are more general. But in the case that both argument expressions are string literals, the macros without the '`_expr`' suffix are more efficient.

11.2.6 Additional functions for plural forms

The functions of the `gettext` family described so far (and all the `catgets` functions as well) have one problem in the real world which have been neglected completely in all existing approaches. What is meant here is the handling of plural forms.

Looking through Unix source code before the time anybody thought about internationalization (and, sadly, even afterwards) one can often find code similar to the following:

```
    printf ("%d file%s deleted", n, n == 1 ? "" : "s");
```

After the first complaints from people internationalizing the code people either completely avoided formulations like this or used strings like `"file(s)"`. Both look unnatural and should be avoided. First tries to solve the problem correctly looked like this:

```
    if (n == 1)
      printf ("%d file deleted", n);
    else
      printf ("%d files deleted", n);
```

But this does not solve the problem. It helps languages where the plural form of a noun is not simply constructed by adding an 's' but that is all. Once again people fell into the trap of believing the rules their language is using are universal. But the handling of plural forms differs widely between the language families. For example, Rafal Maszkowski `<rzm@mat.uni.torun.pl>` reports:

In Polish we use e.g. plik (file) this way:

```
    1 plik
    2,3,4 pliki
    5-21 pliko'w
    22-24 pliki
    25-31 pliko'w
```

and so on (o' means 8859-2 oacute which should be rather okreska, similar to aogonek).

There are two things which can differ between languages (and even inside language families);

- The form how plural forms are built differs. This is a problem with languages which have many irregularities. German, for instance, is a drastic case. Though English and German are part of the same language family (Germanic), the almost regular forming of plural noun forms (appending an 's') is hardly found in German.

- The number of plural forms differ. This is somewhat surprising for those who only have experiences with Romanic and Germanic languages since here the number is the same (there are two).

But other language families have only one form or many forms. More information on this in an extra section.

The consequence of this is that application writers should not try to solve the problem in their code. This would be localization since it is only usable for certain, hardcoded language environments. Instead the extended `gettext` interface should be used.

These extra functions are taking instead of the one key string two strings and a numerical argument. The idea behind this is that using the numerical argument and the first string as a key, the implementation can select using rules specified by the translator the right plural form. The two string arguments then will be used to provide a return value in case no message catalog is found (similar to the normal `gettext` behavior). In this case the rules for Germanic language is used and it is assumed that the first string argument is the singular form, the second the plural form.

This has the consequence that programs without language catalogs can display the correct strings only if the program itself is written using a Germanic language. This is a limitation but since the GNU C library (as well as the GNU `gettext` package) are written as part of the GNU package and the coding standards for the GNU project require program being written in English, this solution nevertheless fulfills its purpose.

char * ngettext (*const char *msgid1, const char *msgid2, unsigned*   [Function]
        long int n)

The `ngettext` function is similar to the `gettext` function as it finds the message catalogs in the same way. But it takes two extra arguments. The *msgid1* parameter must contain the singular form of the string to be converted. It is also used as the key for the search in the catalog. The *msgid2* parameter is the plural form. The parameter *n* is used to determine the plural form. If no message catalog is found *msgid1* is returned if `n == 1`, otherwise `msgid2`.

An example for the use of this function is:

```
printf (ngettext ("%d file removed", "%d files removed", n), n);
```

Please note that the numeric value *n* has to be passed to the `printf` function as well. It is not sufficient to pass it only to `ngettext`.

In the English singular case, the number – always 1 – can be replaced with "one":

```
printf (ngettext ("One file removed", "%d files removed", n), n);
```

This works because the 'printf' function discards excess arguments that are not consumed by the format string.

If this function is meant to yield a format string that takes two or more arguments, you can not use it like this:

```
printf (ngettext ("%d file removed from directory %s",
                  "%d files removed from directory %s",
                n),
        n, dir);
```

because in many languages the translators want to replace the '%d' with an explicit word in the singular case, just like "one" in English, and C format strings cannot consume the second argument but skip the first argument. Instead, you have to reorder the arguments so that 'n' comes last:

```
      printf (ngettext ("%2$d file removed from directory %1$s",
                        "%2$d files removed from directory %1$s",
                        n),
            dir, n);
```

See Section 15.3.1 [c-format], page 161 for details about this argument reordering syntax.

When you know that the value of n is within a given range, you can specify it as a comment directed to the xgettext tool. This information may help translators to use more adequate translations. Like this:

```
   if (days > 7 && days < 14)
     /* xgettext: range: 1..6 */
     printf (ngettext ("one week and one day", "one week and %d days",
                       days - 7),
            days - 7);
```

It is also possible to use this function when the strings don't contain a cardinal number:

```
   puts (ngettext ("Delete the selected file?",
                   "Delete the selected files?",
                   n));
```

In this case the number n is only used to choose the plural form.

char * dngettext (*const char *domain, const char *msgid1, const char*   [Function]
        *msgid2, unsigned long int n)
The dngettext is similar to the dgettext function in the way the message catalog is selected. The difference is that it takes two extra parameter to provide the correct plural form. These two parameters are handled in the same way ngettext handles them.

char * dcngettext (*const char *domain, const char *msgid1, const*   [Function]
        char *msgid2, unsigned long int n, int category)
The dcngettext is similar to the dcgettext function in the way the message catalog is selected. The difference is that it takes two extra parameter to provide the correct plural form. These two parameters are handled in the same way ngettext handles them.

Now, how do these functions solve the problem of the plural forms? Without the input of linguists (which was not available) it was not possible to determine whether there are only a few different forms in which plural forms are formed or whether the number can increase with every new supported language.

Therefore the solution implemented is to allow the translator to specify the rules of how to select the plural form. Since the formula varies with every language this is the only viable solution except for hardcoding the information in the code (which still would require the possibility of extensions to not prevent the use of new languages).

The information about the plural form selection has to be stored in the header entry of the PO file (the one with the empty msgid string). The plural form information looks like this:

```
   Plural-Forms: nplurals=2; plural=n == 1 ? 0 : 1;
```

The nplurals value must be a decimal number which specifies how many different plural forms exist for this language. The string following plural is an expression which is using the C language syntax. Exceptions are that no negative numbers are allowed, numbers must be decimal, and the only variable allowed is **n**. Spaces are allowed in the expression, but backslash-newlines are not; in the examples below the backslash-newlines are present for formatting purposes only. This expression will be evaluated whenever one of the functions **ngettext**, **dngettext**, or **dcngettext** is called. The numeric value passed to these functions is then substituted for all uses of the variable **n** in the expression. The resulting value then must be greater or equal to zero and smaller than the value given as the value of **nplurals**.

The following rules are known at this point. The language with families are listed. But this does not necessarily mean the information can be generalized for the whole family (as can be easily seen in the table below).[3]

Only one form:

> Some languages only require one single form. There is no distinction between the singular and plural form. An appropriate header entry would look like this:
>
> ```
> Plural-Forms: nplurals=1; plural=0;
> ```
>
> Languages with this property include:

Asian family

> Japanese, Vietnamese, Korean

Tai-Kadai family

> Thai

Two forms, singular used for one only

> This is the form used in most existing programs since it is what English is using. A header entry would look like this:
>
> ```
> Plural-Forms: nplurals=2; plural=n != 1;
> ```
>
> (Note: this uses the feature of C expressions that boolean expressions have to value zero or one.)
>
> Languages with this property include:

Germanic family

> English, German, Dutch, Swedish, Danish, Norwegian, Faroese

Romanic family

> Spanish, Portuguese, Italian, Bulgarian

Latin/Greek family

> Greek

Finno-Ugric family

> Finnish, Estonian

Semitic family

> Hebrew

Austronesian family

> Bahasa Indonesian

---

[3] Additions are welcome. Send appropriate information to **bug-gnu-gettext@gnu.org** and **bug-glibc-manual@gnu.org**. The Unicode CLDR Project (**http://cldr.unicode.org**) provides a comprehensive set of plural forms in a different format. The **msginit** program has preliminary support for the format so you can use it as a baseline (see Section 6.1 [msginit Invocation], page 42).

Artificial   Esperanto

Other languages using the same header entry are:

Finno-Ugric family
        Hungarian

Turkic/Altaic family
        Turkish

Hungarian does not appear to have a plural if you look at sentences involving cardinal numbers. For example, "1 apple" is "1 alma", and "123 apples" is "123 alma". But when the number is not explicit, the distinction between singular and plural exists: "the apple" is "az alma", and "the apples" is "az almák". Since `ngettext` has to support both types of sentences, it is classified here, under "two forms".

The same holds for Turkish: "1 apple" is "1 elma", and "123 apples" is "123 elma". But when the number is omitted, the distinction between singular and plural exists: "the apple" is "elma", and "the apples" is "elmalar".

Two forms, singular used for zero and one
        Exceptional case in the language family. The header entry would be:
```
Plural-Forms: nplurals=2; plural=n>1;
```
        Languages with this property include:

Romanic family
        Brazilian Portuguese, French

Three forms, special case for zero
        The header entry would be:
```
Plural-Forms: nplurals=3; plural=n%10==1 && n%100!=11 ? 0 : n != 0 ? 1 : 2;
```
        Languages with this property include:

Baltic family
        Latvian

Three forms, special cases for one and two
        The header entry would be:
```
Plural-Forms: nplurals=3; plural=n==1 ? 0 : n==2 ? 1 : 2;
```
        Languages with this property include:

Celtic   Gaeilge (Irish)

Three forms, special case for numbers ending in 00 or [2-9][0-9]
        The header entry would be:
```
Plural-Forms: nplurals=3; \
    plural=n==1 ? 0 : (n==0 || (n%100 > 0 && n%100 < 20)) ? 1 : 2;
```
        Languages with this property include:

Romanic family
        Romanian

Three forms, special case for numbers ending in 1[2-9]
        The header entry would look like this:

```
Plural-Forms: nplurals=3; \
    plural=n%10==1 && n%100!=11 ? 0 : \
        n%10>=2 && (n%100<10 || n%100>=20) ? 1 : 2;
```

Languages with this property include:

Baltic family

Lithuanian

Three forms, special cases for numbers ending in 1 and 2, 3, 4, except those ending in 1[1-4]

The header entry would look like this:

```
Plural-Forms: nplurals=3; \
    plural=n%10==1 && n%100!=11 ? 0 : \
        n%10>=2 && n%10<=4 && (n%100<10 || n%100>=20) ? 1 : 2;
```

Languages with this property include:

Slavic family

Russian, Ukrainian, Belarusian, Serbian, Croatian

Three forms, special cases for 1 and 2, 3, 4

The header entry would look like this:

```
Plural-Forms: nplurals=3; \
    plural=(n==1) ? 0 : (n>=2 && n<=4) ? 1 : 2;
```

Languages with this property include:

Slavic family

Czech, Slovak

Three forms, special case for one and some numbers ending in 2, 3, or 4

The header entry would look like this:

```
Plural-Forms: nplurals=3; \
    plural=n==1 ? 0 : \
        n%10>=2 && n%10<=4 && (n%100<10 || n%100>=20) ? 1 : 2;
```

Languages with this property include:

Slavic family

Polish

Four forms, special case for one and all numbers ending in 02, 03, or 04

The header entry would look like this:

```
Plural-Forms: nplurals=4; \
    plural=n%100==1 ? 0 : n%100==2 ? 1 : n%100==3 || n%100==4 ? 2 : 3;
```

Languages with this property include:

Slavic family

Slovenian

Six forms, special cases for one, two, all numbers ending in 02, 03, ... 10, all numbers ending in 11 ... 99, and others

The header entry would look like this:

```
Plural-Forms: nplurals=6; \
    plural=n==0 ? 0 : n==1 ? 1 : n==2 ? 2 : n%100>=3 && n%100<=10 ? 3 \
        : n%100>=11 ? 4 : 5;
```

Languages with this property include:

> Afroasiatic family
> Arabic

You might now ask, `ngettext` handles only numbers n of type 'unsigned long'. What about larger integer types? What about negative numbers? What about floating-point numbers?

About larger integer types, such as 'uintmax_t' or 'unsigned long long': they can be handled by reducing the value to a range that fits in an 'unsigned long'. Simply casting the value to 'unsigned long' would not do the right thing, since it would treat ULONG_MAX + 1 like zero, ULONG_MAX + 2 like singular, and the like. Here you can exploit the fact that all mentioned plural form formulas eventually become periodic, with a period that is a divisor of 100 (or 1000 or 1000000). So, when you reduce a large value to another one in the range [1000000, 1999999] that ends in the same 6 decimal digits, you can assume that it will lead to the same plural form selection. This code does this:

```
#include <inttypes.h>
uintmax_t nbytes = ...;
printf (ngettext ("The file has %"PRIuMAX" byte.",
                  "The file has %"PRIuMAX" bytes.",
                  (nbytes > ULONG_MAX
                   ? (nbytes % 1000000) + 1000000
                   : nbytes)),
        nbytes);
```

Negative and floating-point values usually represent physical entities for which singular and plural don't clearly apply. In such cases, there is no need to use `ngettext`; a simple `gettext` call with a form suitable for all values will do. For example:

```
printf (gettext ("Time elapsed: %.3f seconds"),
        num_milliseconds * 0.001);
```

Even if *num_milliseconds* happens to be a multiple of 1000, the output

```
Time elapsed: 1.000 seconds
```

is acceptable in English, and similarly for other languages.

The translators' perspective regarding plural forms is explained in Section 12.6 [Translating plural forms], page 136.

11.2.7 Optimization of the *gettext functions

At this point of the discussion we should talk about an advantage of the GNU `gettext` implementation. Some readers might have pointed out that an internationalized program might have a poor performance if some string has to be translated in an inner loop. While this is unavoidable when the string varies from one run of the loop to the other it is simply a waste of time when the string is always the same. Take the following example:

```
{
  while (...)
    {
      puts (gettext ("Hello world"));
    }
}
```

When the locale selection does not change between two runs the resulting string is always the same. One way to use this is:

```
{
  str = gettext ("Hello world");
  while (...)
    {
      puts (str);
    }
}
```

But this solution is not usable in all situation (e.g. when the locale selection changes) nor does it lead to legible code.

For this reason, GNU gettext caches previous translation results. When the same translation is requested twice, with no new message catalogs being loaded in between, gettext will, the second time, find the result through a single cache lookup.

11.3 Comparing the Two Interfaces

The following discussion is perhaps a little bit colored. As said above we implemented GNU gettext following the Uniforum proposal and this surely has its reasons. But it should show how we came to this decision.

First we take a look at the developing process. When we write an application using NLS provided by gettext we proceed as always. Only when we come to a string which might be seen by the users and thus has to be translated we use gettext("...") instead of "...". At the beginning of each source file (or in a central header file) we define

```
#define gettext(String) (String)
```

Even this definition can be avoided when the system supports the gettext function in its C library. When we compile this code the result is the same as if no NLS code is used. When you take a look at the GNU gettext code you will see that we use _("...") instead of gettext("..."). This reduces the number of additional characters per translatable string to *3* (in words: three).

When now a production version of the program is needed we simply replace the definition

```
#define _(String) (String)
```

by

```
#include <libintl.h>
#define _(String) gettext (String)
```

Additionally we run the program xgettext on all source code file which contain translatable strings and that's it: we have a running program which does not depend on translations to be available, but which can use any that becomes available.

The same procedure can be done for the gettext_noop invocations (see Section 4.7 [Special cases], page 28). One usually defines gettext_noop as a no-op macro. So you should consider the following code for your project:

```
#define gettext_noop(String) String
#define N_(String) gettext_noop (String)
```

N_ is a short form similar to _. The Makefile in the po/ directory of GNU gettext knows by default both of the mentioned short forms so you are invited to follow this proposal for your own ease.

Now to `catgets`. The main problem is the work for the programmer. Every time he comes to a translatable string he has to define a number (or a symbolic constant) which has also be defined in the message catalog file. He also has to take care for duplicate entries, duplicate message IDs etc. If he wants to have the same quality in the message catalog as the GNU `gettext` program provides he also has to put the descriptive comments for the strings and the location in all source code files in the message catalog. This is nearly a Mission: Impossible.

But there are also some points people might call advantages speaking for `catgets`. If you have a single word in a string and this string is used in different contexts it is likely that in one or the other language the word has different translations. Example:

```
printf ("%s: %d", gettext ("number"), number_of_errors)

printf ("you should see %d %s", number_count,
        number_count == 1 ? gettext ("number") : gettext ("numbers"))
```

Here we have to translate two times the string `"number"`. Even if you do not speak a language beside English it might be possible to recognize that the two words have a different meaning. In German the first appearance has to be translated to `"Anzahl"` and the second to `"Zahl"`.

Now you can say that this example is really esoteric. And you are right! This is exactly how we felt about this problem and decide that it does not weight that much. The solution for the above problem could be very easy:

```
printf ("%s %d", gettext ("number:"), number_of_errors)

printf (number_count == 1 ? gettext ("you should see %d number")
                          : gettext ("you should see %d numbers"),
        number_count)
```

We believe that we can solve all conflicts with this method. If it is difficult one can also consider changing one of the conflicting string a little bit. But it is not impossible to overcome.

`catgets` allows same original entry to have different translations, but `gettext` has another, scalable approach for solving ambiguities of this kind: See Section 11.2.2 [Ambiguities], page 115.

11.4 Using libintl.a in own programs

Starting with version 0.9.4 the library `libintl.h` should be self-contained. I.e., you can use it in your own programs without providing additional functions. The `Makefile` will put the header and the library in directories selected using the `$(prefix)`.

11.5 Being a gettext grok

NOTE: This documentation section is outdated and needs to be revised.

To fully exploit the functionality of the GNU `gettext` library it is surely helpful to read the source code. But for those who don't want to spend that much time in reading the (sometimes complicated) code here is a list comments:

- Changing the language at runtime

  For interactive programs it might be useful to offer a selection of the used language at runtime. To understand how to do this one need to know how the used language is determined while executing the `gettext` function. The method which is presented here only works correctly with the GNU implementation of the `gettext` functions.

  In the function `dcgettext` at every call the current setting of the highest priority environment variable is determined and used. Highest priority means here the following list with decreasing priority:

  1. `LANGUAGE`
  2. `LC_ALL`
  3. `LC_xxx`, according to selected locale category
  4. `LANG`

  Afterwards the path is constructed using the found value and the translation file is loaded if available.

  What happens now when the value for, say, `LANGUAGE` changes? According to the process explained above the new value of this variable is found as soon as the `dcgettext` function is called. But this also means the (perhaps) different message catalog file is loaded. In other words: the used language is changed.

  But there is one little hook. The code for gcc-2.7.0 and up provides some optimization. This optimization normally prevents the calling of the `dcgettext` function as long as no new catalog is loaded. But if `dcgettext` is not called the program also cannot find the `LANGUAGE` variable be changed (see Section 11.2.7 [Optimized gettext], page 125). A solution for this is very easy. Include the following code in the language switching function.

  ```
  /* Change language.  */
  setenv ("LANGUAGE", "fr", 1);

  /* Make change known.  */
  {
    extern int  _nl_msg_cat_cntr;
    ++_nl_msg_cat_cntr;
  }
  ```

  The variable `_nl_msg_cat_cntr` is defined in `loadmsgcat.c`. You don't need to know what this is for. But it can be used to detect whether a `gettext` implementation is GNU gettext and not non-GNU system's native gettext implementation.

11.6 Temporary Notes for the Programmers Chapter

NOTE: This documentation section is outdated and needs to be revised.

11.6.1 Temporary - Two Possible Implementations

There are two competing methods for language independent messages: the X/Open `catgets` method, and the Uniforum `gettext` method. The `catgets` method indexes messages by integers; the `gettext` method indexes them by their English translations. The `catgets` method has been around longer and is supported by more vendors. The `gettext` method is supported by Sun, and it has been heard that the COSE multi-vendor initiative is supporting it. Neither method is a POSIX standard; the POSIX.1 committee had a lot of disagreement in this area.

Neither one is in the POSIX standard. There was much disagreement in the POSIX.1 committee about using the `gettext` routines vs. `catgets` (XPG). In the end the committee couldn't agree on anything, so no messaging system was included as part of the standard. I believe the informative annex of the standard includes the XPG3 messaging interfaces, "...as an example of a messaging system that has been implemented..."

They were very careful not to say anywhere that you should use one set of interfaces over the other. For more on this topic please see the Programming for Internationalization FAQ.

11.6.2 Temporary - About `catgets`

There have been a few discussions of late on the use of `catgets` as a base. I think it important to present both sides of the argument and hence am opting to play devil's advocate for a little bit.

I'll not deny the fact that `catgets` could have been designed a lot better. It currently has quite a number of limitations and these have already been pointed out.

However there is a great deal to be said for consistency and standardization. A common recurring problem when writing Unix software is the myriad portability problems across Unix platforms. It seems as if every Unix vendor had a look at the operating system and found parts they could improve upon. Undoubtedly, these modifications are probably innovative and solve real problems. However, software developers have a hard time keeping up with all these changes across so many platforms.

And this has prompted the Unix vendors to begin to standardize their systems. Hence the impetus for Spec1170. Every major Unix vendor has committed to supporting this standard and every Unix software developer waits with glee the day they can write software to this standard and simply recompile (without having to use autoconf) across different platforms.

As I understand it, Spec1170 is roughly based upon version 4 of the X/Open Portability Guidelines (XPG4). Because `catgets` and friends are defined in XPG4, I'm led to believe that `catgets` is a part of Spec1170 and hence will become a standardized component of all Unix systems.

11.6.3 Temporary - Why a single implementation

Now it seems kind of wasteful to me to have two different systems installed for accessing message catalogs. If we do want to remedy `catgets` deficiencies why don't we try to expand `catgets` (in a compatible manner) rather than implement an entirely new system. Otherwise, we'll end up with two message catalog access systems installed with an operating system - one set of routines for packages using GNU `gettext` for their internationalization, and another set of routines (catgets) for all other software. Bloated?

Supposing another catalog access system is implemented. Which do we recommend? At least for Linux, we need to attract as many software developers as possible. Hence we need to make it as easy for them to port their software as possible. Which means supporting catgets. We will be implementing the `libintl` code within our `libc`, but does this mean we also have to incorporate another message catalog access scheme within our `libc` as well? And what about people who are going to be using the `libintl` + non-`catgets` routines. When they port their software to other platforms, they're now going to have to include the front-end (`libintl`) code plus the back-end code (the non-`catgets` access routines) with their software instead of just including the `libintl` code with their software.

Message catalog support is however only the tip of the iceberg. What about the data for the other locale categories? They also have a number of deficiencies. Are we going to abandon them as well and develop another duplicate set of routines (should `libintl` expand beyond message catalog support)?

Like many parts of Unix that can be improved upon, we're stuck with balancing compatibility with the past with useful improvements and innovations for the future.

11.6.4 Temporary - Notes

X/Open agreed very late on the standard form so that many implementations differ from the final form. Both of my system (old Linux catgets and Ultrix-4) have a strange variation.

OK. After incorporating the last changes I have to spend some time on making the GNU/Linux `libc` `gettext` functions. So in future Solaris is not the only system having `gettext`.

12 The Translator's View

12.1 Introduction 0

NOTE: This documentation section is outdated and needs to be revised.

Free software is going international! The Translation Project is a way to get maintainers, translators and users all together, so free software will gradually become able to speak many native languages.

The GNU `gettext` tool set contains *everything* maintainers need for internationalizing their packages for messages. It also contains quite useful tools for helping translators at localizing messages to their native language, once a package has already been internationalized.

To achieve the Translation Project, we need many interested people who like their own language and write it well, and who are also able to synergize with other translators speaking the same language. If you'd like to volunteer to *work* at translating messages, please send mail to your translating team.

Each team has its own mailing list, courtesy of Linux International. You may reach your translating team at the address `ll@li.org`, replacing *ll* by the two-letter ISO 639 code for your language. Language codes are *not* the same as country codes given in ISO 3166. The following translating teams exist:

> Chinese `zh`, Czech `cs`, Danish `da`, Dutch `nl`, Esperanto `eo`, Finnish `fi`, French `fr`, Irish `ga`, German `de`, Greek `el`, Italian `it`, Japanese `ja`, Indonesian `in`, Norwegian `no`, Polish `pl`, Portuguese `pt`, Russian `ru`, Spanish `es`, Swedish `sv` and Turkish `tr`.

For example, you may reach the Chinese translating team by writing to `zh@li.org`. When you become a member of the translating team for your own language, you may subscribe to its list. For example, Swedish people can send a message to `sv-request@li.org`, having this message body:

```
subscribe
```

Keep in mind that team members should be interested in *working* at translations, or at solving translational difficulties, rather than merely lurking around. If your team does not exist yet and you want to start one, please write to `coordinator@translationproject.org`; you will then reach the coordinator for all translator teams.

A handful of GNU packages have already been adapted and provided with message translations for several languages. Translation teams have begun to organize, using these packages as a starting point. But there are many more packages and many languages for which we have no volunteer translators. If you would like to volunteer to work at translating messages, please send mail to `coordinator@translationproject.org` indicating what language(s) you can work on.

12.2 Introduction 1

NOTE: This documentation section is outdated and needs to be revised.

This is now official, GNU is going international! Here is the announcement submitted for the January 1995 GNU Bulletin:

> A handful of GNU packages have already been adapted and provided with message translations for several languages. Translation teams have begun to organize, using these packages as a starting point. But there are many more packages and many languages for which we have no volunteer translators. If you'd like to volunteer to work at translating messages, please send mail to 'coordinator@translationproject.org' indicating what language(s) you can work on.

This document should answer many questions for those who are curious about the process or would like to contribute. Please at least skim over it, hoping to cut down a little of the high volume of e-mail generated by this collective effort towards internationalization of free software.

Most free programming which is widely shared is done in English, and currently, English is used as the main communicating language between national communities collaborating to free software. This very document is written in English. This will not change in the foreseeable future.

However, there is a strong appetite from national communities for having more software able to write using national language and habits, and there is an on-going effort to modify free software in such a way that it becomes able to do so. The experiments driven so far raised an enthusiastic response from pretesters, so we believe that internationalization of free software is dedicated to succeed.

For suggestion clarifications, additions or corrections to this document, please e-mail to coordinator@translationproject.org.

12.3 Discussions

NOTE: This documentation section is outdated and needs to be revised.

Facing this internationalization effort, a few users expressed their concerns. Some of these doubts are presented and discussed, here.

- Smaller groups

  Some languages are not spoken by a very large number of people, so people speaking them sometimes consider that there may not be all that much demand such versions of free software packages. Moreover, many people being *into computers*, in some countries, generally seem to prefer English versions of their software.

  On the other end, people might enjoy their own language a lot, and be very motivated at providing to themselves the pleasure of having their beloved free software speaking their mother tongue. They do themselves a personal favor, and do not pay that much attention to the number of people benefiting of their work.

- Misinterpretation

  Other users are shy to push forward their own language, seeing in this some kind of misplaced propaganda. Someone thought there must be some users of the language over the networks pestering other people with it.

  But any spoken language is worth localization, because there are people behind the language for whom the language is important and dear to their hearts.

- Odd translations

  The biggest problem is to find the right translations so that everybody can understand the messages. Translations are usually a little odd. Some people get used to English, to the extent they may find translations into their own language "rather pushy, obnoxious and sometimes even hilarious." As a French speaking man, I have the experience of those instruction manuals for goods, so poorly translated in French in Korea or Taiwan...

  The fact is that we sometimes have to create a kind of national computer culture, and this is not easy without the collaboration of many people liking their mother tongue. This is why translations are better achieved by people knowing and loving their own language, and ready to work together at improving the results they obtain.

- Dependencies over the GPL or LGPL

  Some people wonder if using GNU `gettext` necessarily brings their package under the protective wing of the GNU General Public License or the GNU Lesser General Public License, when they do not want to make their program free, or want other kinds of freedom. The simplest answer is "normally not".

  The `gettext-runtime` part of GNU `gettext`, i.e. the contents of `libintl`, is covered by the GNU Lesser General Public License. The `gettext-tools` part of GNU `gettext`, i.e. the rest of the GNU `gettext` package, is covered by the GNU General Public License.

  The mere marking of localizable strings in a package, or conditional inclusion of a few lines for initialization, is not really including GPL'ed or LGPL'ed code. However, since the localization routines in `libintl` are under the LGPL, the LGPL needs to be considered. It gives the right to distribute the complete unmodified source of `libintl` even with non-free programs. It also gives the right to use `libintl` as a shared library, even for non-free programs. But it gives the right to use `libintl` as a static library or to incorporate `libintl` into another library only to free software.

12.4 Organization

NOTE: This documentation section is outdated and needs to be revised.

On a larger scale, the true solution would be to organize some kind of fairly precise set up in which volunteers could participate. I gave some thought to this idea lately, and realize there will be some touchy points. I thought of writing to Richard Stallman to launch such a project, but feel it might be good to shake out the ideas between ourselves first. Most probably that Linux International has some experience in the field already, or would like to orchestrate the volunteer work, maybe. Food for thought, in any case!

I guess we have to setup something early, somehow, that will help many possible contributors of the same language to interlock and avoid work duplication, and further be put in contact for solving together problems particular to their tongue (in most languages, there are many difficulties peculiar to translating technical English). My Swedish contributor acknowledged these difficulties, and I'm well aware of them for French.

This is surely not a technical issue, but we should manage so the effort of locale contributors be maximally useful, despite the national team layer interface between contributors and maintainers.

The Translation Project needs some setup for coordinating language coordinators. Localizing evolving programs will surely become a permanent and continuous activity in the free software community, once well started. The setup should be minimally completed and tested before GNU `gettext` becomes an official reality. The e-mail address `coordinator@translationproject.org` has been set up for receiving offers from volunteers and general e-mail on these topics. This address reaches the Translation Project coordinator.

12.4.1 Central Coordination

I also think GNU will need sooner than it thinks, that someone set up a way to organize and coordinate these groups. Some kind of group of groups. My opinion is that it would be good that GNU delegates this task to a small group of collaborating volunteers, shortly. Perhaps in `gnu.announce` a list of this national committee's can be published.

My role as coordinator would simply be to refer to Ulrich any German speaking volunteer interested to localization of free software packages, and maybe helping national groups to initially organize, while maintaining national registries for until national groups are ready to take over. In fact, the coordinator should ease volunteers to get in contact with one another for creating national teams, which should then select one coordinator per language, or country (regionalized language). If well done, the coordination should be useful without being an overwhelming task, the time to put delegations in place.

12.4.2 National Teams

I suggest we look for volunteer coordinators/editors for individual languages. These people will scan contributions of translation files for various programs, for their own languages, and will ensure high and uniform standards of diction.

From my current experience with other people in these days, those who provide localizations are very enthusiastic about the process, and are more interested in the localization process than in the program they localize, and want to do many programs, not just one. This seems to confirm that having a coordinator/editor for each language is a good idea.

We need to choose someone who is good at writing clear and concise prose in the language in question. That is hard—we can't check it ourselves. So we need to ask a few people to judge each others' writing and select the one who is best.

I announce my prerelease to a few dozen people, and you would not believe all the discussions it generated already. I shudder to think what will happen when this will be launched, for true, officially, world wide. Who am I to arbitrate between two Czekolsovak users contradicting each other, for example?

I assume that your German is not much better than my French so that I would not be able to judge about these formulations. What I would suggest is that for each language there is a group for people who maintain the PO files and judge about changes. I suspect there will be cultural differences between how such groups of people will behave. Some will have relaxed ways, reach consensus easily, and have anyone of the group relate to the maintainers, while others will fight to death, organize heavy administrations up to national standards, and use strict channels.

The German team is putting out a good example. Right now, they are maybe half a dozen people revising translations of each other and discussing the linguistic issues. I do not even have all the names. Ulrich Drepper is taking care of coordinating the German team. He subscribed to all my pretest lists, so I do not even have to warn him specifically of incoming releases.

I'm sure, that is a good idea to get teams for each language working on translations. That will make the translations better and more consistent.

12.4.2.1 Sub-Cultures

Taking French for example, there are a few sub-cultures around computers which developed diverging vocabularies. Picking volunteers here and there without addressing this problem in an organized way, soon in the project, might produce a distasteful mix of internationalized programs, and possibly trigger endless quarrels among those who really care.

Keeping some kind of unity in the way French localization of internationalized programs is achieved is a difficult (and delicate) job. Knowing the latin character of French people (:-), if we take this the wrong way, we could end up nowhere, or spoil a lot of energies. Maybe we should begin to address this problem seriously *before* GNU `gettext` become officially published. And I suspect that this means soon!

12.4.2.2 Organizational Ideas

I expect the next big changes after the official release. Please note that I use the German translation of the short GPL message. We need to set a few good examples before the localization goes out for true in the free software community. Here are a few points to discuss:

- Each group should have one FTP server (at least one master).

- The files on the server should reflect the latest version (of course!) and it should also contain a RCS directory with the corresponding archives (I don't have this now).

- There should also be a ChangeLog file (this is more useful than the RCS archive but can be generated automatically from the later by Emacs).

- A *core group* should judge about questionable changes (for now this group consists solely by me but I ask some others occasionally; this also seems to work).

12.4.3 Mailing Lists

If we get any inquiries about GNU `gettext`, send them on to:

> `coordinator@translationproject.org`

The `*-pretest` lists are quite useful to me, maybe the idea could be generalized to many GNU, and non-GNU packages. But each maintainer his/her way!

François, we have a mechanism in place here at `gnu.ai.mit.edu` to track teams, support mailing lists for them and log members. We have a slight preference that you use it. If this is OK with you, I can get you clued in.

Things are changing! A few years ago, when Daniel Fekete and I asked for a mailing list for GNU localization, nested at the FSF, we were politely invited to organize it anywhere else, and so did we. For communicating with my pretesters, I later made a handful of mailing lists located at iro.umontreal.ca and administrated by `majordomo`. These lists have been *very* dependable so far...

I suspect that the German team will organize itself a mailing list located in Germany, and so forth for other countries. But before they organize for true, it could surely be useful to offer mailing lists located at the FSF to each national team. So yes, please explain me how I should proceed to create and handle them.

We should create temporary mailing lists, one per country, to help people organize. Temporary, because once regrouped and structured, it would be fair the volunteers from country bring back *their* list in there and manage it as they want. My feeling is that, in the long run, each team should run its own list, from within their country. There also should be some central list to which all teams could subscribe as they see fit, as long as each team is represented in it.

12.5 Information Flow

NOTE: This documentation section is outdated and needs to be revised.

There will surely be some discussion about this messages after the packages are finally released. If people now send you some proposals for better messages, how do you proceed? Jim, please note that right now, as I put forward nearly a dozen of localizable programs, I receive both the translations and the coordination concerns about them.

If I put one of my things to pretest, Ulrich receives the announcement and passes it on to the German team, who make last minute revisions. Then he submits the translation files to me *as the maintainer*. For free packages I do not maintain, I would not even hear about it. This scheme could be made to work for the whole Translation Project, I think. For security reasons, maybe Ulrich (national coordinators, in fact) should update central registry kept at the Translation Project (Jim, me, or Len's recruits) once in a while.

In December/January, I was aggressively ready to internationalize all of GNU, giving myself the duty of one small GNU package per week or so, taking many weeks or months for bigger packages. But it does not work this way. I first did all the things I'm responsible for. I've nothing against some missionary work on other maintainers, but I'm also losing a lot of energy over it—same debates over again.

And when the first localized packages are released we'll get a lot of responses about ugly translations :-). Surely, and we need to have beforehand a fairly good idea about how to handle the information flow between the national teams and the package maintainers.

Please start saving somewhere a quick history of each PO file. I know for sure that the file format will change, allowing for comments. It would be nice that each file has a kind of log, and references for those who want to submit comments or gripes, or otherwise contribute. I sent a proposal for a fast and flexible format, but it is not receiving acceptance yet by the GNU deciders. I'll tell you when I have more information about this.

12.6 Translating plural forms

Suppose you are translating a PO file, and it contains an entry like this:

```
#, c-format
msgid "One file removed"
msgid_plural "%d files removed"
msgstr[0] ""
msgstr[1] ""
```

What does this mean? How do you fill it in?

Such an entry denotes a message with plural forms, that is, a message where the text depends on a cardinal number. The general form of the message, in English, is the `msgid_plural` line. The `msgid` line is the English singular form, that is, the form for when the number is equal to 1. More details about plural forms are explained in Section 11.2.6 [Plural forms], page 119.

The first thing you need to look at is the `Plural-Forms` line in the header entry of the PO file. It contains the number of plural forms and a formula. If the PO file does not yet have such a line, you have to add it. It only depends on the language into which you are translating. You can get this info by using the `msginit` command (see Chapter 6 [Creating], page 42) – it contains a database of known plural formulas – or by asking other members of your translation team.

Suppose the line looks as follows:

```
"Plural-Forms: nplurals=3; plural=n%10==1 && n%100!=11 ? 0 : n%10>=2 && n"
"%10<=4 && (n%100<10 || n%100>=20) ? 1 : 2;\n"
```

It's logically one line; recall that the PO file formatting is allowed to break long lines so that each physical line fits in 80 monospaced columns.

The value of `nplurals` here tells you that there are three plural forms. The first thing you need to do is to ensure that the entry contains an `msgstr` line for each of the forms:

```
#, c-format
msgid "One file removed"
msgid_plural "%d files removed"
msgstr[0] ""
msgstr[1] ""
msgstr[2] ""
```

Then translate the `msgid_plural` line and fill it in into each `msgstr` line:

```
#, c-format
msgid "One file removed"
msgid_plural "%d files removed"
msgstr[0] "%d slika uklonjenih"
msgstr[1] "%d slika uklonjenih"
msgstr[2] "%d slika uklonjenih"
```

Now you can refine the translation so that it matches the plural form. According to the formula above, `msgstr[0]` is used when the number ends in 1 but does not end in 11; `msgstr[1]` is used when the number ends in 2, 3, 4, but not in 12, 13, 14; and `msgstr[2]` is used in all other cases. With this knowledge, you can refine the translations:

```
#, c-format
msgid "One file removed"
msgid_plural "%d files removed"
msgstr[0] "%d slika je uklonjena"
msgstr[1] "%d datoteke uklonjenih"
msgstr[2] "%d slika uklonjenih"
```

You noticed that in the English singular form (`msgid`) the number placeholder could be omitted and replaced by the numeral word "one". Can you do this in your translation as well?

```
msgstr[0] "jednom datotekom je uklonjen"
```

Well, it depends on whether `msgstr[0]` applies only to the number 1, or to other numbers as well. If, according to the plural formula, `msgstr[0]` applies only to $n == 1$, then you can use the specialized translation without the number placeholder. In our case, however, `msgstr[0]` also applies to the numbers 21, 31, 41, etc., and therefore you cannot omit the placeholder.

12.7 Prioritizing messages: How to determine which messages to translate first

A translator sometimes has only a limited amount of time per week to spend on a package, and some packages have quite large message catalogs (over 1000 messages). Therefore she wishes to translate the messages first that are the most visible to the user, or that occur most frequently. This section describes how to determine these "most urgent" messages. It also applies to determine the "next most urgent" messages after the message catalog has already been partially translated.

In a first step, she uses the programs like a user would do. While she does this, the GNU `gettext` library logs into a file the not yet translated messages for which a translation was requested from the program.

In a second step, she uses the PO mode to translate precisely this set of messages.

Here a more details. The GNU `libintl` library (but not the corresponding functions in GNU `libc`) supports an environment variable `GETTEXT_LOG_UNTRANSLATED`. The GNU `libintl` library will log into this file the messages for which `gettext()` and related functions couldn't find the translation. If the file doesn't exist, it will be created as needed. On systems with GNU `libc` a shared library 'preloadable_libintl.so' is provided that can be used with the ELF 'LD_PRELOAD' mechanism.

So, in the first step, the translator uses these commands on systems with GNU `libc`:

```
$ LD_PRELOAD=/usr/local/lib/preloadable_libintl.so
$ export LD_PRELOAD
$ GETTEXT_LOG_UNTRANSLATED=$HOME/gettextlogused
$ export GETTEXT_LOG_UNTRANSLATED
```

and these commands on other systems:

```
$ GETTEXT_LOG_UNTRANSLATED=$HOME/gettextlogused
$ export GETTEXT_LOG_UNTRANSLATED
```

Then she uses and peruses the programs. (It is a good and recommended practice to use the programs for which you provide translations: it gives you the needed context.) When done, she removes the environment variables:

```
$ unset LD_PRELOAD
$ unset GETTEXT_LOG_UNTRANSLATED
```

The second step starts with removing duplicates:

```
$ msguniq $HOME/gettextlogused > missing.po
```

The result is a PO file, but needs some preprocessing before a PO file editor can be used with it. First, it is a multi-domain PO file, containing messages from many translation domains. Second, it lacks all translator comments and source references. Here is how to get a list of the affected translation domains:

```
$ sed -n -e 's,^domain "\(.*\)"$,\1,p' < missing.po | sort | uniq
```

Then the translator can handle the domains one by one. For simplicity, let's use environment variables to denote the language, domain and source package.

```
$ lang=nl            # your language
$ domain=coreutils   # the name of the domain to be handled
```

```
$ package=/usr/src/gnu/coreutils-4.5.4   # the package where it comes from
```

She takes the latest copy of `$lang.po` from the Translation Project, or from the package (in most cases, `$package/po/$lang.po`), or creates a fresh one if she's the first translator (see Chapter 6 [Creating], page 42). She then uses the following commands to mark the not urgent messages as "obsolete". (This doesn't mean that these messages - translated and untranslated ones - will go away. It simply means that the PO file editor will ignore them in the following editing session.)

```
$ msggrep --domain=$domain missing.po | grep -v '^domain' \
  > $domain-missing.po
$ msgattrib --set-obsolete --ignore-file $domain-missing.po $domain.$lang.po \
  > $domain.$lang-urgent.po
```

The she translates `$domain.$lang-urgent.po` by use of a PO file editor (see Chapter 8 [Editing], page 52). (FIXME: I don't know whether KBabel and gtranslator also preserve obsolete messages, as they should.) Finally she restores the not urgent messages (with their earlier translations, for those which were already translated) through this command:

```
$ msgmerge --no-fuzzy-matching $domain.$lang-urgent.po $package/po/$domain.pot \
  > $domain.$lang.po
```

Then she can submit `$domain.$lang.po` and proceed to the next domain.

13 The Maintainer's View

The maintainer of a package has many responsibilities. One of them is ensuring that the package will install easily on many platforms, and that the magic we described earlier (see Chapter 2 [Users], page 9) will work for installers and end users.

Of course, there are many possible ways by which GNU `gettext` might be integrated in a distribution, and this chapter does not cover them in all generality. Instead, it details one possible approach which is especially adequate for many free software distributions following GNU standards, or even better, Gnits standards, because GNU `gettext` is purposely for helping the internationalization of the whole GNU project, and as many other good free packages as possible. So, the maintainer's view presented here presumes that the package already has a `configure.ac` file and uses GNU Autoconf.

Nevertheless, GNU `gettext` may surely be useful for free packages not following GNU standards and conventions, but the maintainers of such packages might have to show imagination and initiative in organizing their distributions so `gettext` work for them in all situations. There are surely many, out there.

Even if `gettext` methods are now stabilizing, slight adjustments might be needed between successive `gettext` versions, so you should ideally revise this chapter in subsequent releases, looking for changes.

13.1 Flat or Non-Flat Directory Structures

Some free software packages are distributed as `tar` files which unpack in a single directory, these are said to be *flat* distributions. Other free software packages have a one level hierarchy of subdirectories, using for example a subdirectory named `doc/` for the Texinfo manual and man pages, another called `lib/` for holding functions meant to replace or complement C libraries, and a subdirectory `src/` for holding the proper sources for the package. These other distributions are said to be *non-flat*.

We cannot say much about flat distributions. A flat directory structure has the disadvantage of increasing the difficulty of updating to a new version of GNU `gettext`. Also, if you have many PO files, this could somewhat pollute your single directory. Also, GNU `gettext`'s libintl sources consist of C sources, shell scripts, `sed` scripts and complicated Makefile rules, which don't fit well into an existing flat structure. For these reasons, we recommend to use non-flat approach in this case as well.

Maybe because GNU `gettext` itself has a non-flat structure, we have more experience with this approach, and this is what will be described in the remaining of this chapter. Some maintainers might use this as an opportunity to unflatten their package structure.

13.2 Prerequisite Works

There are some works which are required for using GNU `gettext` in one of your package. These works have some kind of generality that escape the point by point descriptions used in the remainder of this chapter. So, we describe them here.

- Before attempting to use `gettextize` you should install some other packages first. Ensure that recent versions of GNU `m4`, GNU Autoconf and GNU `gettext` are already installed at your site, and if not, proceed to do this first. If you get to install these things, beware that GNU m4 must be fully installed before GNU Autoconf is even *configured*.

To further ease the task of a package maintainer the automake package was designed and implemented. GNU gettext now uses this tool and the Makefiles in the intl/ and po/ therefore know about all the goals necessary for using automake and libintl in one project.

Those four packages are only needed by you, as a maintainer; the installers of your own package and end users do not really need any of GNU m4, GNU Autoconf, GNU gettext, or GNU automake for successfully installing and running your package, with messages properly translated. But this is not completely true if you provide internationalized shell scripts within your own package: GNU gettext shall then be installed at the user site if the end users want to see the translation of shell script messages.

- Your package should use Autoconf and have a configure.ac or configure.in file. If it does not, you have to learn how. The Autoconf documentation is quite well written, it is a good idea that you print it and get familiar with it.

- Your C sources should have already been modified according to instructions given earlier in this manual. See Chapter 4 [Sources], page 19.

- Your po/ directory should receive all PO files submitted to you by the translator teams, each having ll.po as a name. This is not usually easy to get translation work done before your package gets internationalized and available! Since the cycle has to start somewhere, the easiest for the maintainer is to start with absolutely no PO files, and wait until various translator teams get interested in your package, and submit PO files.

It is worth adding here a few words about how the maintainer should ideally behave with PO files submissions. As a maintainer, your role is to authenticate the origin of the submission as being the representative of the appropriate translating teams of the Translation Project (forward the submission to coordinator@translationproject.org in case of doubt), to ensure that the PO file format is not severely broken and does not prevent successful installation, and for the rest, to merely put these PO files in po/ for distribution.

As a maintainer, you do not have to take on your shoulders the responsibility of checking if the translations are adequate or complete, and should avoid diving into linguistic matters. Translation teams drive themselves and are fully responsible of their linguistic choices for the Translation Project. Keep in mind that translator teams are *not* driven by maintainers. You can help by carefully redirecting all communications and reports from users about linguistic matters to the appropriate translation team, or explain users how to reach or join their team. The simplest might be to send them the ABOUT-NLS file.

Maintainers should *never ever* apply PO file bug reports themselves, short-cutting translation teams. If some translator has difficulty to get some of her points through her team, it should not be an option for her to directly negotiate translations with maintainers. Teams ought to settle their problems themselves, if any. If you, as a maintainer, ever think there is a real problem with a team, please never try to *solve* a team's problem on your own.

13.3 Invoking the gettextize Program

The gettextize program is an interactive tool that helps the maintainer of a package internationalized through GNU gettext. It is used for two purposes:

- As a wizard, when a package is modified to use GNU `gettext` for the first time.
- As a migration tool, for upgrading the GNU `gettext` support in a package from a previous to a newer version of GNU `gettext`.

This program performs the following tasks:

- It copies into the package some files that are consistently and identically needed in every package internationalized through GNU `gettext`.
- It performs as many of the tasks mentioned in the next section Section 13.4 [Adjusting Files], page 144 as can be performed automatically.
- It removes obsolete files and idioms used for previous GNU `gettext` versions to the form recommended for the current GNU `gettext` version.
- It prints a summary of the tasks that ought to be done manually and could not be done automatically by `gettextize`.

It can be invoked as follows:

```
gettextize [ option... ] [ directory ]
```

and accepts the following options:

`'-f'`
`'--force'`   Force replacement of files which already exist.

`'--intl'`   Install the libintl sources in a subdirectory named `intl/`. This libintl will be used to provide internationalization on systems that don't have GNU libintl installed. If this option is omitted, the call to `AM_GNU_GETTEXT` in `configure.ac` should read: `'AM_GNU_GETTEXT([external])'`, and internationalization will not be enabled on systems lacking GNU gettext.

`'--po-dir=dir'`
    Specify a directory containing PO files. Such a directory contains the translations into various languages of a particular POT file. This option can be specified multiple times, once for each translation domain. If it is not specified, the directory named `po/` is updated.

`'--no-changelog'`
    Don't update or create ChangeLog files. By default, `gettextize` logs all changes (file additions, modifications and removals) in a file called '`ChangeLog`' in each affected directory.

`'--symlink'`
    Make symbolic links instead of copying the needed files. This can be useful to save a few kilobytes of disk space, but it requires extra effort to create self-contained tarballs, it may disturb some mechanism the maintainer applies to the sources, and it is likely to introduce bugs when a newer version of `gettext` is installed on the system.

`'-n'`
`'--dry-run'`
    Print modifications but don't perform them. All actions that `gettextize` would normally execute are inhibited and instead only listed on standard output.

'--help'   Display this help and exit.

'--version'

Output version information and exit.

If *directory* is given, this is the top level directory of a package to prepare for using GNU gettext. If not given, it is assumed that the current directory is the top level directory of such a package.

The program gettextize provides the following files. However, no existing file will be replaced unless the option --force (-f) is specified.

1. The ABOUT-NLS file is copied in the main directory of your package, the one being at the top level. This file gives the main indications about how to install and use the Native Language Support features of your program. You might elect to use a more recent copy of this ABOUT-NLS file than the one provided through gettextize, if you have one handy. You may also fetch a more recent copy of file ABOUT-NLS from Translation Project sites, and from most GNU archive sites.

2. A po/ directory is created for eventually holding all translation files, but initially only containing the file po/Makefile.in.in from the GNU gettext distribution (beware the double '.in' in the file name) and a few auxiliary files. If the po/ directory already exists, it will be preserved along with the files it contains, and only Makefile.in.in and the auxiliary files will be overwritten.

   If '--po-dir' has been specified, this holds for every directory specified through '--po-dir', instead of po/.

3. Only if '--intl' has been specified: A intl/ directory is created and filled with most of the files originally in the intl/ directory of the GNU gettext distribution. Also, if option --force (-f) is given, the intl/ directory is emptied first.

4. The file config.rpath is copied into the directory containing configuration support files. It is needed by the AM_GNU_GETTEXT autoconf macro.

5. Only if the project is using GNU automake: A set of autoconf macro files is copied into the package's autoconf macro repository, usually in a directory called m4/.

If your site support symbolic links, gettextize will not actually copy the files into your package, but establish symbolic links instead. This avoids duplicating the disk space needed in all packages. Merely using the '-h' option while creating the tar archive of your distribution will resolve each link by an actual copy in the distribution archive. So, to insist, you really should use '-h' option with tar within your dist goal of your main Makefile.in.

Furthermore, gettextize will update all Makefile.am files in each affected directory, as well as the top level configure.ac or configure.in file.

It is interesting to understand that most new files for supporting GNU gettext facilities in one package go in intl/, po/ and m4/ subdirectories. One distinction between intl/ and the two other directories is that intl/ is meant to be completely identical in all packages using GNU gettext, while the other directories will mostly contain package dependent files.

The gettextize program makes backup files for all files it replaces or changes, and also write ChangeLog entries about these changes. This way, the careful maintainer can check after running gettextize whether its changes are acceptable to him, and possibly adjust them. An exception to this rule is the intl/ directory, which is added or replaced or removed as a whole.

It is important to understand that `gettextize` can not do the entire job of adapting a package for using GNU `gettext`. The amount of remaining work depends on whether the package uses GNU `automake` or not. But in any case, the maintainer should still read the section Section 13.4 [Adjusting Files], page 144 after invoking `gettextize`.

In particular, if after using 'gettexize', you get an error 'AC_COMPILE_IFELSE was called before AC_GNU_SOURCE' or 'AC_RUN_IFELSE was called before AC_GNU_SOURCE', you can fix it by modifying `configure.ac`, as described in Section 13.4.5 [configure.ac], page 146.

It is also important to understand that `gettextize` is not part of the GNU build system, in the sense that it should not be invoked automatically, and not be invoked by someone who doesn't assume the responsibilities of a package maintainer. For the latter purpose, a separate tool is provided, see Section 13.6.4 [autopoint Invocation], page 157.

13.4 Files You Must Create or Alter

Besides files which are automatically added through `gettextize`, there are many files needing revision for properly interacting with GNU `gettext`. If you are closely following GNU standards for Makefile engineering and auto-configuration, the adaptations should be easier to achieve. Here is a point by point description of the changes needed in each.

So, here comes a list of files, each one followed by a description of all alterations it needs. Many examples are taken out from the GNU `gettext` 0.19.5 distribution itself, or from the GNU `hello` distribution (`http://www.gnu.org/software/hello`). You may indeed refer to the source code of the GNU `gettext` and GNU `hello` packages, as they are intended to be good examples for using GNU gettext functionality.

13.4.1 POTFILES.in in po/

The `po/` directory should receive a file named `POTFILES.in`. This file tells which files, among all program sources, have marked strings needing translation. Here is an example of such a file:

```
# List of source files containing translatable strings.
# Copyright (C) 1995 Free Software Foundation, Inc.

# Common library files
lib/error.c
lib/getopt.c
lib/xmalloc.c

# Package source files
src/gettext.c
src/msgfmt.c
src/xgettext.c
```

Hash-marked comments and white lines are ignored. All other lines list those source files containing strings marked for translation (see Section 4.4 [Mark Keywords], page 23), in a notation relative to the top level of your whole distribution, rather than the location of the `POTFILES.in` file itself.

When a C file is automatically generated by a tool, like `flex` or `bison`, that doesn't introduce translatable strings by itself, it is recommended to list in `po/POTFILES.in` the real source file (ending in `.l` in the case of `flex`, or in `.y` in the case of `bison`), not the generated C file.

13.4.2 LINGUAS in po/

The `po/` directory should also receive a file named `LINGUAS`. This file contains the list of available translations. It is a whitespace separated list. Hash-marked comments and white lines are ignored. Here is an example file:

```
# Set of available languages.
de fr
```

This example means that German and French PO files are available, so that these languages are currently supported by your package. If you want to further restrict, at installation time, the set of installed languages, this should not be done by modifying the `LINGUAS` file, but rather by using the `LINGUAS` environment variable (see Chapter 14 [Installers], page 159).

It is recommended that you add the "languages" 'en@quot' and 'en@boldquot' to the `LINGUAS` file. en@quot is a variant of English message catalogs (en) which uses real quotation marks instead of the ugly looking asymmetric ASCII substitutes '`' and '''. en@boldquot is a variant of `en@quot` that additionally outputs quoted pieces of text in a bold font, when used in a terminal emulator which supports the VT100 escape sequences (such as `xterm` or the Linux console, but not Emacs in *M-x shell* mode).

These extra message catalogs 'en@quot' and 'en@boldquot' are constructed automatically, not by translators; to support them, you need the files `Rules-quot`, `quot.sed`, `boldquot.sed`, `en@quot.header`, `en@boldquot.header`, `insert-header.sin` in the `po/` directory. You can copy them from GNU gettext's `po/` directory; they are also installed by running `gettextize`.

13.4.3 Makevars in po/

The `po/` directory also has a file named `Makevars`. It contains variables that are specific to your project. `po/Makevars` gets inserted into the `po/Makefile` when the latter is created. The variables thus take effect when the POT file is created or updated, and when the message catalogs get installed.

The first three variables can be left unmodified if your package has a single message domain and, accordingly, a single `po/` directory. Only packages which have multiple `po/` directories at different locations need to adjust the three first variables defined in `Makevars`.

As an alternative to the `XGETTEXT_OPTIONS` variables, it is also possible to specify `xgettext` options through the `AM_XGETTEXT_OPTION` autoconf macro. See Section 13.5.6 [AM_XGETTEXT_OPTION], page 154.

13.4.4 Extending Makefile in po/

All files called `Rules-*` in the `po/` directory get appended to the `po/Makefile` when it is created. They present an opportunity to add rules for special PO files to the Makefile, without needing to mess with `po/Makefile.in.in`.

GNU gettext comes with a `Rules-quot` file, containing rules for building catalogs `en@quot.po` and `en@boldquot.po`. The effect of `en@quot.po` is that people who set their `LANGUAGE` environment variable to 'en@quot' will get messages with proper looking symmetric Unicode quotation marks instead of abusing the ASCII grave accent and the ASCII apostrophe for indicating quotations. To enable this catalog, simply add `en@quot` to the `po/LINGUAS` file. The effect of `en@boldquot.po` is that people who set `LANGUAGE` to 'en@boldquot' will get not only proper quotation marks, but also the quoted text will be shown in a bold font on terminals and consoles. This catalog is useful only for command-line programs, not GUI programs. To enable it, similarly add `en@boldquot` to the `po/LINGUAS` file.

Similarly, you can create rules for building message catalogs for the `sr@latin` locale – Serbian written with the Latin alphabet – from those for the `sr` locale – Serbian written with Cyrillic letters. See Section 9.4 [msgfilter Invocation], page 78.

13.4.5 `configure.ac` at top level

`configure.ac` or `configure.in` - this is the source from which `autoconf` generates the `configure` script.

1. Declare the package and version.

   This is done by a set of lines like these:

   ```
   PACKAGE=gettext
   VERSION=0.19.5
   AC_DEFINE_UNQUOTED(PACKAGE, "$PACKAGE")
   AC_DEFINE_UNQUOTED(VERSION, "$VERSION")
   AC_SUBST(PACKAGE)
   AC_SUBST(VERSION)
   ```

   or, if you are using GNU `automake`, by a line like this:

   ```
   AM_INIT_AUTOMAKE(gettext, 0.19.5)
   ```

   Of course, you replace 'gettext' with the name of your package, and '0.19.5' by its version numbers, exactly as they should appear in the packaged `tar` file name of your distribution (`gettext-0.19.5.tar.gz`, here).

2. Check for internationalization support.

   Here is the main `m4` macro for triggering internationalization support. Just add this line to `configure.ac`:

   ```
   AM_GNU_GETTEXT
   ```

   This call is purposely simple, even if it generates a lot of configure time checking and actions.

   If you have suppressed the `intl/` subdirectory by calling `gettextize` without '--intl' option, this call should read

   ```
   AM_GNU_GETTEXT([external])
   ```

3. Have output files created.

   The `AC_OUTPUT` directive, at the end of your `configure.ac` file, needs to be modified in two ways:

   ```
   AC_OUTPUT([existing configuration files intl/Makefile po/Makefile.in],
   [existing additional actions])
   ```

The modification to the first argument to `AC_OUTPUT` asks for substitution in the `intl/` and `po/` directories. Note the '`.in`' suffix used for `po/` only. This is because the distributed file is really `po/Makefile.in.in`.

If you have suppressed the `intl/` subdirectory by calling `gettextize` without '`--intl`' option, then you don't need to add `intl/Makefile` to the `AC_OUTPUT` line.

If, after doing the recommended modifications, a command like '`aclocal -I m4`' or '`autoconf`' or '`autoreconf`' fails with a trace similar to this:

```
configure.ac:44: warning: AC_COMPILE_IFELSE was called before AC_GNU_SOURCE
../../lib/autoconf/specific.m4:335: AC_GNU_SOURCE is expanded from...
m4/lock.m4:224: gl_LOCK is expanded from...
m4/gettext.m4:571: gt_INTL_SUBDIR_CORE is expanded from...
m4/gettext.m4:472: AM_INTL_SUBDIR is expanded from...
m4/gettext.m4:347: AM_GNU_GETTEXT is expanded from...
configure.ac:44: the top level
configure.ac:44: warning: AC_RUN_IFELSE was called before AC_GNU_SOURCE
```

you need to add an explicit invocation of '`AC_GNU_SOURCE`' in the `configure.ac` file - after '`AC_PROG_CC`' but before '`AM_GNU_GETTEXT`', most likely very close to the '`AC_PROG_CC`' invocation. This is necessary because of ordering restrictions imposed by GNU autoconf.

13.4.6 `config.guess`, `config.sub` at top level

If you haven't suppressed the `intl/` subdirectory, you need to add the GNU `config.guess` and `config.sub` files to your distribution. They are needed because the `intl/` directory has platform dependent support for determining the locale's character encoding and therefore needs to identify the platform.

You can obtain the newest version of `config.guess` and `config.sub` from the '`config`' project at `http://savannah.gnu.org/`. The commands to fetch them are

```
$ wget -O config.guess 'http://git.savannah.gnu.org/gitweb/?p=config.git;a=blob_plain;f=config.guess;hb=H
$ wget -O config.sub 'http://git.savannah.gnu.org/gitweb/?p=config.git;a=blob_plain;f=config.sub;hb=HEAD'
```

Less recent versions are also contained in the GNU `automake` and GNU `libtool` packages.

Normally, `config.guess` and `config.sub` are put at the top level of a distribution. But it is also possible to put them in a subdirectory, altogether with other configuration support files like `install-sh`, `ltconfig`, `ltmain.sh` or `missing`. All you need to do, other than moving the files, is to add the following line to your `configure.ac`.

```
AC_CONFIG_AUX_DIR([subdir])
```

13.4.7 `mkinstalldirs` at top level

With earlier versions of GNU gettext, you needed to add the GNU `mkinstalldirs` script to your distribution. This is not needed any more. You can remove it if you not also using an automake version older than automake 1.9.

13.4.8 `aclocal.m4` at top level

If you do not have an `aclocal.m4` file in your distribution, the simplest is to concatenate the files `codeset.m4`, `fcntl-o.m4`, `gettext.m4`, `glibc2.m4`, `glibc21.m4`, `iconv.m4`, `intdiv0.m4`, `intl.m4`, `intldir.m4`, `intlmacosx.m4`, `intmax.m4`, `inttypes_h.m4`, `inttypes-pri.m4`, `lcmessage.m4`, `lib-ld.m4`, `lib-link.m4`, `lib-prefix.m4`, `lock.m4`, `longlong.m4`, `nls.m4`, `po.m4`, `printf-posix.m4`, `progtest.m4`, `size_max.m4`, stdint_h.m4, threadlib.m4, uintmax_t.m4, visibility.m4, wchar_t.m4, wint_t.m4, xsize.m4 from GNU gettext's m4/ directory into a single file. If you have suppressed the intl/ directory, only gettext.m4, iconv.m4, lib-ld.m4, lib-link.m4, lib-prefix.m4, nls.m4, po.m4, progtest.m4 need to be concatenated.

If you are not using GNU automake 1.8 or newer, you will need to add a file mkdirp.m4 from a newer automake distribution to the list of files above.

If you already have an aclocal.m4 file, then you will have to merge the said macro files into your aclocal.m4. Note that if you are upgrading from a previous release of GNU gettext, you should most probably *replace* the macros (AM_GNU_GETTEXT, etc.), as they usually change a little from one release of GNU gettext to the next. Their contents may vary as we get more experience with strange systems out there.

If you are using GNU automake 1.5 or newer, it is enough to put these macro files into a subdirectory named m4/ and add the line

```
ACLOCAL_AMFLAGS = -I m4
```

to your top level Makefile.am.

If you are using GNU automake 1.10 or newer, it is even easier: Add the line

```
ACLOCAL_AMFLAGS = --install -I m4
```

to your top level Makefile.am, and run 'aclocal --install -I m4'. This will copy the needed files to the m4/ subdirectory automatically, before updating aclocal.m4.

These macros check for the internationalization support functions and related informations. Hopefully, once stabilized, these macros might be integrated in the standard Autoconf set, because this piece of m4 code will be the same for all projects using GNU gettext.

13.4.9 acconfig.h at top level

Earlier GNU gettext releases required to put definitions for ENABLE_NLS, HAVE_GETTEXT and HAVE_LC_MESSAGES, HAVE_STPCPY, PACKAGE and VERSION into an acconfig.h file. This is not needed any more; you can remove them from your acconfig.h file unless your package uses them independently from the intl/ directory.

13.4.10 config.h.in at top level

The include file template that holds the C macros to be defined by configure is usually called config.h.in and may be maintained either manually or automatically.

If gettextize has created an intl/ directory, this file must be called config.h.in and must be at the top level. If, however, you have suppressed the intl/ directory by calling gettextize without '--intl' option, then you can choose the name of this file and its location freely.

If it is maintained automatically, by use of the 'autoheader' program, you need to do nothing about it. This is the case in particular if you are using GNU automake.

If it is maintained manually, and if gettextize has created an intl/ directory, you should switch to using 'autoheader'. The list of C macros to be added for the sake of the intl/ directory is just too long to be maintained manually; it also changes between different versions of GNU gettext.

If it is maintained manually, and if on the other hand you have suppressed the intl/ directory by calling gettextize without '--intl' option, then you can get away by adding the following lines to config.h.in:

```
/* Define to 1 if translation of program messages to the user's
   native language is requested. */
#undef ENABLE_NLS
```

13.4.11 `Makefile.in` at top level

Here are a few modifications you need to make to your main, top-level `Makefile.in` file.

1. Add the following lines near the beginning of your `Makefile.in`, so the 'dist:' goal will work properly (as explained further down):

   ```
   PACKAGE = @PACKAGE@
   VERSION = @VERSION@
   ```

2. Add file `ABOUT-NLS` to the `DISTFILES` definition, so the file gets distributed.

3. Wherever you process subdirectories in your `Makefile.in`, be sure you also process the subdirectories 'intl' and 'po'. Special rules in the `Makefiles` take care for the case where no internationalization is wanted.

   If you are using Makefiles, either generated by automake, or hand-written so they carefully follow the GNU coding standards, the effected goals for which the new sub-directories must be handled include 'installdirs', 'install', 'uninstall', 'clean', 'distclean'.

   Here is an example of a canonical order of processing. In this example, we also define `SUBDIRS` in `Makefile.in` for it to be further used in the 'dist:' goal.

   ```
   SUBDIRS = doc intl lib src po
   ```

   Note that you must arrange for 'make' to descend into the `intl` directory before descending into other directories containing code which make use of the `libintl.h` header file. For this reason, here we mention `intl` before `lib` and `src`.

4. A delicate point is the 'dist:' goal, as both `intl/Makefile` and `po/Makefile` will later assume that the proper directory has been set up from the main `Makefile`. Here is an example at what the 'dist:' goal might look like:

   ```
   distdir = $(PACKAGE)-$(VERSION)
   dist: Makefile
   rm -fr $(distdir)
   mkdir $(distdir)
   chmod 777 $(distdir)
   for file in $(DISTFILES); do \
     ln $$file $(distdir) 2>/dev/null || cp -p $$file $(distdir); \
   done
   for subdir in $(SUBDIRS); do \
     mkdir $(distdir)/$$subdir || exit 1; \
     chmod 777 $(distdir)/$$subdir; \
     (cd $$subdir && $(MAKE) $@) || exit 1; \
   done
   tar chozf $(distdir).tar.gz $(distdir)
   rm -fr $(distdir)
   ```

Note that if you are using GNU `automake`, `Makefile.in` is automatically generated from `Makefile.am`, and all needed changes to `Makefile.am` are already made by running 'gettextize'.

13.4.12 Makefile.in in src/

Some of the modifications made in the main `Makefile.in` will also be needed in the `Makefile.in` from your package sources, which we assume here to be in the `src/` subdirectory. Here are all the modifications needed in `src/Makefile.in`:

1. In view of the 'dist:' goal, you should have these lines near the beginning of `src/Makefile.in`:

   ```
   PACKAGE = @PACKAGE@
   VERSION = @VERSION@
   ```

2. If not done already, you should guarantee that `top_srcdir` gets defined. This will serve for `cpp` include files. Just add the line:

   ```
   top_srcdir = @top_srcdir@
   ```

3. You might also want to define `subdir` as 'src', later allowing for almost uniform 'dist:' goals in all your `Makefile.in`. At list, the 'dist:' goal below assume that you used:

   ```
   subdir = src
   ```

4. The `main` function of your program will normally call `bindtextdomain` (see see Section 4.2 [Triggering], page 19), like this:

   ```
   bindtextdomain (PACKAGE, LOCALEDIR);
   textdomain (PACKAGE);
   ```

   To make LOCALEDIR known to the program, add the following lines to `Makefile.in` if you are using Autoconf version 2.60 or newer:

   ```
   datadir = @datadir@
   datarootdir= @datarootdir@
   localedir = @localedir@
   DEFS = -DLOCALEDIR=\"$(localedir)\" @DEFS@
   ```

   or these lines if your version of Autoconf is older than 2.60:

   ```
   datadir = @datadir@
   localedir = $(datadir)/locale
   DEFS = -DLOCALEDIR=\"$(localedir)\" @DEFS@
   ```

   Note that `@datadir@` defaults to '`$(prefix)/share`', thus `$(localedir)` defaults to '`$(prefix)/share/locale`'.

5. You should ensure that the final linking will use `@LIBINTL@` or `@LTLIBINTL@` as a library. `@LIBINTL@` is for use without `libtool`, `@LTLIBINTL@` is for use with `libtool`. An easy way to achieve this is to manage that it gets into LIBS, like this:

   ```
   LIBS = @LIBINTL@ @LIBS@
   ```

   In most packages internationalized with GNU `gettext`, one will find a directory `lib/` in which a library containing some helper functions will be build. (You need at least the few functions which the GNU `gettext` Library itself needs.) However some of the functions in the `lib/` also give messages to the user which of course should be translated, too. Taking care of this, the support library (say `libsupport.a`) should be placed before `@LIBINTL@` and `@LIBS@` in the above example. So one has to write this:

   ```
   LIBS = ../lib/libsupport.a @LIBINTL@ @LIBS@
   ```

6. You should also ensure that directory `intl/` will be searched for C preprocessor include files in all circumstances. So, you have to manage so both '`-I../intl`' and '`-I$(top_srcdir)/intl`' will be given to the C compiler.

7. Your '`dist:`' goal has to conform with others. Here is a reasonable definition for it:

```
distdir = ../$(PACKAGE)-$(VERSION)/$(subdir)
dist: Makefile $(DISTFILES)
for file in $(DISTFILES); do \
  ln $$file $(distdir) 2>/dev/null || cp -p $$file $(distdir) || exit 1; \
done
```

Note that if you are using GNU `automake`, `Makefile.in` is automatically generated from `Makefile.am`, and the first three changes and the last change are not necessary. The remaining needed `Makefile.am` modifications are the following:

1. To make LOCALEDIR known to the program, add the following to `Makefile.am`:

```
<module>_CPPFLAGS = -DLOCALEDIR=\"$(localedir)\"
```

for each specific module or compilation unit, or

```
AM_CPPFLAGS = -DLOCALEDIR=\"$(localedir)\"
```

for all modules and compilation units together. Furthermore, if you are using an Autoconf version older then 2.60, add this line to define '`localedir`':

```
localedir = $(datadir)/locale
```

2. To ensure that the final linking will use @LIBINTL@ or @LTLIBINTL@ as a library, add the following to `Makefile.am`:

```
<program>_LDADD = @LIBINTL@
```

for each specific program, or

```
LDADD = @LIBINTL@
```

for all programs together. Remember that when you use `libtool` to link a program, you need to use @LTLIBINTL@ instead of @LIBINTL@ for that program.

3. If you have an `intl/` directory, whose contents is created by `gettextize`, then to ensure that it will be searched for C preprocessor include files in all circumstances, add something like this to `Makefile.am`:

```
AM_CPPFLAGS = -I../intl -I$(top_srcdir)/intl
```

13.4.13 `gettext.h` in `lib/`

Internationalization of packages, as provided by GNU `gettext`, is optional. It can be turned off in two situations:

- When the installer has specified '`./configure --disable-nls`'. This can be useful when small binaries are more important than features, for example when building utilities for boot diskettes. It can also be useful in order to get some specific C compiler warnings about code quality with some older versions of GCC (older than 3.0).

- When the package does not include the `intl/` subdirectory, and the libintl.h header (with its associated libintl library, if any) is not already installed on the system, it is preferable that the package builds without internationalization support, rather than to give a compilation error.

A C preprocessor macro can be used to detect these two cases. Usually, when `libintl.h` was found and not explicitly disabled, the `ENABLE_NLS` macro will be defined to 1 in the autoconf generated configuration file (usually called `config.h`). In the two negative situations, however, this macro will not be defined, thus it will evaluate to 0 in C preprocessor expressions.

`gettext.h` is a convenience header file for conditional use of `<libintl.h>`, depending on the `ENABLE_NLS` macro. If `ENABLE_NLS` is set, it includes `<libintl.h>`; otherwise it defines no-op substitutes for the libintl.h functions. We recommend the use of `"gettext.h"` over direct use of `<libintl.h>`, so that portability to older systems is guaranteed and installers can turn off internationalization if they want to. In the C code, you will then write

```
#include "gettext.h"
```

instead of

```
#include <libintl.h>
```

The location of `gettext.h` is usually in a directory containing auxiliary include files. In many GNU packages, there is a directory `lib/` containing helper functions; `gettext.h` fits there. In other packages, it can go into the `src` directory.

Do not install the `gettext.h` file in public locations. Every package that needs it should contain a copy of it on its own.

13.5 Autoconf macros for use in `configure.ac`

GNU `gettext` installs macros for use in a package's `configure.ac` or `configure.in`. See Section "Introduction" in *The Autoconf Manual*. The primary macro is, of course, `AM_GNU_GETTEXT`.

13.5.1 AM_GNU_GETTEXT in `gettext.m4`

The `AM_GNU_GETTEXT` macro tests for the presence of the GNU gettext function family in either the C library or a separate `libintl` library (shared or static libraries are both supported) or in the package's `intl/` directory. It also invokes `AM_PO_SUBDIRS`, thus preparing the `po/` directories of the package for building.

`AM_GNU_GETTEXT` accepts up to three optional arguments. The general syntax is

```
AM_GNU_GETTEXT([intlsymbol], [needsymbol], [intldir])
```

intlsymbol can be 'external' or 'no-libtool'. The default (if it is not specified or empty) is 'no-libtool'. *intlsymbol* should be 'external' for packages with no `intl/` directory. For packages with an `intl/` directory, you can either use an *intlsymbol* equal to 'no-libtool', or you can use 'external' and override by using the macro `AM_GNU_GETTEXT_INTL_SUBDIR` elsewhere. The two ways to specify the existence of an `intl/` directory are equivalent. At build time, a static library `$(top_builddir)/intl/libintl.a` will then be created.

If *needsymbol* is specified and is 'need-ngettext', then GNU gettext implementations (in libc or libintl) without the `ngettext()` function will be ignored. If *needsymbol* is specified and is 'need-formatstring-macros', then GNU gettext implementations that don't support the ISO C 99 `<inttypes.h>` formatstring macros will be ignored. Only one *needsymbol* can be specified. These requirements can also be specified by using the macro `AM_GNU_GETTEXT_NEED` elsewhere. To specify more than one requirement, just specify the strongest one among them, or invoke the `AM_GNU_GETTEXT_NEED` macro several times. The hierarchy among the various alternatives is as follows: 'need-formatstring-macros' implies 'need-ngettext'.

intldir is used to find the intl libraries. If empty, the value '$(top_builddir)/intl/' is used.

The `AM_GNU_GETTEXT` macro determines whether GNU gettext is available and should be used. If so, it sets the `USE_NLS` variable to 'yes'; it defines `ENABLE_NLS` to 1 in the autoconf generated configuration file (usually called `config.h`); it sets the variables `LIBINTL` and `LTLIBINTL` to the linker options for use in a Makefile (`LIBINTL` for use without libtool, `LTLIBINTL` for use with libtool); it adds an '-I' option to `CPPFLAGS` if necessary. In the negative case, it sets `USE_NLS` to 'no'; it sets `LIBINTL` and `LTLIBINTL` to empty and doesn't change `CPPFLAGS`.

The complexities that `AM_GNU_GETTEXT` deals with are the following:

- Some operating systems have `gettext` in the C library, for example glibc. Some have it in a separate library `libintl`. GNU `libintl` might have been installed as part of the GNU `gettext` package.

- GNU `libintl`, if installed, is not necessarily already in the search path (`CPPFLAGS` for the include file search path, `LDFLAGS` for the library search path).

- Except for glibc, the operating system's native `gettext` cannot exploit the GNU mo files, doesn't have the necessary locale dependency features, and cannot convert messages from the catalog's text encoding to the user's locale encoding.

- GNU `libintl`, if installed, is not necessarily already in the run time library search path. To avoid the need for setting an environment variable like `LD_LIBRARY_PATH`, the macro adds the appropriate run time search path options to the `LIBINTL` and `LTLIBINTL` variables. This works on most systems, but not on some operating systems with limited shared library support, like SCO.

- GNU `libintl` relies on POSIX/XSI `iconv`. The macro checks for linker options needed to use iconv and appends them to the `LIBINTL` and `LTLIBINTL` variables.

13.5.2 AM_GNU_GETTEXT_VERSION in gettext.m4

The `AM_GNU_GETTEXT_VERSION` macro declares the version number of the GNU gettext infrastructure that is used by the package.

The use of this macro is optional; only the `autopoint` program makes use of it (see Section 13.6 [Version Control Issues], page 155).

13.5.3 AM_GNU_GETTEXT_NEED in gettext.m4

The `AM_GNU_GETTEXT_NEED` macro declares a constraint regarding the GNU gettext implementation. The syntax is

    AM_GNU_GETTEXT_NEED([needsymbol])

If *needsymbol* is 'need-ngettext', then GNU gettext implementations (in libc or libintl) without the `ngettext()` function will be ignored. If *needsymbol* is 'need-formatstring-macros', then GNU gettext implementations that don't support the ISO C 99 `<inttypes.h>` formatstring macros will be ignored.

The optional second argument of `AM_GNU_GETTEXT` is also taken into account.

The `AM_GNU_GETTEXT_NEED` invocations can occur before or after the `AM_GNU_GETTEXT` invocation; the order doesn't matter.

13.5.4 AM_GNU_GETTEXT_INTL_SUBDIR in `intldir.m4`

The `AM_GNU_GETTEXT_INTL_SUBDIR` macro specifies that the `AM_GNU_GETTEXT` macro, although invoked with the first argument 'external', should also prepare for building the `intl/` subdirectory.

The `AM_GNU_GETTEXT_INTL_SUBDIR` invocation can occur before or after the `AM_GNU_GETTEXT` invocation; the order doesn't matter.

The use of this macro requires GNU automake 1.10 or newer and GNU autoconf 2.61 or newer.

13.5.5 AM_PO_SUBDIRS in `po.m4`

The `AM_PO_SUBDIRS` macro prepares the `po/` directories of the package for building. This macro should be used in internationalized programs written in other programming languages than C, C++, Objective C, for example `sh`, `Python`, `Lisp`. See Chapter 15 [Programming Languages], page 160 for a list of programming languages that support localization through PO files.

The `AM_PO_SUBDIRS` macro determines whether internationalization should be used. If so, it sets the `USE_NLS` variable to 'yes', otherwise to 'no'. It also determines the right values for Makefile variables in each `po/` directory.

13.5.6 AM_XGETTEXT_OPTION in `po.m4`

The `AM_XGETTEXT_OPTION` macro registers a command-line option to be used in the invocations of `xgettext` in the `po/` directories of the package.

For example, if you have a source file that defines a function 'error_at_line' whose fifth argument is a format string, you can use

```
AM_XGETTEXT_OPTION([--flag=error_at_line:5:c-format])
```

to instruct `xgettext` to mark all translatable strings in 'gettext' invocations that occur as fifth argument to this function as 'c-format'.

See Section 5.1 [xgettext Invocation], page 33 for the list of options that `xgettext` accepts.

The use of this macro is an alternative to the use of the 'XGETTEXT_OPTIONS' variable in `po/Makevars`.

13.5.7 AM_ICONV in `iconv.m4`

The `AM_ICONV` macro tests for the presence of the POSIX/XSI `iconv` function family in either the C library or a separate `libiconv` library. If found, it sets the `am_cv_func_iconv` variable to 'yes'; it defines `HAVE_ICONV` to 1 in the autoconf generated configuration file (usually called `config.h`); it defines `ICONV_CONST` to 'const' or to empty, depending on whether the second argument of `iconv()` is of type 'const char **' or 'char **'; it sets the variables `LIBICONV` and `LTLIBICONV` to the linker options for use in a Makefile (`LIBICONV` for use without libtool, `LTLIBICONV` for use with libtool); it adds an '-I' option to `CPPFLAGS` if necessary. If not found, it sets `LIBICONV` and `LTLIBICONV` to empty and doesn't change `CPPFLAGS`.

The complexities that `AM_ICONV` deals with are the following:

- Some operating systems have `iconv` in the C library, for example glibc. Some have it in a separate library `libiconv`, for example OSF/1 or FreeBSD. Regardless of the operating system, GNU `libiconv` might have been installed. In that case, it should be used instead of the operating system's native `iconv`.

- GNU `libiconv`, if installed, is not necessarily already in the search path (`CPPFLAGS` for the include file search path, `LDFLAGS` for the library search path).

- GNU `libiconv` is binary incompatible with some operating system's native `iconv`, for example on FreeBSD. Use of an `iconv.h` and `libiconv.so` that don't fit together would produce program crashes.

- GNU `libiconv`, if installed, is not necessarily already in the run time library search path. To avoid the need for setting an environment variable like `LD_LIBRARY_PATH`, the macro adds the appropriate run time search path options to the `LIBICONV` variable. This works on most systems, but not on some operating systems with limited shared library support, like SCO.

`iconv.m4` is distributed with the GNU gettext package because `gettext.m4` relies on it.

13.6 Integrating with Version Control Systems

Many projects use version control systems for distributed development and source backup. This section gives some advice how to manage the uses of `gettextize`, `autopoint` and `autoconf` on version controlled files.

13.6.1 Avoiding version mismatch in distributed development

In a project development with multiple developers, there should be a single developer who occasionally - when there is desire to upgrade to a new `gettext` version - runs `gettextize` and performs the changes listed in Section 13.4 [Adjusting Files], page 144, and then commits his changes to the repository.

It is highly recommended that all developers on a project use the same version of GNU `gettext` in the package. In other words, if a developer runs `gettextize`, he should go the whole way, make the necessary remaining changes and commit his changes to the repository. Otherwise the following damages will likely occur:

- Apparent version mismatch between developers. Since some `gettext` specific portions in `configure.ac`, `configure.in` and `Makefile.am`, `Makefile.in` files depend on the `gettext` version, the use of infrastructure files belonging to different `gettext` versions can easily lead to build errors.

- Hidden version mismatch. Such version mismatch can also lead to malfunctioning of the package, that may be undiscovered by the developers. The worst case of hidden version mismatch is that internationalization of the package doesn't work at all.

- Release risks. All developers implicitly perform constant testing on a package. This is important in the days and weeks before a release. If the guy who makes the release tar files uses a different version of GNU `gettext` than the other developers, the distribution will be less well tested than if all had been using the same `gettext` version. For example, it is possible that a platform specific bug goes undiscovered due to this constellation.

13.6.2 Files to put under version control

There are basically three ways to deal with generated files in the context of a version controlled repository, such as `configure` generated from `configure.ac`, *parser.c* generated from *parser.y*, or `po/Makefile.in.in` autoinstalled by `gettextize` or `autopoint`.

1. All generated files are always committed into the repository.

2. All generated files are committed into the repository occasionally, for example each time a release is made.

3. Generated files are never committed into the repository.

Each of these three approaches has different advantages and drawbacks.

1. The advantage is that anyone can check out the source at any moment and gets a working build. The drawbacks are: 1a. It requires some frequent "push" actions by the maintainers. 1b. The repository grows in size quite fast.

2. The advantage is that anyone can check out the source, and the usual "./configure; make" will work. The drawbacks are: 2a. The one who checks out the repository needs tools like GNU `automake`, GNU `autoconf`, GNU `m4` installed in his PATH; sometimes he even needs particular versions of them. 2b. When a release is made and a commit is made on the generated files, the other developers get conflicts on the generated files when merging the local work back to the repository. Although these conflicts are easy to resolve, they are annoying.

3. The advantage is less work for the maintainers. The drawback is that anyone who checks out the source not only needs tools like GNU `automake`, GNU `autoconf`, GNU `m4` installed in his PATH, but also that he needs to perform a package specific pre-build step before being able to "./configure; make".

For the first and second approach, all files modified or brought in by the occasional `gettextize` invocation and update should be committed into the repository.

For the third approach, the maintainer can omit from the repository all the files that `gettextize` mentions as "copy". Instead, he adds to the `configure.ac` or `configure.in` a line of the form

```
AM_GNU_GETTEXT_VERSION(0.19.5)
```

and adds to the package's pre-build script an invocation of 'autopoint'. For everyone who checks out the source, this `autopoint` invocation will copy into the right place the `gettext` infrastructure files that have been omitted from the repository.

The version number used as argument to `AM_GNU_GETTEXT_VERSION` is the version of the `gettext` infrastructure that the package wants to use. It is also the minimum version number of the 'autopoint' program. So, if you write `AM_GNU_GETTEXT_VERSION(0.11.5)` then the developers can have any version >= 0.11.5 installed; the package will work with the 0.11.5 infrastructure in all developers' builds. When the maintainer then runs gettextize from, say, version 0.12.1 on the package, the occurrence of `AM_GNU_GETTEXT_VERSION(0.11.5)` will be changed into `AM_GNU_GETTEXT_VERSION(0.12.1)`, and all other developers that use the CVS will henceforth need to have GNU `gettext` 0.12.1 or newer installed.

13.6.3 Put PO Files under Version Control

Since translations are valuable assets as well as the source code, it would make sense to put them under version control. The GNU gettext infrastructure supports two ways to deal with translations in the context of a version controlled repository.

1. Both POT file and PO files are committed into the repository.

2. Only PO files are committed into the repository.

If a POT file is absent when building, it will be generated by scanning the source files with `xgettext`, and then the PO files are regenerated as a dependency. On the other hand, some maintainers want to keep the POT file unchanged during the development phase. So, even if a POT file is present and older than the source code, it won't be updated automatically. You can manually update it with `make $(DOMAIN).pot-update`, and commit it at certain point.

Special advices for particular version control systems:

- Recent version control systems, Git for instance, ignore file's timestamp. In that case, PO files can be accidentally updated even if a POT file is not updated. To prevent this, you can set 'PO_DEPENDS_ON_POT' variable to `no` in the `Makevars` file and do `make update-po` manually.

- Location comments such as `#: lib/error.c:116` are sometimes annoying, since these comments are volatile and may introduce unwanted change to the working copy when building. To mitigate this, you can decide to omit those comments from the PO files in the repository.

  This is possible with the `--no-location` option of the `msgmerge` command[1]. The drawback is that, if the location information is needed, translators have to recover the location comments by running `msgmerge` again.

13.6.4 Invoking the `autopoint` Program

```
autopoint [option]...
```

The `autopoint` program copies standard gettext infrastructure files into a source package. It extracts from a macro call of the form `AM_GNU_GETTEXT_VERSION(version)`, found in the package's `configure.in` or `configure.ac` file, the gettext version used by the package, and copies the infrastructure files belonging to this version into the package.

13.6.4.1 Options

'`-f`'
'`--force`'   Force overwriting of files that already exist.

'`-n`'
'`--dry-run`'

> Print modifications but don't perform them. All file copying actions that `autopoint` would normally execute are inhibited and instead only listed on standard output.

---

[1] you can also use it through the 'MSGMERGE_OPTIONS' option from `Makevars`

13.6.4.2 Informative output

'--help'   Display this help and exit.

'--version'

> Output version information and exit.

autopoint supports the GNU gettext versions from 0.10.35 to the current one, 0.19.5. In order to apply autopoint to a package using a gettext version newer than 0.19.5, you need to install this same version of GNU gettext at least.

In packages using GNU automake, an invocation of autopoint should be followed by invocations of aclocal and then autoconf and autoheader. The reason is that autopoint installs some autoconf macro files, which are used by aclocal to create aclocal.m4, and the latter is used by autoconf to create the package's configure script and by autoheader to create the package's config.h.in include file template.

The name 'autopoint' is an abbreviation of 'auto-po-intl-m4'; the tool copies or updates mostly files in the po, intl, m4 directories.

13.7 Creating a Distribution Tarball

In projects that use GNU automake, the usual commands for creating a distribution tarball, 'make dist' or 'make distcheck', automatically update the PO files as needed.

If GNU automake is not used, the maintainer needs to perform this update before making a release:

```
$ ./configure
$ (cd po; make update-po)
$ make distclean
```

14 The Installer's and Distributor's View

By default, packages fully using GNU `gettext`, internally, are installed in such a way as to allow translation of messages. At *configuration* time, those packages should automatically detect whether the underlying host system already provides the GNU `gettext` functions. If not, the GNU `gettext` library should be automatically prepared and used. Installers may use special options at configuration time for changing this behavior. The command '`./configure --with-included-gettext`' bypasses system `gettext` to use the included GNU `gettext` instead, while '`./configure --disable-nls`' produces programs totally unable to translate messages.

Internationalized packages have usually many `ll.po` files. Unless translations are disabled, all those available are installed together with the package. However, the environment variable `LINGUAS` may be set, prior to configuration, to limit the installed set. `LINGUAS` should then contain a space separated list of two-letter codes, stating which languages are allowed.

15 Other Programming Languages

While the presentation of `gettext` focuses mostly on C and implicitly applies to C++ as well, its scope is far broader than that: Many programming languages, scripting languages and other textual data like GUI resources or package descriptions can make use of the gettext approach.

15.1 The Language Implementor's View

All programming and scripting languages that have the notion of strings are eligible to supporting `gettext`. Supporting `gettext` means the following:

1. You should add to the language a syntax for translatable strings. In principle, a function call of `gettext` would do, but a shorthand syntax helps keeping the legibility of internationalized programs. For example, in C we use the syntax `_("string")`, and in GNU awk we use the shorthand `_"string"`.

2. You should arrange that evaluation of such a translatable string at runtime calls the `gettext` function, or performs equivalent processing.

3. Similarly, you should make the functions `ngettext`, `dcgettext`, `dcngettext` available from within the language. These functions are less often used, but are nevertheless necessary for particular purposes: `ngettext` for correct plural handling, and `dcgettext` and `dcngettext` for obeying other locale-related environment variables than `LC_MESSAGES`, such as `LC_TIME` or `LC_MONETARY`. For these latter functions, you need to make the `LC_*` constants, available in the C header `<locale.h>`, referenceable from within the language, usually either as enumeration values or as strings.

4. You should allow the programmer to designate a message domain, either by making the `textdomain` function available from within the language, or by introducing a magic variable called `TEXTDOMAIN`. Similarly, you should allow the programmer to designate where to search for message catalogs, by providing access to the `bindtextdomain` function.

5. You should either perform a `setlocale (LC_ALL, "")` call during the startup of your language runtime, or allow the programmer to do so. Remember that gettext will act as a no-op if the `LC_MESSAGES` and `LC_CTYPE` locale categories are not both set.

6. A programmer should have a way to extract translatable strings from a program into a PO file. The GNU `xgettext` program is being extended to support very different programming languages. Please contact the GNU `gettext` maintainers to help them doing this. If the string extractor is best integrated into your language's parser, GNU `xgettext` can function as a front end to your string extractor.

7. The language's library should have a string formatting facility where the arguments of a format string are denoted by a positional number or a name. This is needed because for some languages and some messages with more than one substitutable argument, the translation will need to output the substituted arguments in different order. See Section 4.6 [c-format Flag], page 27.

8. If the language has more than one implementation, and not all of the implementations use `gettext`, but the programs should be portable across implementations, you should provide a no-i18n emulation, that makes the other implementations accept programs written for yours, without actually translating the strings.

9. To help the programmer in the task of marking translatable strings, which is sometimes performed using the Emacs PO mode (see Section 4.5 [Marking], page 24), you are welcome to contact the GNU `gettext` maintainers, so they can add support for your language to `po-mode.el`.

On the implementation side, three approaches are possible, with different effects on portability and copyright:

- You may integrate the GNU `gettext`'s `intl/` directory in your package, as described in Chapter 13 [Maintainers], page 140. This allows you to have internationalization on all kinds of platforms. Note that when you then distribute your package, it legally falls under the GNU General Public License, and the GNU project will be glad about your contribution to the Free Software pool.

- You may link against GNU `gettext` functions if they are found in the C library. For example, an autoconf test for `gettext()` and `ngettext()` will detect this situation. For the moment, this test will succeed on GNU systems and not on other platforms. No severe copyright restrictions apply.

- You may emulate or reimplement the GNU `gettext` functionality. This has the advantage of full portability and no copyright restrictions, but also the drawback that you have to reimplement the GNU `gettext` features (such as the `LANGUAGE` environment variable, the locale aliases database, the automatic charset conversion, and plural handling).

15.2 The Programmer's View

For the programmer, the general procedure is the same as for the C language. The Emacs PO mode marking supports other languages, and the GNU `xgettext` string extractor recognizes other languages based on the file extension or a command-line option. In some languages, `setlocale` is not needed because it is already performed by the underlying language runtime.

15.3 The Translator's View

The translator works exactly as in the C language case. The only difference is that when translating format strings, she has to be aware of the language's particular syntax for positional arguments in format strings.

15.3.1 C Format Strings

C format strings are described in POSIX (IEEE P1003.1 2001), section XSH 3 fprintf(), `http://www.opengroup.org/onlinepubs/007904975/functions/fprintf.html`. See also the fprintf() manual page, `http://www.linuxvalley.it/encyclopedia/ldp/manpage/man3/printf.3.php`, `http://informatik.fh-wuerzburg.de/student/i510/man/printf.html`.

Although format strings with positions that reorder arguments, such as

```
"Only %2$d bytes free on '%1$s'."
```
which is semantically equivalent to

```
"'%s' has only %d bytes free."
```

are a POSIX/XSI feature and not specified by ISO C 99, translators can rely on this reordering ability: On the few platforms where `printf()`, `fprintf()` etc. don't support this feature natively, `libintl.a` or `libintl.so` provides replacement functions, and GNU `<libintl.h>` activates these replacement functions automatically.

As a special feature for Farsi (Persian) and maybe Arabic, translators can insert an 'I' flag into numeric format directives. For example, the translation of `"%d"` can be `"%Id"`. The effect of this flag, on systems with GNU `libc`, is that in the output, the ASCII digits are replaced with the 'outdigits' defined in the `LC_CTYPE` locale category. On other systems, the `gettext` function removes this flag, so that it has no effect.

Note that the programmer should *not* put this flag into the untranslated string. (Putting the 'I' format directive flag into an *msgid* string would lead to undefined behaviour on platforms without glibc when NLS is disabled.)

15.3.2 Objective C Format Strings

Objective C format strings are like C format strings. They support an additional format directive: `"%@"`, which when executed consumes an argument of type `Object *`.

15.3.3 Shell Format Strings

Shell format strings, as supported by GNU gettext and the 'envsubst' program, are strings with references to shell variables in the form $*variable* or ${*variable*}. References of the form ${*variable-default*}, ${*variable:-default*}, ${*variable=default*}, ${*variable:=default*}, ${*variable+replacement*}, ${*variable:+replacement*}, ${*variable?ignored*}, ${*variable:?ignored*}, that would be valid inside shell scripts, are not supported. The *variable* names must consist solely of alphanumeric or underscore ASCII characters, not start with a digit and be nonempty; otherwise such a variable reference is ignored.

15.3.4 Python Format Strings

There are two kinds of format strings in Python: those acceptable to the Python built-in format operator `%`, labelled as 'python-format', and those acceptable to the `format` method of the 'str' object.

Python `%` format strings are described in Python Library reference / 5. Built-in Types / 5.6. Sequence Types / 5.6.2. String Formatting Operations. `http://docs.python.org/2/library/stdtypes.html#string-formatting-operations`.

Python brace format strings are described in PEP 3101 – Advanced String Formatting, `http://www.python.org/dev/peps/pep-3101/`.

15.3.5 Lisp Format Strings

Lisp format strings are described in the Common Lisp HyperSpec, chapter 22.3 Formatted Output, `http://www.lisp.org/HyperSpec/Body/sec_22-3.html`.

15.3.6 Emacs Lisp Format Strings

Emacs Lisp format strings are documented in the Emacs Lisp reference, section Formatting Strings, `http://www.gnu.org/manual/elisp-manual-21-2.8/html_chapter/elisp_4.html#SEC75`. Note that as of version 21, XEmacs supports numbered argument specifications in format strings while FSF Emacs doesn't.

15.3.7 librep Format Strings

librep format strings are documented in the librep manual, section Formatted Output, `http://librep.sourceforge.net/librep-manual.html#Formatted%20Output`, `http://www.gwinnup.org/research/docs/librep.html#SEC122`.

15.3.8 Scheme Format Strings

Scheme format strings are documented in the SLIB manual, section Format Specification.

15.3.9 Smalltalk Format Strings

Smalltalk format strings are described in the GNU Smalltalk documentation, class `CharArray`, methods 'bindWith:' and 'bindWithArguments:'. `http://www.gnu.org/software/smalltalk/gst-manual/gst_68.html#SEC238`. In summary, a directive starts with '%' and is followed by '%' or a nonzero digit ('1' to '9').

15.3.10 Java Format Strings

Java format strings are described in the JDK documentation for class `java.text.MessageFormat`, `http://java.sun.com/j2se/1.4/docs/api/java/text/MessageFormat.html`. See also the ICU documentation `http://oss.software.ibm.com/icu/apiref/classMessageFormat.html`.

15.3.11 C# Format Strings

C# format strings are described in the .NET documentation for class `System.String` and in `http://msdn.microsoft.com/library/default.asp?url=/library/en-us/cpguide/html/cpConFormattingOverview.asp`.

15.3.12 awk Format Strings

awk format strings are described in the gawk documentation, section Printf, `http://www.gnu.org/manual/gawk/html_node/Printf.html#Printf`.

15.3.13 Object Pascal Format Strings

Object Pascal format strings are described in the documentation of the Free Pascal runtime library, section Format, `http://www.freepascal.org/docs-html/rtl/sysutils/format.html`.

15.3.14 YCP Format Strings

YCP sformat strings are described in the libycp documentation `file:/usr/share/doc/packages/libycp/YCP-builtins.html`. In summary, a directive starts with '%' and is followed by '%' or a nonzero digit ('1' to '9').

15.3.15 Tcl Format Strings

Tcl format strings are described in the `format.n` manual page, `http://www.scriptics.com/man/tcl8.3/TclCmd/format.htm`.

15.3.16 Perl Format Strings

There are two kinds format strings in Perl: those acceptable to the Perl built-in function `printf`, labelled as 'perl-format', and those acceptable to the `libintl-perl` function `__x`, labelled as 'perl-brace-format'.

Perl `printf` format strings are described in the `sprintf` section of 'man perlfunc'.

Perl brace format strings are described in the `Locale::TextDomain(3pm)` manual page of the CPAN package libintl-perl. In brief, Perl format uses placeholders put between braces ('{' and '}'). The placeholder must have the syntax of simple identifiers.

15.3.17 PHP Format Strings

PHP format strings are described in the documentation of the PHP function `sprintf`, in `phpdoc/manual/function.sprintf.html` or `http://www.php.net/manual/en/function.sprintf.php`.

15.3.18 GCC internal Format Strings

These format strings are used inside the GCC sources. In such a format string, a directive starts with '%', is optionally followed by a size specifier 'l', an optional flag '+', another optional flag '#', and is finished by a specifier: '%' denotes a literal percent sign, 'c' denotes a character, 's' denotes a string, 'i' and 'd' denote an integer, 'o', 'u', 'x' denote an unsigned integer, '.*s' denotes a string preceded by a width specification, 'H' denotes a 'location_t *' pointer, 'D' denotes a general declaration, 'F' denotes a function declaration, 'T' denotes a type, 'A' denotes a function argument, 'C' denotes a tree code, 'E' denotes an expression, 'L' denotes a programming language, 'O' denotes a binary operator, 'P' denotes a function parameter, 'Q' denotes an assignment operator, 'V' denotes a const/volatile qualifier.

15.3.19 GFC internal Format Strings

These format strings are used inside the GNU Fortran Compiler sources, that is, the Fortran frontend in the GCC sources. In such a format string, a directive starts with '%' and is finished by a specifier: '%' denotes a literal percent sign, 'C' denotes the current source location, 'L' denotes a source location, 'c' denotes a character, 's' denotes a string, 'i' and 'd' denote an integer, 'u' denotes an unsigned integer. 'i', 'd', and 'u' may be preceded by a size specifier 'l'.

15.3.20 Qt Format Strings

Qt format strings are described in the documentation of the QString class `file:/usr/lib/qt-4.3.0/doc/html/qstring.html`. In summary, a directive consists of a '%' followed by a digit. The same directive cannot occur more than once in a format string.

15.3.21 Qt Format Strings

Qt format strings are described in the documentation of the QObject::tr method `file:/usr/lib/qt-4.3.0/doc/html/qobject.html`. In summary, the only allowed directive is '%n'.

15.3.22 KDE Format Strings

KDE 4 format strings are defined as follows: A directive consists of a '%' followed by a non-zero decimal number. If a '%n' occurs in a format strings, all of '%1', ..., '%(n-1)' must occur as well, except possibly one of them.

15.3.23 KUIT Format Strings

KUIT (KDE User Interface Text) is compatible with KDE 4 format strings, while it also allows programmers to add semantic information to a format string, through XML markup tags. For example, if the first format directive in a string is a filename, programmers could indicate that with a 'filename' tag, like '<filename>%1</filename>'.

KUIT format strings are described in `http: / / api . kde . org / frameworks-api / frameworks5-apidocs/ki18n/html/prg_guide.html#kuit_markup`.

15.3.24 Boost Format Strings

Boost format strings are described in the documentation of the `boost::format` class, at `http://www.boost.org/libs/format/doc/format.html`. In summary, a directive has either the same syntax as in a C format string, such as '%1$+5d', or may be surrounded by vertical bars, such as '%|1$+5d|' or '%|1$+5|', or consists of just an argument number between percent signs, such as '%1%'.

15.3.25 Lua Format Strings

Lua format strings are described in the Lua reference manual, section String Manipulation, `http: / / www . lua . org / manual / 5 . 1 / manual . html # pdf-string.format`.

15.3.26 JavaScript Format Strings

Although JavaScript specification itself does not define any format strings, many JavaScript implementations provide printf-like functions. `xgettext` understands a set of common format strings used in popular JavaScript implementations including Gjs, Seed, and Node.JS. In such a format string, a directive starts with '%' and is finished by a specifier: '%' denotes a literal percent sign, 'c' denotes a character, 's' denotes a string, 'b', 'd', 'o', 'x', 'X' denote an integer, 'f' denotes floating-point number, 'j' denotes a JSON object.

15.4 The Maintainer's View

For the maintainer, the general procedure differs from the C language case in two ways.

- For those languages that don't use GNU gettext, the `intl/` directory is not needed and can be omitted. This means that the maintainer calls the `gettextize` program without the '`--intl`' option, and that he invokes the `AM_GNU_GETTEXT` autoconf macro via '`AM_GNU_GETTEXT([external])`'.

- If only a single programming language is used, the `XGETTEXT_OPTIONS` variable in `po/Makevars` (see Section 13.4.3 [po/Makevars], page 145) should be adjusted to match the `xgettext` options for that particular programming language. If the package uses more than one programming language with `gettext` support, it becomes necessary to change the POT file construction rule in `po/Makefile.in.in`. It is recommended to make one `xgettext` invocation per programming language, each with the options appropriate for that language, and to combine the resulting files using `msgcat`.

15.5 Individual Programming Languages

15.5.1 C, C++, Objective C

RPMs gcc, gpp, gobjc, glibc, gettext

File extension
> For C: `c`, `h`.
> For C++: `C`, `c++`, `cc`, `cxx`, `cpp`, `hpp`.
> For Objective C: `m`.

String syntax
> `"abc"`

gettext shorthand
> `_("abc")`

gettext/ngettext functions
> `gettext`, `dgettext`, `dcgettext`, `ngettext`, `dngettext`, `dcngettext`

textdomain
> `textdomain` function

bindtextdomain
> `bindtextdomain` function

setlocale Programmer must call `setlocale (LC_ALL, "")`

Prerequisite
> `#include <libintl.h>`
> `#include <locale.h>`
> `#define _(string) gettext (string)`

Use or emulate GNU gettext
> Use

Extractor `xgettext -k_`

Formatting with positions
> `fprintf "%2$d %1$d"`
> In C++: `autosprintf "%2$d %1$d"` (see Section "Introduction" in *GNU autosprintf*)

Portability
> autoconf (gettext.m4) and #if ENABLE_NLS

po-mode marking
> yes

The following examples are available in the `examples` directory: `hello-c`, `hello-c-gnome`, `hello-c++`, `hello-c++-qt`, `hello-c++-kde`, `hello-c++-gnome`, `hello-c++-wxwidgets`, `hello-objc`, `hello-objc-gnustep`, `hello-objc-gnome`.

15.5.2 sh - Shell Script

RPMs   bash, gettext

File extension
        sh

String syntax
        "abc", 'abc', abc

gettext shorthand
        "`gettext \"abc\"`"

gettext/ngettext functions
        gettext, ngettext programs
        eval_gettext, eval_ngettext shell functions

textdomain
        environment variable TEXTDOMAIN

bindtextdomain
        environment variable TEXTDOMAINDIR

setlocale   automatic

Prerequisite
        . gettext.sh

Use or emulate GNU gettext
        use

Extractor   xgettext

Formatting with positions
        —

Portability
        fully portable

po-mode marking
        —

An example is available in the examples directory: hello-sh.

15.5.2.1 Preparing Shell Scripts for Internationalization

Preparing a shell script for internationalization is conceptually similar to the steps described in Chapter 4 [Sources], page 19. The concrete steps for shell scripts are as follows.

1. Insert the line

        . gettext.sh

   near the top of the script. gettext.sh is a shell function library that provides the functions eval_gettext (see Section 15.5.2.6 [eval_gettext Invocation], page 171) and eval_ngettext (see Section 15.5.2.7 [eval_ngettext Invocation], page 171). You have to ensure that gettext.sh can be found in the PATH.

2. Set and export the `TEXTDOMAIN` and `TEXTDOMAINDIR` environment variables. Usually `TEXTDOMAIN` is the package or program name, and `TEXTDOMAINDIR` is the absolute pathname corresponding to `$prefix/share/locale`, where `$prefix` is the installation location.

```
TEXTDOMAIN=@PACKAGE@
export TEXTDOMAIN
TEXTDOMAINDIR=@LOCALEDIR@
export TEXTDOMAINDIR
```

3. Prepare the strings for translation, as described in Section 4.3 [Preparing Strings], page 20.

4. Simplify translatable strings so that they don't contain command substitution (`"`...`"` or `"$(...)"`), variable access with defaulting (like `${variable-default}`), access to positional arguments (like `$0`, `$1`, ...) or highly volatile shell variables (like `$?`). This can always be done through simple local code restructuring. For example,

```
echo "Usage: $0 [OPTION] FILE..."
```

becomes

```
program_name=$0
echo "Usage: $program_name [OPTION] FILE..."
```

Similarly,

```
echo "Remaining files: `ls | wc -l`"
```

becomes

```
filecount="`ls | wc -l`"
echo "Remaining files: $filecount"
```

5. For each translatable string, change the output command 'echo' or '$echo' to 'gettext' (if the string contains no references to shell variables) or to 'eval_gettext' (if it refers to shell variables), followed by a no-argument 'echo' command (to account for the terminating newline). Similarly, for cases with plural handling, replace a conditional 'echo' command with an invocation of 'ngettext' or 'eval_ngettext', followed by a no-argument 'echo' command.

When doing this, you also need to add an extra backslash before the dollar sign in references to shell variables, so that the 'eval_gettext' function receives the translatable string before the variable values are substituted into it. For example,

```
echo "Remaining files: $filecount"
```

becomes

```
eval_gettext "Remaining files: \$filecount"; echo
```

If the output command is not 'echo', you can make it use 'echo' nevertheless, through the use of backquotes. However, note that inside backquotes, backslashes must be doubled to be effective (because the backquoting eats one level of backslashes). For example, assuming that 'error' is a shell function that signals an error,

```
error "file not found: $filename"
```

is first transformed into

```
error "`echo \"file not found: \$filename\"`"
```

which then becomes

```
error "`eval_gettext \"file not found: \\\$filename\"`"
```

15.5.2.2 Contents of `gettext.sh`

`gettext.sh`, contained in the run-time package of GNU gettext, provides the following:

- $echo The variable `echo` is set to a command that outputs its first argument and a newline, without interpreting backslashes in the argument string.

- eval_gettext See Section 15.5.2.6 [eval_gettext Invocation], page 171.

- eval_ngettext See Section 15.5.2.7 [eval_ngettext Invocation], page 171.

15.5.2.3 Invoking the `gettext` program

```
gettext [option] [[textdomain] msgid]
gettext [option] -s [msgid]...
```

The `gettext` program displays the native language translation of a textual message.

Arguments

'-d *textdomain*'
'--domain=*textdomain*'

> Retrieve translated messages from *textdomain*. Usually a *textdomain* corresponds to a package, a program, or a module of a program.

'-e'

> Enable expansion of some escape sequences. This option is for compatibility with the 'echo' program or shell built-in. The escape sequences '\a', '\b', '\c', '\f', '\n', '\r', '\t', '\v', '\\', and '\' followed by one to three octal digits, are interpreted like the System V 'echo' program did.

'-E'

> This option is only for compatibility with the 'echo' program or shell built-in. It has no effect.

'-h'
'--help' Display this help and exit.

'-n' Suppress trailing newline. By default, `gettext` adds a newline to the output.

'-V'
'--version'

> Output version information and exit.

'[*textdomain*] *msgid*'

> Retrieve translated message corresponding to *msgid* from *textdomain*.

If the *textdomain* parameter is not given, the domain is determined from the environment variable TEXTDOMAIN. If the message catalog is not found in the regular directory, another location can be specified with the environment variable TEXTDOMAINDIR.

When used with the -s option the program behaves like the 'echo' command. But it does not simply copy its arguments to stdout. Instead those messages found in the selected catalog are translated.

Note: `xgettext` supports only the one-argument form of the `gettext` invocation, where no options are present and the *textdomain* is implicit, from the environment.

15.5.2.4 Invoking the `ngettext` program

```
ngettext [option] [textdomain] msgid msgid-plural count
```

The `ngettext` program displays the native language translation of a textual message whose grammatical form depends on a number.

Arguments

'-d *textdomain*'

'--domain=*textdomain*'

> Retrieve translated messages from *textdomain*. Usually a *textdomain* corresponds to a package, a program, or a module of a program.

'-e'

> Enable expansion of some escape sequences. This option is for compatibility with the 'gettext' program. The escape sequences '\a', '\b', '\c', '\f', '\n', '\r', '\t', '\v', '\\', and '\' followed by one to three octal digits, are interpreted like the System V 'echo' program did.

'-E'

> This option is only for compatibility with the 'gettext' program. It has no effect.

'-h'

'--help'   Display this help and exit.

'-V'

'--version'

> Output version information and exit.

'*textdomain*'

> Retrieve translated message from *textdomain*.

'*msgid msgid-plural*'

> Translate *msgid* (English singular) / *msgid-plural* (English plural).

'*count*'   Choose singular/plural form based on this value.

If the *textdomain* parameter is not given, the domain is determined from the environment variable TEXTDOMAIN. If the message catalog is not found in the regular directory, another location can be specified with the environment variable TEXTDOMAINDIR.

Note: xgettext supports only the three-arguments form of the `ngettext` invocation, where no options are present and the *textdomain* is implicit, from the environment.

15.5.2.5 Invoking the `envsubst` program

```
envsubst [option] [shell-format]
```

The `envsubst` program substitutes the values of environment variables.

Operation mode

'-v'

'--variables'

> Output the variables occurring in *shell-format*.

Informative output

'-h'

'--help'   Display this help and exit.

'-V'
'--version'
                Output version information and exit.

In normal operation mode, standard input is copied to standard output, with references
to environment variables of the form `$VARIABLE` or `${VARIABLE}` being replaced with the
corresponding values. If a *shell-format* is given, only those environment variables that are
referenced in *shell-format* are substituted; otherwise all environment variables references
occurring in standard input are substituted.

These substitutions are a subset of the substitutions that a shell performs on unquoted and double-quoted strings. Other kinds of substitutions done by a shell, such as
`${variable-default}` or `$(command-list)` or `command-list`, are not performed by the
`envsubst` program, due to security reasons.

When `--variables` is used, standard input is ignored, and the output consists of the
environment variables that are referenced in *shell-format*, one per line.

15.5.2.6 Invoking the `eval_gettext` function

        `eval_gettext` *msgid*

This function outputs the native language translation of a textual message, performing
dollar-substitution on the result. Note that only shell variables mentioned in *msgid* will be
dollar-substituted in the result.

15.5.2.7 Invoking the `eval_ngettext` function

        `eval_ngettext` *msgid msgid-plural count*

This function outputs the native language translation of a textual message whose grammatical form depends on a number, performing dollar-substitution on the result. Note that
only shell variables mentioned in *msgid* or *msgid-plural* will be dollar-substituted in the
result.

15.5.3 bash - Bourne-Again Shell Script

GNU `bash` 2.0 or newer has a special shorthand for translating a string and substituting
variable values in it: `$"msgid"`. But the use of this construct is **discouraged**, due to the
security holes it opens and due to its portability problems.

The security holes of `$"..."` come from the fact that after looking up the translation of
the string, `bash` processes it like it processes any double-quoted string: dollar and backquote
processing, like 'eval' does.

1. In a locale whose encoding is one of BIG5, BIG5-HKSCS, GBK, GB18030, SHIFT_JIS,
   JOHAB, some double-byte characters have a second byte whose value is `0x60`. For
   example, the byte sequence `\xe0\x60` is a single character in these locales. Many
   versions of `bash` (all versions up to bash-2.05, and newer versions on platforms without
   `mbsrtowcs()` function) don't know about character boundaries and see a backquote
   character where there is only a particular Chinese character. Thus it can start executing
   part of the translation as a command list. This situation can occur even without
   the translator being aware of it: if the translator provides translations in the UTF-
   8 encoding, it is the `gettext()` function which will, during its conversion from the
   translator's encoding to the user's locale's encoding, produce the dangerous `\x60` bytes.

2. A translator could - voluntarily or inadvertently - use backquotes "`...`" or dollar-parentheses "$(...)" in her translations. The enclosed strings would be executed as command lists by the shell.

The portability problem is that bash must be built with internationalization support; this is normally not the case on systems that don't have the gettext() function in libc.

15.5.4 Python

RPMs   python

File extension

> py

String syntax

> 'abc', u'abc', r'abc', ur'abc',
> "abc", u"abc", r"abc", ur"abc",
> '''abc''', u'''abc''', r'''abc''', ur'''abc''',
> """abc""", u"""abc""", r"""abc""", ur"""abc"""

gettext shorthand

> _('abc') etc.

gettext/ngettext functions

> gettext.gettext, gettext.dgettext, gettext.ngettext, gettext.dngettext, also ugettext, ungettext

textdomain

> gettext.textdomain function, or gettext.install(domain) function

bindtextdomain

> gettext.bindtextdomain function, or gettext.install(domain, localedir) function

setlocale   not used by the gettext emulation

Prerequisite

> import gettext

Use or emulate GNU gettext

> emulate

Extractor   xgettext

Formatting with positions

> '...%(ident)d...' % { 'ident': value }

Portability

> fully portable

po-mode marking

> ---

An example is available in the examples directory: hello-python.

A note about format strings: Python supports format strings with unnamed arguments, such as '...%d...', and format strings with named arguments, such as

'...%(ident)d...'. The latter are preferable for internationalized programs, for two
reasons:

- When a format string takes more than one argument, the translator can provide a
  translation that uses the arguments in a different order, if the format string uses named
  arguments. For example, the translator can reformulate

    ```
    "'%(volume)s' has only %(freespace)d bytes free."
    ```

  to

    ```
    "Only %(freespace)d bytes free on '%(volume)s'."
    ```

  Additionally, the identifiers also provide some context to the translator.

- In the context of plural forms, the format string used for the singular form does not
  use the numeric argument in many languages. Even in English, one prefers to write
  "one hour" instead of "1 hour". Omitting individual arguments from format strings
  like this is only possible with the named argument syntax. (With unnamed arguments,
  Python – unlike C – verifies that the format string uses all supplied arguments.)

15.5.5 GNU clisp - Common Lisp

RPMs   clisp 2.28 or newer

File extension
              lisp

String syntax
              "abc"

gettext shorthand
              (_ "abc"), (ENGLISH "abc")

gettext/ngettext functions
              i18n:gettext, i18n:ngettext

textdomain
              i18n:textdomain

bindtextdomain
              i18n:textdomaindir

setlocale   automatic

Prerequisite
              —

Use or emulate GNU gettext
              use

Extractor   xgettext -k_ -kENGLISH

Formatting with positions
              format "~1@*~D ~0@*~D"

Portability
              On platforms without gettext, no translation.

po-mode marking
              —

An example is available in the examples directory: hello-clisp.

15.5.6 GNU clisp C sources

RPMs   clisp

File extension
> `d`

String syntax
> `"abc"`

gettext shorthand
> `ENGLISH ? "abc" : ""`
> `GETTEXT("abc")`
> `GETTEXTL("abc")`

gettext/ngettext functions
> `clgettext, clgettextl`

textdomain
> ——

bindtextdomain
> ——

setlocale   automatic

Prerequisite
> `#include "lispbibl.c"`

Use or emulate GNU gettext
> use

Extractor   `clisp-xgettext`

Formatting with positions
> `fprintf "%2$d %1$d"`

Portability
> On platforms without gettext, no translation.

po-mode marking
> ——

15.5.7 Emacs Lisp

RPMs   emacs, xemacs

File extension
> `el`

String syntax
> `"abc"`

gettext shorthand
> `(_"abc")`

gettext/ngettext functions
> `gettext, dgettext` (xemacs only)

textdomain
    `domain` special form (xemacs only)

bindtextdomain
    `bind-text-domain` function (xemacs only)

setlocale   automatic

Prerequisite
    —

Use or emulate GNU gettext
    use

Extractor   `xgettext`

Formatting with positions
    `format "%2$d %1$d"`

Portability
    Only XEmacs. Without `I18N3` defined at build time, no translation.

po-mode marking
    —

15.5.8 librep

RPMs   librep 0.15.3 or newer

File extension
    `jl`

String syntax
    `"abc"`

gettext shorthand
    `(_"abc")`

gettext/ngettext functions
    `gettext`

textdomain
    `textdomain` function

bindtextdomain
    `bindtextdomain` function

setlocale   —

Prerequisite
    `(require 'rep.i18n.gettext)`

Use or emulate GNU gettext
    use

Extractor   `xgettext`

Formatting with positions
    `format "%2$d %1$d"`

Portability

> On platforms without gettext, no translation.

po-mode marking

> —

An example is available in the examples directory: hello-librep.

15.5.9 GNU guile - Scheme

RPMs
> guile

File extension

> scm

String syntax

> "abc"

gettext shorthand

> (_ "abc"), _"abc" (GIMP script-fu extension)

gettext/ngettext functions

> gettext, ngettext

textdomain

> textdomain

bindtextdomain

> bindtextdomain

setlocale   (catch #t (lambda () (setlocale LC_ALL "")) (lambda args #f))

Prerequisite

> (use-modules (ice-9 format))

Use or emulate GNU gettext

> use

Extractor   xgettext -k_

Formatting with positions

> —

Portability

> On platforms without gettext, no translation.

po-mode marking

> —

An example is available in the examples directory: hello-guile.

15.5.10 GNU Smalltalk

RPMs
> smalltalk

File extension

> st

String syntax
> 'abc'

gettext shorthand
> NLS ? 'abc'

gettext/ngettext functions
> LcMessagesDomain>>#at:, LcMessagesDomain>>#at:plural:with:

textdomain
> LcMessages>>#domain:localeDirectory: (returns a LcMessagesDomain object).
>
> Example: I18N Locale default messages domain: 'gettext'
> localeDirectory: /usr/local/share/locale'

bindtextdomain
> LcMessages>>#domain:localeDirectory:, see above.

setlocale   Automatic if you use I18N Locale default.

Prerequisite
> PackageLoader fileInPackage: 'I18N'!

Use or emulate GNU gettext
> emulate

Extractor   xgettext

Formatting with positions
> '%1 %2' bindWith: 'Hello' with: 'world'

Portability
> fully portable

po-mode marking
> —

An example is available in the **examples** directory: `hello-smalltalk`.

15.5.11 Java

RPMs   java, java2

File extension
> `java`

String syntax
> "abc"

gettext shorthand
> _("abc")

gettext/ngettext functions
> GettextResource.gettext, GettextResource.ngettext, GettextResource.pgettext,
> GettextResource.npgettext

textdomain
> —, use `ResourceBundle.getResource` instead

bindtextdomain
> —, use CLASSPATH instead

setlocale automatic

Prerequisite
> —

Use or emulate GNU gettext
> —, uses a Java specific message catalog format

Extractor `xgettext -k_`

Formatting with positions
> `MessageFormat.format "{1,number} {0,number}"`

Portability
> fully portable

po-mode marking
> —

Before marking strings as internationalizable, uses of the string concatenation operator need to be converted to `MessageFormat` applications. For example, `"file "+filename+" not found"` becomes `MessageFormat.format("file {0} not found", new Object[] { filename })`. Only after this is done, can the strings be marked and extracted.

GNU gettext uses the native Java internationalization mechanism, namely `ResourceBundles`. There are two formats of `ResourceBundles`: `.properties` files and `.class` files. The `.properties` format is a text file which the translators can directly edit, like PO files, but which doesn't support plural forms. Whereas the `.class` format is compiled from `.java` source code and can support plural forms (provided it is accessed through an appropriate API, see below).

To convert a PO file to a `.properties` file, the `msgcat` program can be used with the option `--properties-output`. To convert a `.properties` file back to a PO file, the `msgcat` program can be used with the option `--properties-input`. All the tools that manipulate PO files can work with `.properties` files as well, if given the `--properties-input` and/or `--properties-output` option.

To convert a PO file to a ResourceBundle class, the `msgfmt` program can be used with the option `--java` or `--java2`. To convert a ResourceBundle back to a PO file, the `msgunfmt` program can be used with the option `--java`.

Two different programmatic APIs can be used to access ResourceBundles. Note that both APIs work with all kinds of ResourceBundles, whether GNU gettext generated classes, or other `.class` or `.properties` files.

1. The `java.util.ResourceBundle` API.

   In particular, its `getString` function returns a string translation. Note that a missing translation yields a `MissingResourceException`.

   This has the advantage of being the standard API. And it does not require any additional libraries, only the `msgcat` generated `.properties` files or the `msgfmt` generated `.class` files. But it cannot do plural handling, even if the resource was generated by `msgfmt` from a PO file with plural handling.

2. The `gnu.gettext.GettextResource` API.

Reference documentation in Javadoc 1.1 style format is in the javadoc2 directory (`javadoc2/index.html`).

Its `gettext` function returns a string translation. Note that when a translation is missing, the *msgid* argument is returned unchanged.

This has the advantage of having the `ngettext` function for plural handling and the `pgettext` and `npgettext` for strings constraint to a particular context.

To use this API, one needs the `libintl.jar` file which is part of the GNU gettext package and distributed under the LGPL.

Four examples, using the second API, are available in the **examples** directory: `hello-java`, `hello-java-awt`, `hello-java-swing`, `hello-java-qtjambi`.

Now, to make use of the API and define a shorthand for '`getString`', there are three idioms that you can choose from:

- (This one assumes Java 1.5 or newer.) In a unique class of your project, say '`Util`', define a static variable holding the `ResourceBundle` instance and the shorthand:

```
private static ResourceBundle myResources =
  ResourceBundle.getBundle("domain-name");
public static String _(String s) {
  return myResources.getString(s);
}
```

  All classes containing internationalized strings then contain

```
import static Util._;
```

  and the shorthand is used like this:

```
System.out.println(_("Operation completed."));
```

- In a unique class of your project, say '`Util`', define a static variable holding the `ResourceBundle` instance:

```
public static ResourceBundle myResources =
  ResourceBundle.getBundle("domain-name");
```

  All classes containing internationalized strings then contain

```
private static ResourceBundle res = Util.myResources;
private static String _(String s) { return res.getString(s); }
```

  and the shorthand is used like this:

```
System.out.println(_("Operation completed."));
```

- You add a class with a very short name, say '`S`', containing just the definition of the resource bundle and of the shorthand:

```
public class S {
  public static ResourceBundle myResources =
    ResourceBundle.getBundle("domain-name");
  public static String _(String s) {
    return myResources.getString(s);
  }
}
```

  and the shorthand is used like this:

```
System.out.println(S._("Operation completed."));
```

Which of the three idioms you choose, will depend on whether your project requires portability to Java versions prior to Java 1.5 and, if so, whether copying two lines of codes into every class is more acceptable in your project than a class with a single-letter name.

15.5.12 C#

RPMs   pnet, pnetlib 0.6.2 or newer, or mono 0.29 or newer

File extension
>   `cs`

String syntax
>   `"abc"`, `@"abc"`

gettext shorthand
>   `_("abc")`

gettext/ngettext functions
>   `GettextResourceManager.GetString`, `GettextResourceManager.GetPluralString`
>   `GettextResourceManager.GetParticularString GettextResourceManager.GetParticu`

textdomain
>   `new GettextResourceManager(domain)`

bindtextdomain
>   —, compiled message catalogs are located in subdirectories of the directory containing the executable

setlocale   automatic

Prerequisite
>   —

Use or emulate GNU gettext
>   —, uses a C# specific message catalog format

Extractor   `xgettext -k_`

Formatting with positions
>   `String.Format "{1} {0}"`

Portability
>   fully portable

po-mode marking
>   —

Before marking strings as internationalizable, uses of the string concatenation operator need to be converted to `String.Format` invocations. For example, `"file "+filename+" not found"` becomes `String.Format("file {0} not found", filename)`. Only after this is done, can the strings be marked and extracted.

GNU gettext uses the native C#/.NET internationalization mechanism, namely the classes `ResourceManager` and `ResourceSet`. Applications use the `ResourceManager` methods to retrieve the native language translation of strings. An instance of `ResourceSet` is the in-memory representation of a message catalog file. The `ResourceManager` loads and accesses `ResourceSet` instances as needed to look up the translations.

There are two formats of `ResourceSet`s that can be directly loaded by the C# runtime: `.resources` files and `.dll` files.

- The `.resources` format is a binary file usually generated through the `resgen` or `monoresgen` utility, but which doesn't support plural forms. `.resources` files can also be embedded in .NET `.exe` files. This only affects whether a file system access is performed to load the message catalog; it doesn't affect the contents of the message catalog.

- On the other hand, the `.dll` format is a binary file that is compiled from `.cs` source code and can support plural forms (provided it is accessed through the GNU gettext API, see below).

Note that these .NET `.dll` and `.exe` files are not tied to a particular platform; their file format and GNU gettext for C# can be used on any platform.

To convert a PO file to a `.resources` file, the `msgfmt` program can be used with the option '`--csharp-resources`'. To convert a `.resources` file back to a PO file, the `msgunfmt` program can be used with the option '`--csharp-resources`'. You can also, in some cases, use the `resgen` program (from the `pnet` package) or the `monoresgen` program (from the `mono/mcs` package). These programs can also convert a `.resources` file back to a PO file. But beware: as of this writing (January 2004), the `monoresgen` converter is quite buggy and the `resgen` converter ignores the encoding of the PO files.

To convert a PO file to a `.dll` file, the `msgfmt` program can be used with the option `--csharp`. The result will be a `.dll` file containing a subclass of `GettextResourceSet`, which itself is a subclass of `ResourceSet`. To convert a `.dll` file containing a `GettextResourceSet` subclass back to a PO file, the `msgunfmt` program can be used with the option `--csharp`.

The advantages of the `.dll` format over the `.resources` format are:

1. Freedom to localize: Users can add their own translations to an application after it has been built and distributed. Whereas when the programmer uses a `ResourceManager` constructor provided by the system, the set of `.resources` files for an application must be specified when the application is built and cannot be extended afterwards.

2. Plural handling: A message catalog in `.dll` format supports the plural handling function `GetPluralString`. Whereas `.resources` files can only contain data and only support lookups that depend on a single string.

3. Context handling: A message catalog in `.dll` format supports the query-with-context functions `GetParticularString` and `GetParticularPluralString`. Whereas `.resources` files can only contain data and only support lookups that depend on a single string.

4. The `GettextResourceManager` that loads the message catalogs in `.dll` format also provides for inheritance on a per-message basis. For example, in Austrian (`de_AT`) locale, translations from the German (`de`) message catalog will be used for messages not found in the Austrian message catalog. This has the consequence that the Austrian translators need only translate those few messages for which the translation into Austrian differs from the German one. Whereas when working with `.resources` files, each message catalog must provide the translations of all messages by itself.

5. The `GettextResourceManager` that loads the message catalogs in `.dll` format also provides for a fallback: The English *msgid* is returned when no translation can be found. Whereas when working with `.resources` files, a language-neutral `.resources` file must explicitly be provided as a fallback.

On the side of the programmatic APIs, the programmer can use either the standard `ResourceManager` API and the GNU `GettextResourceManager` API. The latter is an extension of the former, because `GettextResourceManager` is a subclass of `ResourceManager`.

1. The `System.Resources.ResourceManager` API.

    This API works with resources in `.resources` format.

    The creation of the `ResourceManager` is done through
    ```
    new ResourceManager(domainname, Assembly.GetExecutingAssembly())
    ```

    The `GetString` function returns a string's translation. Note that this function returns null when a translation is missing (i.e. not even found in the fallback resource file).

2. The `GNU.Gettext.GettextResourceManager` API.

    This API works with resources in `.dll` format.

    Reference documentation is in the csharpdoc directory (`csharpdoc/index.html`).

    The creation of the `ResourceManager` is done through
    ```
    new GettextResourceManager(domainname)
    ```

    The `GetString` function returns a string's translation. Note that when a translation is missing, the *msgid* argument is returned unchanged.

    The `GetPluralString` function returns a string translation with plural handling, like the `ngettext` function in C.

    The `GetParticularString` function returns a string's translation, specific to a particular context, like the `pgettext` function in C. Note that when a translation is missing, the *msgid* argument is returned unchanged.

    The `GetParticularPluralString` function returns a string translation, specific to a particular context, with plural handling, like the `npgettext` function in C.

    To use this API, one needs the `GNU.Gettext.dll` file which is part of the GNU gettext package and distributed under the LGPL.

You can also mix both approaches: use the `GNU.Gettext.GettextResourceManager` constructor, but otherwise use only the `ResourceManager` type and only the `GetString` method. This is appropriate when you want to profit from the tools for PO files, but don't want to change an existing source code that uses `ResourceManager` and don't (yet) need the `GetPluralString` method.

Two examples, using the second API, are available in the `examples` directory: `hello-csharp`, `hello-csharp-forms`.

Now, to make use of the API and define a shorthand for 'GetString', there are two idioms that you can choose from:

- In a unique class of your project, say '`Util`', define a static variable holding the `ResourceManager` instance:
    ```
    public static GettextResourceManager MyResourceManager =
        new GettextResourceManager("domain-name");
    ```

    All classes containing internationalized strings then contain
    ```
    private static GettextResourceManager Res = Util.MyResourceManager;
    private static String _(String s) { return Res.GetString(s); }
    ```

    and the shorthand is used like this:
    ```
    Console.WriteLine(_("Operation completed."));
    ```

- You add a class with a very short name, say 'S', containing just the definition of the resource manager and of the shorthand:

```
public class S {
  public static GettextResourceManager MyResourceManager =
    new GettextResourceManager("domain-name");
  public static String _(String s) {
    return MyResourceManager.GetString(s);
  }
}
```

  and the shorthand is used like this:

```
Console.WriteLine(S._("Operation completed."));
```

Which of the two idioms you choose, will depend on whether copying two lines of codes into every class is more acceptable in your project than a class with a single-letter name.

15.5.13 GNU awk

RPMs   gawk 3.1 or newer

File extension

       `awk`, `gawk`, `twjr`. The file extension `twjr` is used by TexiWeb Jr (`https://github.com/arnoldrobbins/texiwebjr`).

String syntax

       `"abc"`

gettext shorthand

       `_"abc"`

gettext/ngettext functions

       `dcgettext`, missing `dcngettext` in gawk-3.1.0

textdomain

       `TEXTDOMAIN` variable

bindtextdomain

       `bindtextdomain` function

setlocale   automatic, but missing `setlocale (LC_MESSAGES, "")` in gawk-3.1.0

Prerequisite

       —

Use or emulate GNU gettext

       use

Extractor   `xgettext`

Formatting with positions

       `printf "%2$d %1$d"` (GNU awk only)

Portability

       On platforms without gettext, no translation. On non-GNU awks, you must define `dcgettext`, `dcngettext` and `bindtextdomain` yourself.

po-mode marking

       —

An example is available in the **examples** directory: `hello-gawk`.

15.5.14 Pascal - Free Pascal Compiler

RPMs   fpk

File extension
>pp, pas

String syntax
>'abc'

gettext shorthand
>automatic

gettext/ngettext functions
>—, use `ResourceString` data type instead

textdomain
>—, use `TranslateResourceStrings` function instead

bindtextdomain
>—, use `TranslateResourceStrings` function instead

setlocale   automatic, but uses only LANG, not LC_MESSAGES or LC_ALL

Prerequisite
>`{$mode delphi}` or `{$mode objfpc}`
>`uses gettext;`

Use or emulate GNU gettext
>emulate partially

Extractor   `ppc386` followed by `xgettext` or `rstconv`

Formatting with positions
>`uses sysutils;`
>`format "%1:d %0:d"`

Portability
>?

po-mode marking
>—

The Pascal compiler has special support for the `ResourceString` data type. It generates a `.rst` file. This is then converted to a `.pot` file by use of `xgettext` or `rstconv`. At runtime, a `.mo` file corresponding to translations of this `.pot` file can be loaded using the `TranslateResourceStrings` function in the `gettext` unit.

An example is available in the `examples` directory: `hello-pascal`.

15.5.15 wxWidgets library

RPMs   wxGTK, gettext

File extension
>cpp

String syntax
        `"abc"`

gettext shorthand
        `_("abc")`

gettext/ngettext functions
        `wxLocale::GetString`, `wxGetTranslation`

textdomain
        `wxLocale::AddCatalog`

bindtextdomain
        `wxLocale::AddCatalogLookupPathPrefix`

setlocale   `wxLocale::Init`, `wxSetLocale`

Prerequisite
        `#include <wx/intl.h>`

Use or emulate GNU gettext
        emulate, see `include/wx/intl.h` and `src/common/intl.cpp`

Extractor   `xgettext`

Formatting with positions
        wxString::Format supports positions if and only if the system has `wprintf()`,
        `vswprintf()` functions and they support positions according to POSIX.

Portability
        fully portable

po-mode marking
        yes

15.5.16 YCP - YaST2 scripting language

RPMs   libycp, libycp-devel, yast2-core, yast2-core-devel

File extension
        `ycp`

String syntax
        `"abc"`

gettext shorthand
        `_("abc")`

gettext/ngettext functions
        `_()` with 1 or 3 arguments

textdomain
        textdomain statement

bindtextdomain
        ---

setlocale   ---

Prerequisite
>   —

Use or emulate GNU gettext
>   use

Extractor   `xgettext`

Formatting with positions
>   `sformat "%2 %1"`

Portability
>   fully portable

po-mode marking
>   —

An example is available in the `examples` directory: `hello-ycp`.

15.5.17 Tcl - Tk's scripting language

RPMs   tcl

File extension
>   `tcl`

String syntax
>   `"abc"`

gettext shorthand
>   `[_ "abc"]`

gettext/ngettext functions
>   `::msgcat::mc`

textdomain
>   —

bindtextdomain
>   —, use `::msgcat::mcload` instead

setlocale   automatic, uses LANG, but ignores LC_MESSAGES and LC_ALL

Prerequisite
>   `package require msgcat`
>   `proc _ {s} {return [::msgcat::mc $s]}`

Use or emulate GNU gettext
>   —, uses a Tcl specific message catalog format

Extractor   `xgettext -k_`

Formatting with positions
>   `format "%2\$d %1\$d"`

Portability
>   fully portable

po-mode marking

Two examples are available in the `examples` directory: `hello-tcl`, `hello-tcl-tk`.

Before marking strings as internationalizable, substitutions of variables into the string need to be converted to `format` applications. For example, `"file $filename not found"` becomes `[format "file %s not found" $filename]`. Only after this is done, can the strings be marked and extracted. After marking, this example becomes `[format [_ "file %s not found"] $filename]` or `[msgcat::mc "file %s not found" $filename]`. Note that the `msgcat::mc` function implicitly calls `format` when more than one argument is given.

15.5.18 Perl

RPMs   perl

File extension

        pl, PL, pm, perl, cgi

String syntax

- `"abc"`
- `'abc'`
- `qq (abc)`
- `q (abc)`
- `qr /abc/`
- `qx (/bin/date)`
- `/pattern match/`
- `?pattern match?`
- `s/substitution/operators/`
- `$tied_hash{"message"}`
- `$tied_hash_reference->{"message"}`
- etc., issue the command '`man perlsyn`' for details

gettext shorthand

        `__` (double underscore)

gettext/ngettext functions

        `gettext, dgettext, dcgettext, ngettext, dngettext, dcngettext`

textdomain

        `textdomain` function

bindtextdomain

        `bindtextdomain` function

bind_textdomain_codeset

        `bind_textdomain_codeset` function

setlocale   Use `setlocale (LC_ALL, "");`

Prerequisite

> ```
> use POSIX;
> use Locale::TextDomain;
> ```
> (included in the package libintl-perl which
> is available on the Comprehensive Perl Archive Network CPAN,
> http://www.cpan.org/).

Use or emulate GNU gettext

> platform dependent: gettext_pp emulates, gettext_xs uses GNU gettext

Extractor `xgettext -k__ -k\$__ -k%__ -k__x -k__n:1,2 -k__nx:1,2 -k__xn:1,2 -kN__ -k`

Formatting with positions

> Both kinds of format strings support formatting with positions.
> `printf "%2\$d %1\$d", ...` (requires Perl 5.8.0 or newer)
> `__expand("[new] replaces [old]", old => $oldvalue, new => $newvalue)`

Portability

> The `libintl-perl` package is platform independent but is not part of the Perl
> core. The programmer is responsible for providing a dummy implementation
> of the required functions if the package is not installed on the target system.

po-mode marking

> —

Documentation

> Included in `libintl-perl`, available on CPAN (http://www.cpan.org/).

An example is available in the **examples** directory: **hello-perl**.

The **xgettext** parser backend for Perl differs significantly from the parser backends for other programming languages, just as Perl itself differs significantly from other programming languages. The Perl parser backend offers many more string marking facilities than the other backends but it also has some Perl specific limitations, the worst probably being its imperfectness.

15.5.18.1 General Problems Parsing Perl Code

It is often heard that only Perl can parse Perl. This is not true. Perl cannot be *parsed* at all, it can only be *executed*. Perl has various built-in ambiguities that can only be resolved at runtime.

The following example may illustrate one common problem:

```
print gettext "Hello World!";
```

Although this example looks like a bullet-proof case of a function invocation, it is not:

```
open gettext, ">testfile" or die;
print gettext "Hello world!"
```

In this context, the string **gettext** looks more like a file handle. But not necessarily:

```
use Locale::Messages qw (:libintl_h);
open gettext ">testfile" or die;
print gettext "Hello world!";
```

Now, the file is probably syntactically incorrect, provided that the module
Locale::Messages found first in the Perl include path exports a function gettext. But
what if the module Locale::Messages really looks like this?

```
use vars qw (*gettext);


1;
```

In this case, the string gettext will be interpreted as a file handle again, and the above
example will create a file testfile and write the string "Hello world!" into it. Even
advanced control flow analysis will not really help:

```
if (0.5 < rand) {
    eval "use Sane";
} else {
    eval "use InSane";
}
print gettext "Hello world!";
```

If the module Sane exports a function gettext that does what we expect, and the module
InSane opens a file for writing and associates the *handle* gettext with this output stream,
we are clueless again about what will happen at runtime. It is completely unpredictable.
The truth is that Perl has so many ways to fill its symbol table at runtime that it is
impossible to interpret a particular piece of code without executing it.

Of course, xgettext will not execute your Perl sources while scanning for translatable
strings, but rather use heuristics in order to guess what you meant.

Another problem is the ambiguity of the slash and the question mark. Their interpreta-
tion depends on the context:

```
# A pattern match.
print "OK\n" if /foobar/;

# A division.
print 1 / 2;

# Another pattern match.
print "OK\n" if ?foobar?;

# Conditional.
print $x ? "foo" : "bar";
```

The slash may either act as the division operator or introduce a pattern match, whereas
the question mark may act as the ternary conditional operator or as a pattern match, too.
Other programming languages like awk present similar problems, but the consequences of a
misinterpretation are particularly nasty with Perl sources. In awk for instance, a statement
can never exceed one line and the parser can recover from a parsing error at the next newline
and interpret the rest of the input stream correctly. Perl is different, as a pattern match
is terminated by the next appearance of the delimiter (the slash or the question mark) in
the input stream, regardless of the semantic context. If a slash is really a division sign
but mis-interpreted as a pattern match, the rest of the input file is most probably parsed
incorrectly.

There are certain cases, where the ambiguity cannot be resolved at all:

```
$x = wantarray ? 1 : 0;
```

The Perl built-in function `wantarray` does not accept any arguments. The Perl parser therefore knows that the question mark does not start a regular expression but is the ternary conditional operator.

```
sub wantarrays {}
$x = wantarrays ? 1 : 0;
```

Now the situation is different. The function `wantarrays` takes a variable number of arguments (like any non-prototyped Perl function). The question mark is now the delimiter of a pattern match, and hence the piece of code does not compile.

```
sub wantarrays() {}
$x = wantarrays ? 1 : 0;
```

Now the function is prototyped, Perl knows that it does not accept any arguments, and the question mark is therefore interpreted as the ternaray operator again. But that unfortunately outsmarts `xgettext`.

The Perl parser in `xgettext` cannot know whether a function has a prototype and what that prototype would look like. It therefore makes an educated guess. If a function is known to be a Perl built-in and this function does not accept any arguments, a following question mark or slash is treated as an operator, otherwise as the delimiter of a following regular expression. The Perl built-ins that do not accept arguments are `wantarray`, `fork`, `time`, `times`, `getlogin`, `getppid`, `getpwent`, `getgrent`, `gethostent`, `getnetent`, `getprotoent`, `getservent`, `setpwent`, `setgrent`, `endpwent`, `endgrent`, `endhostent`, `endnetent`, `endprotoent`, and `endservent`.

If you find that `xgettext` fails to extract strings from portions of your sources, you should therefore look out for slashes and/or question marks preceding these sections. You may have come across a bug in `xgettext`'s Perl parser (and of course you should report that bug). In the meantime you should consider to reformulate your code in a manner less challenging to `xgettext`.

In particular, if the parser is too dumb to see that a function does not accept arguments, use parentheses:

```
$x = somefunc() ? 1 : 0;
$y = (somefunc) ? 1 : 0;
```

In fact the Perl parser itself has similar problems and warns you about such constructs.

15.5.18.2 Which keywords will xgettext look for?

Unless you instruct `xgettext` otherwise by invoking it with one of the options `--keyword` or `-k`, it will recognize the following keywords in your Perl sources:

- `gettext`
- `dgettext`
- `dcgettext`
- `ngettext:1,2`

  The first (singular) and the second (plural) argument will be extracted.

- `dngettext:1,2`

  The first (singular) and the second (plural) argument will be extracted.

- `dcngettext:1,2`

  The first (singular) and the second (plural) argument will be extracted.

- `gettext_noop`

- `%gettext`

  The keys of lookups into the hash `%gettext` will be extracted.

- `$gettext`

  The keys of lookups into the hash reference `$gettext` will be extracted.

15.5.18.3 How to Extract Hash Keys

Translating messages at runtime is normally performed by looking up the original string in the translation database and returning the translated version. The "natural" Perl implementation is a hash lookup, and, of course, `xgettext` supports such practice.

```
print __"Hello world!";
print $__{"Hello world!"};
print $__->{"Hello world!"};
print $$__{"Hello world!"};
```

The above four lines all do the same thing. The Perl module `Locale::TextDomain` exports by default a hash `%__` that is tied to the function `__()`. It also exports a reference `$__` to `%__`.

If an argument to the `xgettext` option `--keyword`, resp. `-k` starts with a percent sign, the rest of the keyword is interpreted as the name of a hash. If it starts with a dollar sign, the rest of the keyword is interpreted as a reference to a hash.

Note that you can omit the quotation marks (single or double) around the hash key (almost) whenever Perl itself allows it:

```
print $gettext{Error};
```

The exact rule is: You can omit the surrounding quotes, when the hash key is a valid C (!) identifier, i.e. when it starts with an underscore or an ASCII letter and is followed by an arbitrary number of underscores, ASCII letters or digits. Other Unicode characters are *not* allowed, regardless of the `use utf8` pragma.

15.5.18.4 What are Strings And Quote-like Expressions?

Perl offers a plethora of different string constructs. Those that can be used either as arguments to functions or inside braces for hash lookups are generally supported by `xgettext`.

- **double-quoted strings**

  ```
  print gettext "Hello World!";
  ```

- **single-quoted strings**

  ```
  print gettext 'Hello World!';
  ```

- **the operator qq**

```
print gettext qq |Hello World!|;
print gettext qq <E-mail: <guido\@imperia.net>>;
```

The operator qq is fully supported. You can use arbitrary delimiters, including the four bracketing delimiters (round, angle, square, curly) that nest.

- **the operator q**

```
print gettext q |Hello World!|;
print gettext q <E-mail: <guido@imperia.net>>;
```

The operator q is fully supported. You can use arbitrary delimiters, including the four bracketing delimiters (round, angle, square, curly) that nest.

- **the operator qx**

```
print gettext qx ;LANGUAGE=C /bin/date;
print gettext qx [/usr/bin/ls | grep '^[A-Z]*'];
```

The operator qx is fully supported. You can use arbitrary delimiters, including the four bracketing delimiters (round, angle, square, curly) that nest.

The example is actually a useless use of **gettext**. It will invoke the **gettext** function on the output of the command specified with the **qx** operator. The feature was included in order to make the interface consistent (the parser will extract all strings and quote-like expressions).

- **here documents**

```
print gettext <<'EOF';
program not found in $PATH
EOF

print ngettext <<EOF, <<"EOF";
one file deleted
EOF
several files deleted
EOF
```

Here-documents are recognized. If the delimiter is enclosed in single quotes, the string is not interpolated. If it is enclosed in double quotes or has no quotes at all, the string is interpolated.

Delimiters that start with a digit are not supported!

15.5.18.5 Invalid Uses Of String Interpolation

Perl is capable of interpolating variables into strings. This offers some nice features in localized programs but can also lead to problems.

A common error is a construct like the following:

```
print gettext "This is the program $0!\n";
```

Perl will interpolate at runtime the value of the variable $0 into the argument of the
gettext() function. Hence, this argument is not a string constant but a variable argument ($0 is a global variable that holds the name of the Perl script being executed). The
interpolation is performed by Perl before the string argument is passed to gettext() and
will therefore depend on the name of the script which can only be determined at runtime.
Consequently, it is almost impossible that a translation can be looked up at runtime (except
if, by accident, the interpolated string is found in the message catalog).

The xgettext program will therefore terminate parsing with a fatal error if it encounters
a variable inside of an extracted string. In general, this will happen for all kinds of string
interpolations that cannot be safely performed at compile time. If you absolutely know
what you are doing, you can always circumvent this behavior:

```
my $know_what_i_am_doing = "This is program $0!\n";
print gettext $know_what_i_am_doing;
```

Since the parser only recognizes strings and quote-like expressions, but not variables
or other terms, the above construct will be accepted. You will have to find another way,
however, to let your original string make it into your message catalog.

If invoked with the option --extract-all, resp. -a, variable interpolation will be accepted. Rationale: You will generally use this option in order to prepare your sources for
internationalization.

Please see the manual page 'man perlop' for details of strings and quote-like expressions
that are subject to interpolation and those that are not. Safe interpolations (that will not
lead to a fatal error) are:

- the escape sequences \t (tab, HT, TAB), \n (newline, NL), \r (return, CR), \f (form
  feed, FF), \b (backspace, BS), \a (alarm, bell, BEL), and \e (escape, ESC).

- octal chars, like \033
  Note that octal escapes in the range of 400-777 are translated into a UTF-8 representation, regardless of the presence of the use utf8 pragma.

- hex chars, like \x1b

- wide hex chars, like \x{263a}
  Note that this escape is translated into a UTF-8 representation, regardless of the presence of the use utf8 pragma.

- control chars, like \c[(CTRL-[)

- named Unicode chars, like \N{LATIN CAPITAL LETTER C WITH CEDILLA}
  Note that this escape is translated into a UTF-8 representation, regardless of the presence of the use utf8 pragma.

The following escapes are considered partially safe:

- \l lowercase next char

- \u uppercase next char

- \L lowercase till \E

- \U uppercase till \E

- \E end case modification

- \Q quote non-word characters till \E

These escapes are only considered safe if the string consists of ASCII characters only. Translation of characters outside the range defined by ASCII is locale-dependent and can actually only be performed at runtime; xgettext doesn't do these locale-dependent translations at extraction time.

Except for the modifier \Q, these translations, albeit valid, are generally useless and only obfuscate your sources. If a translation can be safely performed at compile time you can just as well write what you mean.

15.5.18.6 Valid Uses Of String Interpolation

Perl is often used to generate sources for other programming languages or arbitrary file formats. Web applications that output HTML code make a prominent example for such usage.

You will often come across situations where you want to intersperse code written in the target (programming) language with translatable messages, like in the following HTML example:

```
print gettext <<EOF;
<h1>My Homepage</h1>
<script language="JavaScript"><!--
for (i = 0; i < 100; ++i) {
    alert ("Thank you so much for visiting my homepage!");
}
//--></script>
EOF
```

The parser will extract the entire here document, and it will appear entirely in the resulting PO file, including the JavaScript snippet embedded in the HTML code. If you exaggerate with constructs like the above, you will run the risk that the translators of your package will look out for a less challenging project. You should consider an alternative expression here:

```
print <<EOF;
<h1>$gettext{"My Homepage"}</h1>
<script language="JavaScript"><!--
for (i = 0; i < 100; ++i) {
    alert ("$gettext{'Thank you so much for visiting my homepage!'}");
}
//--></script>
EOF
```

Only the translatable portions of the code will be extracted here, and the resulting PO file will begrudgingly improve in terms of readability.

You can interpolate hash lookups in all strings or quote-like expressions that are subject to interpolation (see the manual page 'man perlop' for details). Double interpolation is invalid, however:

```
# TRANSLATORS: Replace "the earth" with the name of your planet.
print gettext qq{Welcome to $gettext->{"the earth"}};
```

The qq-quoted string is recognized as an argument to xgettext in the first place, and checked for invalid variable interpolation. The dollar sign of hash-dereferencing will therefore terminate the parser with an "invalid interpolation" error.

It is valid to interpolate hash lookups in regular expressions:

```
if ($var =~ /$gettext{"the earth"}/) {
    print gettext "Match!\n";
}
s/$gettext{"U. S. A."}/$gettext{"U. S. A."} $gettext{"(dial +0)"}/g;
```

15.5.18.7 When To Use Parentheses

In Perl, parentheses around function arguments are mostly optional. xgettext will always assume that all recognized keywords (except for hashes and hash references) are names of properly prototyped functions, and will (hopefully) only require parentheses where Perl itself requires them. All constructs in the following example are therefore ok to use:

```
print gettext ("Hello World!\n");
print gettext "Hello World!\n";
print dgettext ($package => "Hello World!\n");
print dgettext $package, "Hello World!\n";

# The "fat comma" => turns the left-hand side argument into a
# single-quoted string!
print dgettext smellovision => "Hello World!\n";

# The following assignment only works with prototyped functions.
# Otherwise, the functions will act as "greedy" list operators and
# eat up all following arguments.
my $anonymous_hash = {
    planet => gettext "earth",
    cakes => ngettext "one cake", "several cakes", $n,
    still => $works,
};
# The same without fat comma:
my $other_hash = {
    'planet', gettext "earth",
    'cakes', ngettext "one cake", "several cakes", $n,
    'still', $works,
};

# Parentheses are only significant for the first argument.
print dngettext 'package', ("one cake", "several cakes", $n), $discarded;
```

15.5.18.8 How To Grok with Long Lines

The necessity of long messages can often lead to a cumbersome or unreadable coding style. Perl has several options that may prevent you from writing unreadable code, and xgettext does its best to do likewise. This is where the dot operator (the string concatenation operator) may come in handy:

```
print gettext ("This is a very long"
             . " message that is still"
             . " readable, because"
             . " it is split into"
             . " multiple lines.\n");
```

Perl is smart enough to concatenate these constant string fragments into one long string at compile time, and so is `xgettext`. You will only find one long message in the resulting POT file.

Note that the future Perl 6 will probably use the underscore ('_') as the string concatenation operator, and the dot ('.') for dereferencing. This new syntax is not yet supported by `xgettext`.

If embedded newline characters are not an issue, or even desired, you may also insert newline characters inside quoted strings wherever you feel like it:

```
print gettext ("<em>In HTML output
embedded newlines are generally no
problem, since adjacent whitespace
is always rendered into a single
space character.</em>");
```

You may also consider to use here documents:

```
print gettext <<EOF;
<em>In HTML output
embedded newlines are generally no
problem, since adjacent whitespace
is always rendered into a single
space character.</em>
EOF
```

Please do not forget that the line breaks are real, i.e. they translate into newline characters that will consequently show up in the resulting POT file.

15.5.18.9 Bugs, Pitfalls, And Things That Do Not Work

The foregoing sections should have proven that `xgettext` is quite smart in extracting translatable strings from Perl sources. Yet, some more or less exotic constructs that could be expected to work, actually do not work.

One of the more relevant limitations can be found in the implementation of variable interpolation inside quoted strings. Only simple hash lookups can be used there:

```
print <<EOF;
$gettext{"The dot operator"
        . " does not work"
        . "here!"}
Likewise, you cannot @{[ gettext ("interpolate function calls") ]}
inside quoted strings or quote-like expressions.
EOF
```

This is valid Perl code and will actually trigger invocations of the `gettext` function at runtime. Yet, the Perl parser in `xgettext` will fail to recognize the strings. A less obvious example can be found in the interpolation of regular expressions:

```
s/<!--START_OF_WEEK-->/gettext ("Sunday")/e;
```

The modifier e will cause the substitution to be interpreted as an evaluable statement. Consequently, at runtime the function gettext() is called, but again, the parser fails to extract the string "Sunday". Use a temporary variable as a simple workaround if you really happen to need this feature:

```
my $sunday = gettext "Sunday";
s/<!--START_OF_WEEK-->/$sunday/;
```

Hash slices would also be handy but are not recognized:

```
my @weekdays = @gettext{'Sunday', 'Monday', 'Tuesday', 'Wednesday',
                        'Thursday', 'Friday', 'Saturday'};
# Or even:
@weekdays = @gettext{qw (Sunday Monday Tuesday Wednesday Thursday
                        Friday Saturday) };
```

This is perfectly valid usage of the tied hash %gettext but the strings are not recognized and therefore will not be extracted.

Another caveat of the current version is its rudimentary support for non-ASCII characters in identifiers. You may encounter serious problems if you use identifiers with characters outside the range of 'A'-'Z', 'a'-'z', '0'-'9' and the underscore '_'.

Maybe some of these missing features will be implemented in future versions, but since you can always make do without them at minimal effort, these todos have very low priority.

A nasty problem are brace format strings that already contain braces as part of the normal text, for example the usage strings typically encountered in programs:

```
die "usage: $0 {OPTIONS} FILENAME...\n";
```

If you want to internationalize this code with Perl brace format strings, you will run into a problem:

```
die __x ("usage: {program} {OPTIONS} FILENAME...\n", program => $0);
```

Whereas '{program}' is a placeholder, '{OPTIONS}' is not and should probably be translated. Yet, there is no way to teach the Perl parser in xgettext to recognize the first one, and leave the other one alone.

There are two possible work-arounds for this problem. If you are sure that your program will run under Perl 5.8.0 or newer (these Perl versions handle positional parameters in printf()) or if you are sure that the translator will not have to reorder the arguments in her translation – for example if you have only one brace placeholder in your string, or if it describes a syntax, like in this one –, you can mark the string as no-perl-brace-format and use printf():

```
# xgettext: no-perl-brace-format
die sprintf ("usage: %s {OPTIONS} FILENAME...\n", $0);
```

If you want to use the more portable Perl brace format, you will have to do put placeholders in place of the literal braces:

```
die __x ("usage: {program} {[}OPTIONS{]} FILENAME...\n",
        program => $0, '[' => '{', ']' => '}');
```

Perl brace format strings know no escaping mechanism. No matter how this escaping mechanism looked like, it would either give the programmer a hard time, make translating

Perl brace format strings heavy-going, or result in a performance penalty at runtime, when the format directives get executed. Most of the time you will happily get along with `printf()` for this special case.

15.5.19 PHP Hypertext Preprocessor

RPMs   mod_php4, mod_php4-core, phpdoc

File extension

        `php`, `php3`, `php4`

String syntax

        `"abc"`, `'abc'`

gettext shorthand

        `_("abc")`

gettext/ngettext functions

        `gettext`, `dgettext`, `dcgettext`; starting with PHP 4.2.0 also `ngettext`, `dngettext`, `dcngettext`

textdomain

        `textdomain` function

bindtextdomain

        `bindtextdomain` function

setlocale   Programmer must call `setlocale (LC_ALL, "")`

Prerequisite

        —

Use or emulate GNU gettext

        use

Extractor   `xgettext`

Formatting with positions

        `printf "%2\$d %1\$d"`

Portability

        On platforms without gettext, the functions are not available.

po-mode marking

        —

An example is available in the `examples` directory: `hello-php`.

15.5.20 Pike

RPMs   roxen

File extension

        `pike`

String syntax

        `"abc"`

gettext shorthand

—

gettext/ngettext functions

gettext, dgettext, dcgettext

textdomain

textdomain function

bindtextdomain

bindtextdomain function

setlocale   setlocale function

Prerequisite

import Locale.Gettext;

Use or emulate GNU gettext

use

Extractor   —

Formatting with positions

—

Portability

On platforms without gettext, the functions are not available.

po-mode marking

—

15.5.21 GNU Compiler Collection sources

RPMs   gcc

File extension

c, h.

String syntax

"abc"

gettext shorthand

_("abc")

gettext/ngettext functions

gettext, dgettext, dcgettext, ngettext, dngettext, dcngettext

textdomain

textdomain function

bindtextdomain

bindtextdomain function

setlocale   Programmer must call setlocale (LC_ALL, "")

Prerequisite

#include "intl.h"

Use or emulate GNU gettext
        Use

Extractor   `xgettext -k_`

Formatting with positions
        ——

Portability
        Uses autoconf macros

po-mode marking
        yes

15.5.22 Lua

RPMs   lua

File extension
        `lua`

String syntax
   - `"abc"`
   - `'abc'`
   - `[[abc]]`
   - `[=[abc]=]`
   - `[==[abc]==]`
   - ...

gettext shorthand
        `_("abc")`

gettext/ngettext functions
        `gettext.gettext,`   `gettext.dgettext,`   `gettext.dcgettext,`
        `gettext.ngettext, gettext.dngettext, gettext.dcngettext`

textdomain
        `textdomain` function

bindtextdomain
        `bindtextdomain` function

setlocale   automatic

Prerequisite
        `require 'gettext'` or running lua interpreter with `-l gettext` option

Use or emulate GNU gettext
        use

Extractor   `xgettext`

Formatting with positions
        ——

Portability
> On platforms without gettext, the functions are not available.

po-mode marking
> —

15.5.23 JavaScript

RPMs   js

File extension
> `js`

String syntax
> - `"abc"`
> - `'abc'`

gettext shorthand
> `_("abc")`

gettext/ngettext functions
> `gettext`, `dgettext`, `dcgettext`, `ngettext`, `dngettext`

textdomain
> `textdomain` function

bindtextdomain
> `bindtextdomain` function

setlocale   automatic

Prerequisite
> —

Use or emulate GNU gettext
> use, or emulate

Extractor   `xgettext`

Formatting with positions
> —

Portability
> On platforms without gettext, the functions are not available.

po-mode marking
> —

15.5.24 Vala

RPMs   vala

File extension
> `vala`

String syntax
> - `"abc"`

- `"""abc"""`

gettext shorthand
> `_("abc")`

gettext/ngettext functions
> `gettext`, `dgettext`, `dcgettext`, `ngettext`, `dngettext`, `dpgettext`, `dpgettext2`

textdomain
> `textdomain` function, defined under the `Intl` namespace

bindtextdomain
> `bindtextdomain` function, defined under the `Intl` namespace

setlocale   Programmer must call `Intl.setlocale (LocaleCategory.ALL, "")`

Prerequisite
> —

Use or emulate GNU gettext
> Use

Extractor   `xgettext`

Formatting with positions
> Same as for the C language.

Portability
> autoconf (gettext.m4) and #if ENABLE_NLS

po-mode marking
> yes

15.6 Internationalizable Data

Here is a list of other data formats which can be internationalized using GNU gettext.

15.6.1 POT - Portable Object Template

RPMs   gettext

File extension
> `pot, po`

Extractor   `xgettext`

15.6.2 Resource String Table

RPMs   fpk

File extension
> `rst`

Extractor   `xgettext, rstconv`

15.6.3 Glade - GNOME user interface description

RPMs   glade, libglade, glade2, libglade2, intltool

File extension
            `glade, glade2, ui`

Extractor   `xgettext, libglade-xgettext, xml-i18n-extract, intltool-extract`

15.6.4 GSettings - GNOME user configuration schema

RPMs   glib2

File extension
            `gschema.xml`

Extractor   `xgettext, intltool-extract`

16 Concluding Remarks

We would like to conclude this GNU `gettext` manual by presenting an history of the Translation Project so far. We finally give a few pointers for those who want to do further research or readings about Native Language Support matters.

16.1 History of GNU `gettext`

Internationalization concerns and algorithms have been informally and casually discussed for years in GNU, sometimes around GNU `libc`, maybe around the incoming `Hurd`, or otherwise (nobody clearly remembers). And even then, when the work started for real, this was somewhat independently of these previous discussions.

This all began in July 1994, when Patrick D'Cruze had the idea and initiative of internationalizing version 3.9.2 of GNU `fileutils`. He then asked Jim Meyering, the maintainer, how to get those changes folded into an official release. That first draft was full of `#ifdefs` and somewhat disconcerting, and Jim wanted to find nicer ways. Patrick and Jim shared some tries and experimentations in this area. Then, feeling that this might eventually have a deeper impact on GNU, Jim wanted to know what standards were, and contacted Richard Stallman, who very quickly and verbally described an overall design for what was meant to become `glocale`, at that time.

Jim implemented `glocale` and got a lot of exhausting feedback from Patrick and Richard, of course, but also from Mitchum DSouza (who wrote a `catgets`-like package), Roland McGrath, maybe David MacKenzie, François Pinard, and Paul Eggert, all pushing and pulling in various directions, not always compatible, to the extent that after a couple of test releases, `glocale` was torn apart. In particular, Paul Eggert – always keeping an eye on developments in Solaris – advocated the use of the `gettext` API over `glocale`'s `catgets`-based API.

While Jim took some distance and time and became dad for a second time, Roland wanted to get GNU `libc` internationalized, and got Ulrich Drepper involved in that project. Instead of starting from `glocale`, Ulrich rewrote something from scratch, but more conforming to the set of guidelines who emerged out of the `glocale` effort. Then, Ulrich got people from the previous forum to involve themselves into this new project, and the switch from `glocale` to what was first named `msgutils`, renamed `nlsutils`, and later `gettext`, became officially accepted by Richard in May 1995 or so.

Let's summarize by saying that Ulrich Drepper wrote GNU `gettext` in April 1995. The first official release of the package, including PO mode, occurred in July 1995, and was numbered 0.7. Other people contributed to the effort by providing a discussion forum around Ulrich, writing little pieces of code, or testing. These are quoted in the `THANKS` file which comes with the GNU `gettext` distribution.

While this was being done, François adapted half a dozen of GNU packages to `glocale` first, then later to `gettext`, putting them in pretest, so providing along the way an effective user environment for fine tuning the evolving tools. He also took the responsibility of organizing and coordinating the Translation Project. After nearly a year of informal exchanges between people from many countries, translator teams started to exist in May 1995, through the creation and support by Patrick D'Cruze of twenty unmoderated mailing lists for that many native languages, and two moderated lists: one for reaching all teams at once, the other for reaching all willing maintainers of internationalized free software packages.

François also wrote PO mode in June 1995 with the collaboration of Greg McGary, as a kind of contribution to Ulrich's package. He also gave a hand with the GNU `gettext` Texinfo manual.

In 1997, Ulrich Drepper released the GNU libc 2.0, which included the `gettext`, `textdomain` and `bindtextdomain` functions.

In 2000, Ulrich Drepper added plural form handling (the `ngettext` function) to GNU libc. Later, in 2001, he released GNU libc 2.2.x, which is the first free C library with full internationalization support.

Ulrich being quite busy in his role of General Maintainer of GNU libc, he handed over the GNU `gettext` maintenance to Bruno Haible in 2000. Bruno added the plural form handling to the tools as well, added support for UTF-8 and CJK locales, and wrote a few new tools for manipulating PO files.

16.2 Related Readings

NOTE: This documentation section is outdated and needs to be revised.

Eugene H. Dorr (`dorre@well.com`) maintains an interesting bibliography on internationalization matters, called *Internationalization Reference List*, which is available as:

> `ftp://ftp.ora.com/pub/examples/nutshell/ujip/doc/i18n-books.txt`

Michael Gschwind (`mike@vlsivie.tuwien.ac.at`) maintains a Frequently Asked Questions (FAQ) list, entitled *Programming for Internationalisation*. This FAQ discusses writing programs which can handle different language conventions, character sets, etc.; and is applicable to all character set encodings, with particular emphasis on ISO 8859-1. It is regularly published in Usenet groups `comp.unix.questions`, `comp.std.internat`, `comp.software.international`, `comp.lang.c`, `comp.windows.x`, `comp.std.c`, `comp.answers` and `news.answers`. The home location of this document is:

> `ftp://ftp.vlsivie.tuwien.ac.at/pub/8bit/ISO-programming`

Patrick D'Cruze (`pdcruze@li.org`) wrote a tutorial about NLS matters, and Jochen Hein (`Hein@student.tu-clausthal.de`) took over the responsibility of maintaining it. It may be found as:

> `ftp://sunsite.unc.edu/pub/Linux/utils/nls/catalogs/Incoming/...`
> `...locale-tutorial-0.8.txt.gz`

This site is mirrored in:

> `ftp://ftp.ibp.fr/pub/linux/sunsite/`

A French version of the same tutorial should be findable at:

> `ftp://ftp.ibp.fr/pub/linux/french/docs/`

together with French translations of many Linux-related documents.

Appendix A Language Codes

The ISO 639 standard defines two-letter codes for many languages, and three-letter codes for more rarely used languages. All abbreviations for languages used in the Translation Project should come from this standard.

A.1 Usual Language Codes

For the commonly used languages, the ISO 639-1 standard defines two-letter codes.

'aa'   Afar.

'ab'   Abkhazian.

'ae'   Avestan.

'af'   Afrikaans.

'ak'   Akan.

'am'   Amharic.

'an'   Aragonese.

'ar'   Arabic.

'as'   Assamese.

'av'   Avaric.

'ay'   Aymara.

'az'   Azerbaijani.

'ba'   Bashkir.

'be'   Belarusian.

'bg'   Bulgarian.

'bh'   Bihari.

'bi'   Bislama.

'bm'   Bambara.

'bn'   Bengali; Bangla.

'bo'   Tibetan.

'br'   Breton.

'bs'   Bosnian.

'ca'   Catalan.

'ce'   Chechen.

'ch'   Chamorro.

'co'   Corsican.

'cr'	Cree.
'cs'	Czech.
'cu'	Church Slavic.
'cv'	Chuvash.
'cy'	Welsh.
'da'	Danish.
'de'	German.
'dv'	Divehi; Maldivian.
'dz'	Dzongkha; Bhutani.
'ee'	Éwé.
'el'	Greek.
'en'	English.
'eo'	Esperanto.
'es'	Spanish.
'et'	Estonian.
'eu'	Basque.
'fa'	Persian.
'ff'	Fulah.
'fi'	Finnish.
'fj'	Fijian; Fiji.
'fo'	Faroese.
'fr'	French.
'fy'	Western Frisian.
'ga'	Irish.
'gd'	Scottish Gaelic.
'gl'	Galician.
'gn'	Guarani.
'gu'	Gujarati.
'gv'	Manx.
'ha'	Hausa.
'he'	Hebrew (formerly iw).
'hi'	Hindi.
'ho'	Hiri Motu.

'hr'	Croatian.
'ht'	Haitian; Haitian Creole.
'hu'	Hungarian.
'hy'	Armenian.
'hz'	Herero.
'ia'	Interlingua.
'id'	Indonesian (formerly in).
'ie'	Interlingue; Occidental.
'ig'	Igbo.
'ii'	Sichuan Yi; Nuosu.
'ik'	Inupiak; Inupiaq.
'io'	Ido.
'is'	Icelandic.
'it'	Italian.
'iu'	Inuktitut.
'ja'	Japanese.
'jv'	Javanese.
'ka'	Georgian.
'kg'	Kongo.
'ki'	Kikuyu; Gikuyu.
'kj'	Kuanyama; Kwanyama.
'kk'	Kazakh.
'kl'	Kalaallisut; Greenlandic.
'km'	Central Khmer; Cambodian.
'kn'	Kannada.
'ko'	Korean.
'kr'	Kanuri.
'ks'	Kashmiri.
'ku'	Kurdish.
'kv'	Komi.
'kw'	Cornish.
'ky'	Kirghiz.
'la'	Latin.

'lb'	Letzeburgesch; Luxembourgish.
'lg'	Ganda.
'li'	Limburgish; Limburger; Limburgan.
'ln'	Lingala.
'lo'	Lao; Laotian.
'lt'	Lithuanian.
'lu'	Luba-Katanga.
'lv'	Latvian; Lettish.
'mg'	Malagasy.
'mh'	Marshallese.
'mi'	Maori.
'mk'	Macedonian.
'ml'	Malayalam.
'mn'	Mongolian.
'mo'	Moldavian.
'mr'	Marathi.
'ms'	Malay.
'mt'	Maltese.
'my'	Burmese.
'na'	Nauru.
'nb'	Norwegian Bokmål.
'nd'	Ndebele, North.
'ne'	Nepali.
'ng'	Ndonga.
'nl'	Dutch.
'nn'	Norwegian Nynorsk.
'no'	Norwegian.
'nr'	Ndebele, South.
'nv'	Navajo; Navaho.
'ny'	Chichewa; Nyanja.
'oc'	Occitan; Provençal.
'oj'	Ojibwa.
'om'	(Afan) Oromo.

'or'	Oriya.
'os'	Ossetian; Ossetic.
'pa'	Panjabi; Punjabi.
'pi'	Pali.
'pl'	Polish.
'ps'	Pashto; Pushto.
'pt'	Portuguese.
'qu'	Quechua.
'rm'	Romansh.
'rn'	Rundi; Kirundi.
'ro'	Romanian.
'ru'	Russian.
'rw'	Kinyarwanda.
'sa'	Sanskrit.
'sc'	Sardinian.
'sd'	Sindhi.
'se'	Northern Sami.
'sg'	Sango; Sangro.
'si'	Sinhala; Sinhalese.
'sk'	Slovak.
'sl'	Slovenian.
'sm'	Samoan.
'sn'	Shona.
'so'	Somali.
'sq'	Albanian.
'sr'	Serbian.
'ss'	Swati; Siswati.
'st'	Sesotho; Sotho, Southern.
'su'	Sundanese.
'sv'	Swedish.
'sw'	Swahili.
'ta'	Tamil.
'te'	Telugu.

‘tg’   Tajik.

‘th’   Thai.

‘ti’   Tigrinya.

‘tk’   Turkmen.

‘tl’   Tagalog.

‘tn’   Tswana; Setswana.

‘to’   Tonga.

‘tr’   Turkish.

‘ts’   Tsonga.

‘tt’   Tatar.

‘tw’   Twi.

‘ty’   Tahitian.

‘ug’   Uighur.

‘uk’   Ukrainian.

‘ur’   Urdu.

‘uz’   Uzbek.

‘ve’   Venda.

‘vi’   Vietnamese.

‘vo’   Volapük; Volapuk.

‘wa’   Walloon.

‘wo’   Wolof.

‘xh’   Xhosa.

‘yi’   Yiddish (formerly ji).

‘yo’   Yoruba.

‘za’   Zhuang.

‘zh’   Chinese.

‘zu’   Zulu.

A.2 Rare Language Codes

For rarely used languages, the ISO 639-2 standard defines three-letter codes. Here is the current list, reduced to only living languages with at least one million of speakers.

'ace'   Achinese.

'awa'   Awadhi.

'bal'   Baluchi.

'ban'   Balinese.

'bej'   Beja; Bedawiyet.

'bem'   Bemba.

'bho'   Bhojpuri.

'bik'   Bikol.

'bin'   Bini; Edo.

'bug'   Buginese.

'ceb'   Cebuano.

'din'   Dinka.

'doi'   Dogri.

'fil'   Filipino; Pilipino.

'fon'   Fon.

'gon'   Gondi.

'gsw'   Swiss German; Alemannic; Alsatian.

'hil'   Hiligaynon.

'hmn'   Hmong.

'ilo'   Iloko.

'kab'   Kabyle.

'kam'   Kamba.

'kbd'   Kabardian.

'kmb'   Kimbundu.

'kok'   Konkani.

'kru'   Kurukh.

'lua'   Luba-Lulua.

'luo'   Luo (Kenya and Tanzania).

'mad'   Madurese.

'mag'   Magahi.

'mai'	Maithili.
'mak'	Makasar.
'man'	Mandingo.
'men'	Mende.
'min'	Minangkabau.
'mni'	Manipuri.
'mos'	Mossi.
'mwr'	Marwari.
'nap'	Neapolitan.
'nso'	Pedi; Sepedi; Northern Sotho.
'nym'	Nyamwezi.
'nyn'	Nyankole.
'pag'	Pangasinan.
'pam'	Pampanga; Kapampangan.
'raj'	Rajasthani.
'sas'	Sasak.
'sat'	Santali.
'scn'	Sicilian.
'shn'	Shan.
'sid'	Sidamo.
'srr'	Serer.
'suk'	Sukuma.
'sus'	Susu.
'tem'	Timne.
'tiv'	Tiv.
'tum'	Tumbuka.
'umb'	Umbundu.
'wal'	Walamo.
'war'	Waray.
'yao'	Yao.

Appendix B Country Codes

The ISO 3166 standard defines two character codes for many countries and territories. All abbreviations for countries used in the Translation Project should come from this standard.

'AD'   Andorra.

'AE'   United Arab Emirates.

'AF'   Afghanistan.

'AG'   Antigua and Barbuda.

'AI'   Anguilla.

'AL'   Albania.

'AM'   Armenia.

'AO'   Angola.

'AQ'   Antarctica.

'AR'   Argentina.

'AS'   American Samoa.

'AT'   Austria.

'AU'   Australia.

'AW'   Aruba.

'AX'   Aaland Islands.

'AZ'   Azerbaijan.

'BA'   Bosnia and Herzegovina.

'BB'   Barbados.

'BD'   Bangladesh.

'BE'   Belgium.

'BF'   Burkina Faso.

'BG'   Bulgaria.

'BH'   Bahrain.

'BI'   Burundi.

'BJ'   Benin.

'BL'   Saint Barthelemy.

'BM'   Bermuda.

'BN'   Brunei Darussalam.

'BO'   Bolivia, Plurinational State of.

'BQ'	Bonaire, Sint Eustatius and Saba.
'BR'	Brazil.
'BS'	Bahamas.
'BT'	Bhutan.
'BV'	Bouvet Island.
'BW'	Botswana.
'BY'	Belarus.
'BZ'	Belize.
'CA'	Canada.
'CC'	Cocos (Keeling) Islands.
'CD'	Congo, The Democratic Republic of the.
'CF'	Central African Republic.
'CG'	Congo.
'CH'	Switzerland.
'CI'	Côte d'Ivoire.
'CK'	Cook Islands.
'CL'	Chile.
'CM'	Cameroon.
'CN'	China.
'CO'	Colombia.
'CR'	Costa Rica.
'CU'	Cuba.
'CV'	Cape Verde.
'CW'	Curaao.
'CX'	Christmas Island.
'CY'	Cyprus.
'CZ'	Czech Republic.
'DE'	Germany.
'DJ'	Djibouti.
'DK'	Denmark.
'DM'	Dominica.
'DO'	Dominican Republic.
'DZ'	Algeria.

'EC'	Ecuador.
'EE'	Estonia.
'EG'	Egypt.
'EH'	Western Sahara.
'ER'	Eritrea.
'ES'	Spain.
'ET'	Ethiopia.
'FI'	Finland.
'FJ'	Fiji.
'FK'	Falkland Islands (Malvinas).
'FM'	Micronesia, Federated States of.
'FO'	Faroe Islands.
'FR'	France.
'GA'	Gabon.
'GB'	United Kingdom.
'GD'	Grenada.
'GE'	Georgia.
'GF'	French Guiana.
'GG'	Guernsey.
'GH'	Ghana.
'GI'	Gibraltar.
'GL'	Greenland.
'GM'	Gambia.
'GN'	Guinea.
'GP'	Guadeloupe.
'GQ'	Equatorial Guinea.
'GR'	Greece.
'GS'	South Georgia and the South Sandwich Islands.
'GT'	Guatemala.
'GU'	Guam.
'GW'	Guinea-Bissau.
'GY'	Guyana.
'HK'	Hong Kong.

'HM'	Heard Island and McDonald Islands.
'HN'	Honduras.
'HR'	Croatia.
'HT'	Haiti.
'HU'	Hungary.
'ID'	Indonesia.
'IE'	Ireland.
'IL'	Israel.
'IM'	Isle of Man.
'IN'	India.
'IO'	British Indian Ocean Territory.
'IQ'	Iraq.
'IR'	Iran, Islamic Republic of.
'IS'	Iceland.
'IT'	Italy.
'JE'	Jersey.
'JM'	Jamaica.
'JO'	Jordan.
'JP'	Japan.
'KE'	Kenya.
'KG'	Kyrgyzstan.
'KH'	Cambodia.
'KI'	Kiribati.
'KM'	Comoros.
'KN'	Saint Kitts and Nevis.
'KP'	Korea, Democratic People's Republic of.
'KR'	Korea, Republic of.
'KW'	Kuwait.
'KY'	Cayman Islands.
'KZ'	Kazakhstan.
'LA'	Lao People's Democratic Republic.
'LB'	Lebanon.
'LC'	Saint Lucia.

'LI'	Liechtenstein.
'LK'	Sri Lanka.
'LR'	Liberia.
'LS'	Lesotho.
'LT'	Lithuania.
'LU'	Luxembourg.
'LV'	Latvia.
'LY'	Libya.
'MA'	Morocco.
'MC'	Monaco.
'MD'	Moldova, Republic of.
'ME'	Montenegro.
'MF'	Saint Martin (French part).
'MG'	Madagascar.
'MH'	Marshall Islands.
'MK'	Macedonia, The Former Yugoslav Republic of.
'ML'	Mali.
'MM'	Myanmar.
'MN'	Mongolia.
'MO'	Macao.
'MP'	Northern Mariana Islands.
'MQ'	Martinique.
'MR'	Mauritania.
'MS'	Montserrat.
'MT'	Malta.
'MU'	Mauritius.
'MV'	Maldives.
'MW'	Malawi.
'MX'	Mexico.
'MY'	Malaysia.
'MZ'	Mozambique.
'NA'	Namibia.
'NC'	New Caledonia.

'NE'	Niger.
'NF'	Norfolk Island.
'NG'	Nigeria.
'NI'	Nicaragua.
'NL'	Netherlands.
'NO'	Norway.
'NP'	Nepal.
'NR'	Nauru.
'NU'	Niue.
'NZ'	New Zealand.
'OM'	Oman.
'PA'	Panama.
'PE'	Peru.
'PF'	French Polynesia.
'PG'	Papua New Guinea.
'PH'	Philippines.
'PK'	Pakistan.
'PL'	Poland.
'PM'	Saint Pierre and Miquelon.
'PN'	Pitcairn.
'PR'	Puerto Rico.
'PS'	Palestine, State of.
'PT'	Portugal.
'PW'	Palau.
'PY'	Paraguay.
'QA'	Qatar.
'RE'	Reunion.
'RO'	Romania.
'RS'	Serbia.
'RU'	Russian Federation.
'RW'	Rwanda.
'SA'	Saudi Arabia.
'SB'	Solomon Islands.

'SC'	Seychelles.
'SD'	Sudan.
'SE'	Sweden.
'SG'	Singapore.
'SH'	Saint Helena, Ascension and Tristan da Cunha.
'SI'	Slovenia.
'SJ'	Svalbard and Jan Mayen.
'SK'	Slovakia.
'SL'	Sierra Leone.
'SM'	San Marino.
'SN'	Senegal.
'SO'	Somalia.
'SR'	Suriname.
'SS'	South Sudan.
'ST'	Sao Tome and Principe.
'SV'	El Salvador.
'SX'	Sint Maarten (Dutch part).
'SY'	Syrian Arab Republic.
'SZ'	Swaziland.
'TC'	Turks and Caicos Islands.
'TD'	Chad.
'TF'	French Southern Territories.
'TG'	Togo.
'TH'	Thailand.
'TJ'	Tajikistan.
'TK'	Tokelau.
'TL'	Timor-Leste.
'TM'	Turkmenistan.
'TN'	Tunisia.
'TO'	Tonga.
'TR'	Turkey.
'TT'	Trinidad and Tobago.
'TV'	Tuvalu.

'TW'	Taiwan, Province of China.
'TZ'	Tanzania, United Republic of.
'UA'	Ukraine.
'UG'	Uganda.
'UM'	United States Minor Outlying Islands.
'US'	United States.
'UY'	Uruguay.
'UZ'	Uzbekistan.
'VA'	Holy See (Vatican City State).
'VC'	Saint Vincent and the Grenadines.
'VE'	Venezuela, Bolivarian Republic of.
'VG'	Virgin Islands, British.
'VI'	Virgin Islands, U.S..
'VN'	Viet Nam.
'VU'	Vanuatu.
'WF'	Wallis and Futuna.
'WS'	Samoa.
'YE'	Yemen.
'YT'	Mayotte.
'ZA'	South Africa.
'ZM'	Zambia.
'ZW'	Zimbabwe.

Appendix C Licenses

The files of this package are covered by the licenses indicated in each particular file or directory. Here is a summary:

- The `libintl` and `libasprintf` libraries are covered by the GNU Lesser General Public License (LGPL). A copy of the license is included in Section C.2 [GNU LGPL], page 229.

- The executable programs of this package and the `libgettextpo` library are covered by the GNU General Public License (GPL). A copy of the license is included in Section C.1 [GNU GPL], page 223.

- This manual is free documentation. It is dually licensed under the GNU FDL and the GNU GPL. This means that you can redistribute this manual under either of these two licenses, at your choice.

  This manual is covered by the GNU FDL. Permission is granted to copy, distribute and/or modify this document under the terms of the GNU Free Documentation License (FDL), either version 1.2 of the License, or (at your option) any later version published by the Free Software Foundation (FSF); with no Invariant Sections, with no Front-Cover Text, and with no Back-Cover Texts. A copy of the license is included in Section C.3 [GNU FDL], page 238.

  This manual is covered by the GNU GPL. You can redistribute it and/or modify it under the terms of the GNU General Public License (GPL), either version 2 of the License, or (at your option) any later version published by the Free Software Foundation (FSF). A copy of the license is included in Section C.1 [GNU GPL], page 223.

C.1 GNU GENERAL PUBLIC LICENSE

Version 2, June 1991

Copyright © 1989, 1991 Free Software Foundation, Inc.
51 Franklin Street, Fifth Floor, Boston, MA 02110-1301, USA

Everyone is permitted to copy and distribute verbatim copies
of this license document, but changing it is not allowed.

Preamble

The licenses for most software are designed to take away your freedom to share and change it. By contrast, the GNU General Public License is intended to guarantee your freedom to share and change free software—to make sure the software is free for all its users. This General Public License applies to most of the Free Software Foundation's software and to any other program whose authors commit to using it. (Some other Free Software Foundation software is covered by the GNU Lesser General Public License instead.) You can apply it to your programs, too.

When we speak of free software, we are referring to freedom, not price. Our General Public Licenses are designed to make sure that you have the freedom to distribute copies of free software (and charge for this service if you wish), that you receive source code or can get it if you want it, that you can change the software or use pieces of it in new free programs; and that you know you can do these things.

To protect your rights, we need to make restrictions that forbid anyone to deny you these rights or to ask you to surrender the rights. These restrictions translate to certain responsibilities for you if you distribute copies of the software, or if you modify it.

For example, if you distribute copies of such a program, whether gratis or for a fee, you must give the recipients all the rights that you have. You must make sure that they, too, receive or can get the source code. And you must show them these terms so they know their rights.

We protect your rights with two steps: (1) copyright the software, and (2) offer you this license which gives you legal permission to copy, distribute and/or modify the software.

Also, for each author's protection and ours, we want to make certain that everyone understands that there is no warranty for this free software. If the software is modified by someone else and passed on, we want its recipients to know that what they have is not the original, so that any problems introduced by others will not reflect on the original authors' reputations.

Finally, any free program is threatened constantly by software patents. We wish to avoid the danger that redistributors of a free program will individually obtain patent licenses, in effect making the program proprietary. To prevent this, we have made it clear that any patent must be licensed for everyone's free use or not licensed at all.

The precise terms and conditions for copying, distribution and modification follow.

TERMS AND CONDITIONS FOR COPYING, DISTRIBUTION AND MODIFICATION

0. This License applies to any program or other work which contains a notice placed

by the copyright holder saying it may be distributed under the terms of this General Public License. The "Program", below, refers to any such program or work, and a "work based on the Program" means either the Program or any derivative work under copyright law: that is to say, a work containing the Program or a portion of it, either verbatim or with modifications and/or translated into another language. (Hereinafter, translation is included without limitation in the term "modification".) Each licensee is addressed as "you".

Activities other than copying, distribution and modification are not covered by this License; they are outside its scope. The act of running the Program is not restricted, and the output from the Program is covered only if its contents constitute a work based on the Program (independent of having been made by running the Program). Whether that is true depends on what the Program does.

1. You may copy and distribute verbatim copies of the Program's source code as you receive it, in any medium, provided that you conspicuously and appropriately publish on each copy an appropriate copyright notice and disclaimer of warranty; keep intact all the notices that refer to this License and to the absence of any warranty; and give any other recipients of the Program a copy of this License along with the Program.

   You may charge a fee for the physical act of transferring a copy, and you may at your option offer warranty protection in exchange for a fee.

2. You may modify your copy or copies of the Program or any portion of it, thus forming a work based on the Program, and copy and distribute such modifications or work under the terms of Section 1 above, provided that you also meet all of these conditions:

   a. You must cause the modified files to carry prominent notices stating that you changed the files and the date of any change.

   b. You must cause any work that you distribute or publish, that in whole or in part contains or is derived from the Program or any part thereof, to be licensed as a whole at no charge to all third parties under the terms of this License.

   c. If the modified program normally reads commands interactively when run, you must cause it, when started running for such interactive use in the most ordinary way, to print or display an announcement including an appropriate copyright notice and a notice that there is no warranty (or else, saying that you provide a warranty) and that users may redistribute the program under these conditions, and telling the user how to view a copy of this License. (Exception: if the Program itself is interactive but does not normally print such an announcement, your work based on the Program is not required to print an announcement.)

   These requirements apply to the modified work as a whole. If identifiable sections of that work are not derived from the Program, and can be reasonably considered independent and separate works in themselves, then this License, and its terms, do not apply to those sections when you distribute them as separate works. But when you distribute the same sections as part of a whole which is a work based on the Program, the distribution of the whole must be on the terms of this License, whose permissions for other licensees extend to the entire whole, and thus to each and every part regardless of who wrote it.

Thus, it is not the intent of this section to claim rights or contest your rights to work written entirely by you; rather, the intent is to exercise the right to control the distribution of derivative or collective works based on the Program.

In addition, mere aggregation of another work not based on the Program with the Program (or with a work based on the Program) on a volume of a storage or distribution medium does not bring the other work under the scope of this License.

3. You may copy and distribute the Program (or a work based on it, under Section 2) in object code or executable form under the terms of Sections 1 and 2 above provided that you also do one of the following:

   a. Accompany it with the complete corresponding machine-readable source code, which must be distributed under the terms of Sections 1 and 2 above on a medium customarily used for software interchange; or,

   b. Accompany it with a written offer, valid for at least three years, to give any third party, for a charge no more than your cost of physically performing source distribution, a complete machine-readable copy of the corresponding source code, to be distributed under the terms of Sections 1 and 2 above on a medium customarily used for software interchange; or,

   c. Accompany it with the information you received as to the offer to distribute corresponding source code. (This alternative is allowed only for noncommercial distribution and only if you received the program in object code or executable form with such an offer, in accord with Subsection b above.)

The source code for a work means the preferred form of the work for making modifications to it. For an executable work, complete source code means all the source code for all modules it contains, plus any associated interface definition files, plus the scripts used to control compilation and installation of the executable. However, as a special exception, the source code distributed need not include anything that is normally distributed (in either source or binary form) with the major components (compiler, kernel, and so on) of the operating system on which the executable runs, unless that component itself accompanies the executable.

If distribution of executable or object code is made by offering access to copy from a designated place, then offering equivalent access to copy the source code from the same place counts as distribution of the source code, even though third parties are not compelled to copy the source along with the object code.

4. You may not copy, modify, sublicense, or distribute the Program except as expressly provided under this License. Any attempt otherwise to copy, modify, sublicense or distribute the Program is void, and will automatically terminate your rights under this License. However, parties who have received copies, or rights, from you under this License will not have their licenses terminated so long as such parties remain in full compliance.

5. You are not required to accept this License, since you have not signed it. However, nothing else grants you permission to modify or distribute the Program or its derivative works. These actions are prohibited by law if you do not accept this License. Therefore, by modifying or distributing the Program (or any work based on the Program), you indicate your acceptance of this License to do so, and all its terms and conditions for copying, distributing or modifying the Program or works based on it.

6. Each time you redistribute the Program (or any work based on the Program), the recipient automatically receives a license from the original licensor to copy, distribute or modify the Program subject to these terms and conditions. You may not impose any further restrictions on the recipients' exercise of the rights granted herein. You are not responsible for enforcing compliance by third parties to this License.

7. If, as a consequence of a court judgment or allegation of patent infringement or for any other reason (not limited to patent issues), conditions are imposed on you (whether by court order, agreement or otherwise) that contradict the conditions of this License, they do not excuse you from the conditions of this License. If you cannot distribute so as to satisfy simultaneously your obligations under this License and any other pertinent obligations, then as a consequence you may not distribute the Program at all. For example, if a patent license would not permit royalty-free redistribution of the Program by all those who receive copies directly or indirectly through you, then the only way you could satisfy both it and this License would be to refrain entirely from distribution of the Program.

   If any portion of this section is held invalid or unenforceable under any particular circumstance, the balance of the section is intended to apply and the section as a whole is intended to apply in other circumstances.

   It is not the purpose of this section to induce you to infringe any patents or other property right claims or to contest validity of any such claims; this section has the sole purpose of protecting the integrity of the free software distribution system, which is implemented by public license practices. Many people have made generous contributions to the wide range of software distributed through that system in reliance on consistent application of that system; it is up to the author/donor to decide if he or she is willing to distribute software through any other system and a licensee cannot impose that choice.

   This section is intended to make thoroughly clear what is believed to be a consequence of the rest of this License.

8. If the distribution and/or use of the Program is restricted in certain countries either by patents or by copyrighted interfaces, the original copyright holder who places the Program under this License may add an explicit geographical distribution limitation excluding those countries, so that distribution is permitted only in or among countries not thus excluded. In such case, this License incorporates the limitation as if written in the body of this License.

9. The Free Software Foundation may publish revised and/or new versions of the General Public License from time to time. Such new versions will be similar in spirit to the present version, but may differ in detail to address new problems or concerns.

   Each version is given a distinguishing version number. If the Program specifies a version number of this License which applies to it and "any later version", you have the option of following the terms and conditions either of that version or of any later version published by the Free Software Foundation. If the Program does not specify a version number of this License, you may choose any version ever published by the Free Software Foundation.

10. If you wish to incorporate parts of the Program into other free programs whose distribution conditions are different, write to the author to ask for permission. For software

which is copyrighted by the Free Software Foundation, write to the Free Software Foundation; we sometimes make exceptions for this. Our decision will be guided by the two goals of preserving the free status of all derivatives of our free software and of promoting the sharing and reuse of software generally.

NO WARRANTY

11. BECAUSE THE PROGRAM IS LICENSED FREE OF CHARGE, THERE IS NO WARRANTY FOR THE PROGRAM, TO THE EXTENT PERMITTED BY APPLICABLE LAW. EXCEPT WHEN OTHERWISE STATED IN WRITING THE COPYRIGHT HOLDERS AND/OR OTHER PARTIES PROVIDE THE PROGRAM "AS IS" WITHOUT WARRANTY OF ANY KIND, EITHER EXPRESSED OR IMPLIED, INCLUDING, BUT NOT LIMITED TO, THE IMPLIED WARRANTIES OF MERCHANTABILITY AND FITNESS FOR A PARTICULAR PURPOSE. THE ENTIRE RISK AS TO THE QUALITY AND PERFORMANCE OF THE PROGRAM IS WITH YOU. SHOULD THE PROGRAM PROVE DEFECTIVE, YOU ASSUME THE COST OF ALL NECESSARY SERVICING, REPAIR OR CORRECTION.

12. IN NO EVENT UNLESS REQUIRED BY APPLICABLE LAW OR AGREED TO IN WRITING WILL ANY COPYRIGHT HOLDER, OR ANY OTHER PARTY WHO MAY MODIFY AND/OR REDISTRIBUTE THE PROGRAM AS PERMITTED ABOVE, BE LIABLE TO YOU FOR DAMAGES, INCLUDING ANY GENERAL, SPECIAL, INCIDENTAL OR CONSEQUENTIAL DAMAGES ARISING OUT OF THE USE OR INABILITY TO USE THE PROGRAM (INCLUDING BUT NOT LIMITED TO LOSS OF DATA OR DATA BEING RENDERED INACCURATE OR LOSSES SUSTAINED BY YOU OR THIRD PARTIES OR A FAILURE OF THE PROGRAM TO OPERATE WITH ANY OTHER PROGRAMS), EVEN IF SUCH HOLDER OR OTHER PARTY HAS BEEN ADVISED OF THE POSSIBILITY OF SUCH DAMAGES.

END OF TERMS AND CONDITIONS

Appendix: How to Apply These Terms to Your New Programs

If you develop a new program, and you want it to be of the greatest possible use to the public, the best way to achieve this is to make it free software which everyone can redistribute and change under these terms.

To do so, attach the following notices to the program. It is safest to attach them to the start of each source file to most effectively convey the exclusion of warranty; and each file should have at least the "copyright" line and a pointer to where the full notice is found.

```
one line to give the program's name and a brief idea of what it does.
Copyright (C) yyyy  name of author

This program is free software; you can redistribute it and/or modify
it under the terms of the GNU General Public License as published by
the Free Software Foundation; either version 2 of the License, or
(at your option) any later version.

This program is distributed in the hope that it will be useful,
but WITHOUT ANY WARRANTY; without even the implied warranty of
MERCHANTABILITY or FITNESS FOR A PARTICULAR PURPOSE.  See the
GNU General Public License for more details.

You should have received a copy of the GNU General Public License
along with this program; if not, write to the Free Software
Foundation, Inc., 51 Franklin Street, Fifth Floor, Boston, MA  02110-1301, USA.
```

Also add information on how to contact you by electronic and paper mail.

If the program is interactive, make it output a short notice like this when it starts in an interactive mode:

```
Gnomovision version 69, Copyright (C) year name of author
Gnomovision comes with ABSOLUTELY NO WARRANTY; for details type 'show w'.
This is free software, and you are welcome to redistribute it
under certain conditions; type 'show c' for details.
```

The hypothetical commands 'show w' and 'show c' should show the appropriate parts of the General Public License. Of course, the commands you use may be called something other than 'show w' and 'show c'; they could even be mouse-clicks or menu items—whatever suits your program.

You should also get your employer (if you work as a programmer) or your school, if any, to sign a "copyright disclaimer" for the program, if necessary. Here is a sample; alter the names:

```
Yoyodyne, Inc., hereby disclaims all copyright interest in the program
'Gnomovision' (which makes passes at compilers) written by James Hacker.

signature of Ty Coon, 1 April 1989
Ty Coon, President of Vice
```

This General Public License does not permit incorporating your program into proprietary programs. If your program is a subroutine library, you may consider it more useful to permit linking proprietary applications with the library. If this is what you want to do, use the GNU Lesser General Public License instead of this License.

C.2 GNU LESSER GENERAL PUBLIC LICENSE

Version 2.1, February 1999

Copyright © 1991, 1999 Free Software Foundation, Inc.
51 Franklin Street, Fifth Floor, Boston, MA 02110-1301, USA

Everyone is permitted to copy and distribute verbatim copies
of this license document, but changing it is not allowed.

[This is the first released version of the Lesser GPL. It also counts
as the successor of the GNU Library Public License, version 2, hence the
version number 2.1.]

Preamble

The licenses for most software are designed to take away your freedom to share and change it. By contrast, the GNU General Public Licenses are intended to guarantee your freedom to share and change free software—to make sure the software is free for all its users.

This license, the Lesser General Public License, applies to some specially designated software—typically libraries—of the Free Software Foundation and other authors who decide to use it. You can use it too, but we suggest you first think carefully about whether this license or the ordinary General Public License is the better strategy to use in any particular case, based on the explanations below.

When we speak of free software, we are referring to freedom of use, not price. Our General Public Licenses are designed to make sure that you have the freedom to distribute copies of free software (and charge for this service if you wish); that you receive source code or can get it if you want it; that you can change the software and use pieces of it in new free programs; and that you are informed that you can do these things.

To protect your rights, we need to make restrictions that forbid distributors to deny you these rights or to ask you to surrender these rights. These restrictions translate to certain responsibilities for you if you distribute copies of the library or if you modify it.

For example, if you distribute copies of the library, whether gratis or for a fee, you must give the recipients all the rights that we gave you. You must make sure that they, too, receive or can get the source code. If you link other code with the library, you must provide complete object files to the recipients, so that they can relink them with the library after making changes to the library and recompiling it. And you must show them these terms so they know their rights.

We protect your rights with a two-step method: (1) we copyright the library, and (2) we offer you this license, which gives you legal permission to copy, distribute and/or modify the library.

To protect each distributor, we want to make it very clear that there is no warranty for the free library. Also, if the library is modified by someone else and passed on, the recipients should know that what they have is not the original version, so that the original author's reputation will not be affected by problems that might be introduced by others.

Finally, software patents pose a constant threat to the existence of any free program. We wish to make sure that a company cannot effectively restrict the users of a free program by obtaining a restrictive license from a patent holder. Therefore, we insist that any patent license obtained for a version of the library must be consistent with the full freedom of use specified in this license.

Most GNU software, including some libraries, is covered by the ordinary GNU General Public License. This license, the GNU Lesser General Public License, applies to certain designated libraries, and is quite different from the ordinary General Public License. We use this license for certain libraries in order to permit linking those libraries into non-free programs.

When a program is linked with a library, whether statically or using a shared library, the combination of the two is legally speaking a combined work, a derivative of the original library. The ordinary General Public License therefore permits such linking only if the entire combination fits its criteria of freedom. The Lesser General Public License permits more lax criteria for linking other code with the library.

We call this license the *Lesser* General Public License because it does *Less* to protect the user's freedom than the ordinary General Public License. It also provides other free software developers Less of an advantage over competing non-free programs. These disadvantages are the reason we use the ordinary General Public License for many libraries. However, the Lesser license provides advantages in certain special circumstances.

For example, on rare occasions, there may be a special need to encourage the widest possible use of a certain library, so that it becomes a de-facto standard. To achieve this, non-free programs must be allowed to use the library. A more frequent case is that a free library does the same job as widely used non-free libraries. In this case, there is little to gain by limiting the free library to free software only, so we use the Lesser General Public License.

In other cases, permission to use a particular library in non-free programs enables a greater number of people to use a large body of free software. For example, permission to use the GNU C Library in non-free programs enables many more people to use the whole GNU operating system, as well as its variant, the GNU/Linux operating system.

Although the Lesser General Public License is Less protective of the users' freedom, it does ensure that the user of a program that is linked with the Library has the freedom and the wherewithal to run that program using a modified version of the Library.

The precise terms and conditions for copying, distribution and modification follow. Pay close attention to the difference between a "work based on the library" and a "work that uses the library". The former contains code derived from the library, whereas the latter must be combined with the library in order to run.

TERMS AND CONDITIONS FOR COPYING, DISTRIBUTION AND MODIFICATION

0. This License Agreement applies to any software library or other program which contains a notice placed by the copyright holder or other authorized party saying it may be distributed under the terms of this Lesser General Public License (also called "this License"). Each licensee is addressed as "you".

    A "library" means a collection of software functions and/or data prepared so as to be conveniently linked with application programs (which use some of those functions and data) to form executables.

The "Library", below, refers to any such software library or work which has been distributed under these terms. A "work based on the Library" means either the Library or any derivative work under copyright law: that is to say, a work containing the Library or a portion of it, either verbatim or with modifications and/or translated straightforwardly into another language. (Hereinafter, translation is included without limitation in the term "modification".)

"Source code" for a work means the preferred form of the work for making modifications to it. For a library, complete source code means all the source code for all modules it contains, plus any associated interface definition files, plus the scripts used to control compilation and installation of the library.

Activities other than copying, distribution and modification are not covered by this License; they are outside its scope. The act of running a program using the Library is not restricted, and output from such a program is covered only if its contents constitute a work based on the Library (independent of the use of the Library in a tool for writing it). Whether that is true depends on what the Library does and what the program that uses the Library does.

1. You may copy and distribute verbatim copies of the Library's complete source code as you receive it, in any medium, provided that you conspicuously and appropriately publish on each copy an appropriate copyright notice and disclaimer of warranty; keep intact all the notices that refer to this License and to the absence of any warranty; and distribute a copy of this License along with the Library.

   You may charge a fee for the physical act of transferring a copy, and you may at your option offer warranty protection in exchange for a fee.

2. You may modify your copy or copies of the Library or any portion of it, thus forming a work based on the Library, and copy and distribute such modifications or work under the terms of Section 1 above, provided that you also meet all of these conditions:

   a. The modified work must itself be a software library.

   b. You must cause the files modified to carry prominent notices stating that you changed the files and the date of any change.

   c. You must cause the whole of the work to be licensed at no charge to all third parties under the terms of this License.

   d. If a facility in the modified Library refers to a function or a table of data to be supplied by an application program that uses the facility, other than as an argument passed when the facility is invoked, then you must make a good faith effort to ensure that, in the event an application does not supply such function or table, the facility still operates, and performs whatever part of its purpose remains meaningful.

      (For example, a function in a library to compute square roots has a purpose that is entirely well-defined independent of the application. Therefore, Subsection 2d requires that any application-supplied function or table used by this function must be optional: if the application does not supply it, the square root function must still compute square roots.)

These requirements apply to the modified work as a whole. If identifiable sections of that work are not derived from the Library, and can be reasonably considered independent and separate works in themselves, then this License, and its terms, do not apply to those sections when you distribute them as separate works. But when you distribute the same sections as part of a whole which is a work based on the Library, the distribution of the whole must be on the terms of this License, whose permissions for other licensees extend to the entire whole, and thus to each and every part regardless of who wrote it.

Thus, it is not the intent of this section to claim rights or contest your rights to work written entirely by you; rather, the intent is to exercise the right to control the distribution of derivative or collective works based on the Library.

In addition, mere aggregation of another work not based on the Library with the Library (or with a work based on the Library) on a volume of a storage or distribution medium does not bring the other work under the scope of this License.

3. You may opt to apply the terms of the ordinary GNU General Public License instead of this License to a given copy of the Library. To do this, you must alter all the notices that refer to this License, so that they refer to the ordinary GNU General Public License, version 2, instead of to this License. (If a newer version than version 2 of the ordinary GNU General Public License has appeared, then you can specify that version instead if you wish.) Do not make any other change in these notices.

Once this change is made in a given copy, it is irreversible for that copy, so the ordinary GNU General Public License applies to all subsequent copies and derivative works made from that copy.

This option is useful when you wish to copy part of the code of the Library into a program that is not a library.

4. You may copy and distribute the Library (or a portion or derivative of it, under Section 2) in object code or executable form under the terms of Sections 1 and 2 above provided that you accompany it with the complete corresponding machine-readable source code, which must be distributed under the terms of Sections 1 and 2 above on a medium customarily used for software interchange.

If distribution of object code is made by offering access to copy from a designated place, then offering equivalent access to copy the source code from the same place satisfies the requirement to distribute the source code, even though third parties are not compelled to copy the source along with the object code.

5. A program that contains no derivative of any portion of the Library, but is designed to work with the Library by being compiled or linked with it, is called a "work that uses the Library". Such a work, in isolation, is not a derivative work of the Library, and therefore falls outside the scope of this License.

However, linking a "work that uses the Library" with the Library creates an executable that is a derivative of the Library (because it contains portions of the Library), rather than a "work that uses the library". The executable is therefore covered by this License. Section 6 states terms for distribution of such executables.

When a "work that uses the Library" uses material from a header file that is part of the Library, the object code for the work may be a derivative work of the Library even though the source code is not. Whether this is true is especially significant if the work can be linked without the Library, or if the work is itself a library. The threshold for this to be true is not precisely defined by law.

If such an object file uses only numerical parameters, data structure layouts and accessors, and small macros and small inline functions (ten lines or less in length), then the use of the object file is unrestricted, regardless of whether it is legally a derivative work. (Executables containing this object code plus portions of the Library will still fall under Section 6.)

Otherwise, if the work is a derivative of the Library, you may distribute the object code for the work under the terms of Section 6. Any executables containing that work also fall under Section 6, whether or not they are linked directly with the Library itself.

6. As an exception to the Sections above, you may also combine or link a "work that uses the Library" with the Library to produce a work containing portions of the Library, and distribute that work under terms of your choice, provided that the terms permit modification of the work for the customer's own use and reverse engineering for debugging such modifications.

You must give prominent notice with each copy of the work that the Library is used in it and that the Library and its use are covered by this License. You must supply a copy of this License. If the work during execution displays copyright notices, you must include the copyright notice for the Library among them, as well as a reference directing the user to the copy of this License. Also, you must do one of these things:

   a. Accompany the work with the complete corresponding machine-readable source code for the Library including whatever changes were used in the work (which must be distributed under Sections 1 and 2 above); and, if the work is an executable linked with the Library, with the complete machine-readable "work that uses the Library", as object code and/or source code, so that the user can modify the Library and then relink to produce a modified executable containing the modified Library. (It is understood that the user who changes the contents of definitions files in the Library will not necessarily be able to recompile the application to use the modified definitions.)

   b. Use a suitable shared library mechanism for linking with the Library. A suitable mechanism is one that (1) uses at run time a copy of the library already present on the user's computer system, rather than copying library functions into the executable, and (2) will operate properly with a modified version of the library, if the user installs one, as long as the modified version is interface-compatible with the version that the work was made with.

   c. Accompany the work with a written offer, valid for at least three years, to give the same user the materials specified in Subsection 6a, above, for a charge no more than the cost of performing this distribution.

   d. If distribution of the work is made by offering access to copy from a designated place, offer equivalent access to copy the above specified materials from the same place.

   e. Verify that the user has already received a copy of these materials or that you have already sent this user a copy.

For an executable, the required form of the "work that uses the Library" must include any data and utility programs needed for reproducing the executable from it. However, as a special exception, the materials to be distributed need not include anything that is normally distributed (in either source or binary form) with the major components (compiler, kernel, and so on) of the operating system on which the executable runs, unless that component itself accompanies the executable.

It may happen that this requirement contradicts the license restrictions of other proprietary libraries that do not normally accompany the operating system. Such a contradiction means you cannot use both them and the Library together in an executable that you distribute.

7. You may place library facilities that are a work based on the Library side-by-side in a single library together with other library facilities not covered by this License, and distribute such a combined library, provided that the separate distribution of the work based on the Library and of the other library facilities is otherwise permitted, and provided that you do these two things:

   a. Accompany the combined library with a copy of the same work based on the Library, uncombined with any other library facilities. This must be distributed under the terms of the Sections above.

   b. Give prominent notice with the combined library of the fact that part of it is a work based on the Library, and explaining where to find the accompanying uncombined form of the same work.

8. You may not copy, modify, sublicense, link with, or distribute the Library except as expressly provided under this License. Any attempt otherwise to copy, modify, sublicense, link with, or distribute the Library is void, and will automatically terminate your rights under this License. However, parties who have received copies, or rights, from you under this License will not have their licenses terminated so long as such parties remain in full compliance.

9. You are not required to accept this License, since you have not signed it. However, nothing else grants you permission to modify or distribute the Library or its derivative works. These actions are prohibited by law if you do not accept this License. Therefore, by modifying or distributing the Library (or any work based on the Library), you indicate your acceptance of this License to do so, and all its terms and conditions for copying, distributing or modifying the Library or works based on it.

10. Each time you redistribute the Library (or any work based on the Library), the recipient automatically receives a license from the original licensor to copy, distribute, link with or modify the Library subject to these terms and conditions. You may not impose any further restrictions on the recipients' exercise of the rights granted herein. You are not responsible for enforcing compliance by third parties with this License.

11. If, as a consequence of a court judgment or allegation of patent infringement or for any other reason (not limited to patent issues), conditions are imposed on you (whether by court order, agreement or otherwise) that contradict the conditions of this License, they do not excuse you from the conditions of this License. If you cannot distribute so as to satisfy simultaneously your obligations under this License and any other pertinent obligations, then as a consequence you may not distribute the Library at all. For example, if a patent license would not permit royalty-free redistribution of the Library by all those who receive copies directly or indirectly through you, then the only way you could satisfy both it and this License would be to refrain entirely from distribution of the Library.

If any portion of this section is held invalid or unenforceable under any particular circumstance, the balance of the section is intended to apply, and the section as a whole is intended to apply in other circumstances.

It is not the purpose of this section to induce you to infringe any patents or other property right claims or to contest validity of any such claims; this section has the sole purpose of protecting the integrity of the free software distribution system which is implemented by public license practices. Many people have made generous contributions to the wide range of software distributed through that system in reliance on consistent application of that system; it is up to the author/donor to decide if he or she is willing to distribute software through any other system and a licensee cannot impose that choice.

This section is intended to make thoroughly clear what is believed to be a consequence of the rest of this License.

12. If the distribution and/or use of the Library is restricted in certain countries either by patents or by copyrighted interfaces, the original copyright holder who places the Library under this License may add an explicit geographical distribution limitation excluding those countries, so that distribution is permitted only in or among countries not thus excluded. In such case, this License incorporates the limitation as if written in the body of this License.

13. The Free Software Foundation may publish revised and/or new versions of the Lesser General Public License from time to time. Such new versions will be similar in spirit to the present version, but may differ in detail to address new problems or concerns.

Each version is given a distinguishing version number. If the Library specifies a version number of this License which applies to it and "any later version", you have the option of following the terms and conditions either of that version or of any later version published by the Free Software Foundation. If the Library does not specify a license version number, you may choose any version ever published by the Free Software Foundation.

14. If you wish to incorporate parts of the Library into other free programs whose distribution conditions are incompatible with these, write to the author to ask for permission. For software which is copyrighted by the Free Software Foundation, write to the Free Software Foundation; we sometimes make exceptions for this. Our decision will be guided by the two goals of preserving the free status of all derivatives of our free software and of promoting the sharing and reuse of software generally.

NO WARRANTY

15. BECAUSE THE LIBRARY IS LICENSED FREE OF CHARGE, THERE IS NO WARRANTY FOR THE LIBRARY, TO THE EXTENT PERMITTED BY APPLICABLE LAW. EXCEPT WHEN OTHERWISE STATED IN WRITING THE COPYRIGHT HOLDERS AND/OR OTHER PARTIES PROVIDE THE LIBRARY "AS IS" WITHOUT WARRANTY OF ANY KIND, EITHER EXPRESSED OR IMPLIED, INCLUDING, BUT NOT LIMITED TO, THE IMPLIED WARRANTIES OF MERCHANTABILITY AND FITNESS FOR A PARTICULAR PURPOSE. THE ENTIRE RISK AS TO THE QUALITY AND PERFORMANCE OF THE LIBRARY IS WITH YOU. SHOULD THE LIBRARY PROVE DEFECTIVE, YOU ASSUME THE COST OF ALL NECESSARY SERVICING, REPAIR OR CORRECTION.

16. IN NO EVENT UNLESS REQUIRED BY APPLICABLE LAW OR AGREED TO IN

WRITING WILL ANY COPYRIGHT HOLDER, OR ANY OTHER PARTY WHO MAY MODIFY AND/OR REDISTRIBUTE THE LIBRARY AS PERMITTED ABOVE, BE LIABLE TO YOU FOR DAMAGES, INCLUDING ANY GENERAL, SPECIAL, INCIDENTAL OR CONSEQUENTIAL DAMAGES ARISING OUT OF THE USE OR INABILITY TO USE THE LIBRARY (INCLUDING BUT NOT LIMITED TO LOSS OF DATA OR DATA BEING RENDERED INACCURATE OR LOSSES SUSTAINED BY YOU OR THIRD PARTIES OR A FAILURE OF THE LIBRARY TO OPERATE WITH ANY OTHER SOFTWARE), EVEN IF SUCH HOLDER OR OTHER PARTY HAS BEEN ADVISED OF THE POSSIBILITY OF SUCH DAMAGES.

END OF TERMS AND CONDITIONS

How to Apply These Terms to Your New Libraries

If you develop a new library, and you want it to be of the greatest possible use to the public, we recommend making it free software that everyone can redistribute and change. You can do so by permitting redistribution under these terms (or, alternatively, under the terms of the ordinary General Public License).

To apply these terms, attach the following notices to the library. It is safest to attach them to the start of each source file to most effectively convey the exclusion of warranty; and each file should have at least the "copyright" line and a pointer to where the full notice is found.

```
one line to give the library's name and an idea of what it does.
Copyright (C) year  name of author

This library is free software; you can redistribute it and/or modify it
under the terms of the GNU Lesser General Public License as published by
the Free Software Foundation; either version 2.1 of the License, or (at
your option) any later version.

This library is distributed in the hope that it will be useful, but
WITHOUT ANY WARRANTY; without even the implied warranty of
MERCHANTABILITY or FITNESS FOR A PARTICULAR PURPOSE.  See the GNU
Lesser General Public License for more details.

You should have received a copy of the GNU Lesser General Public
License along with this library; if not, write to the Free Software
Foundation, Inc., 51 Franklin Street, Fifth Floor, Boston, MA 02110-1301,
USA.
```

Also add information on how to contact you by electronic and paper mail.

You should also get your employer (if you work as a programmer) or your school, if any, to sign a "copyright disclaimer" for the library, if necessary. Here is a sample; alter the names:

```
Yoyodyne, Inc., hereby disclaims all copyright interest in the library
'Frob' (a library for tweaking knobs) written by James Random Hacker.

signature of Ty Coon, 1 April 1990
Ty Coon, President of Vice
```

That's all there is to it!

C.3 GNU Free Documentation License

Version 1.2, November 2002

Copyright © 2000,2001,2002 Free Software Foundation, Inc.
51 Franklin St, Fifth Floor, Boston, MA 02110-1301, USA

0. PREAMBLE

The purpose of this License is to make a manual, textbook, or other functional and useful document *free* in the sense of freedom: to assure everyone the effective freedom to copy and redistribute it, with or without modifying it, either commercially or non-commercially. Secondarily, this License preserves for the author and publisher a way to get credit for their work, while not being considered responsible for modifications made by others.

This License is a kind of "copyleft", which means that derivative works of the document must themselves be free in the same sense. It complements the GNU General Public License, which is a copyleft license designed for free software.

We have designed this License in order to use it for manuals for free software, because free software needs free documentation: a free program should come with manuals providing the same freedoms that the software does. But this License is not limited to software manuals; it can be used for any textual work, regardless of subject matter or whether it is published as a printed book. We recommend this License principally for works whose purpose is instruction or reference.

1. APPLICABILITY AND DEFINITIONS

This License applies to any manual or other work, in any medium, that contains a notice placed by the copyright holder saying it can be distributed under the terms of this License. Such a notice grants a world-wide, royalty-free license, unlimited in duration, to use that work under the conditions stated herein. The "Document", below, refers to any such manual or work. Any member of the public is a licensee, and is addressed as "you". You accept the license if you copy, modify or distribute the work in a way requiring permission under copyright law.

A "Modified Version" of the Document means any work containing the Document or a portion of it, either copied verbatim, or with modifications and/or translated into another language.

A "Secondary Section" is a named appendix or a front-matter section of the Document that deals exclusively with the relationship of the publishers or authors of the Document to the Document's overall subject (or to related matters) and contains nothing that could fall directly within that overall subject. (Thus, if the Document is in part a textbook of mathematics, a Secondary Section may not explain any mathematics.) The relationship could be a matter of historical connection with the subject or with related matters, or of legal, commercial, philosophical, ethical or political position regarding them.

The "Invariant Sections" are certain Secondary Sections whose titles are designated, as being those of Invariant Sections, in the notice that says that the Document is released under this License. If a section does not fit the above definition of Secondary then it is not allowed to be designated as Invariant. The Document may contain zero Invariant Sections. If the Document does not identify any Invariant Sections then there are none.

The "Cover Texts" are certain short passages of text that are listed, as Front-Cover Texts or Back-Cover Texts, in the notice that says that the Document is released under this License. A Front-Cover Text may be at most 5 words, and a Back-Cover Text may be at most 25 words.

A "Transparent" copy of the Document means a machine-readable copy, represented in a format whose specification is available to the general public, that is suitable for revising the document straightforwardly with generic text editors or (for images composed of pixels) generic paint programs or (for drawings) some widely available drawing editor, and that is suitable for input to text formatters or for automatic translation to a variety of formats suitable for input to text formatters. A copy made in an otherwise Transparent file format whose markup, or absence of markup, has been arranged to thwart or discourage subsequent modification by readers is not Transparent. An image format is not Transparent if used for any substantial amount of text. A copy that is not "Transparent" is called "Opaque".

Examples of suitable formats for Transparent copies include plain ASCII without markup, Texinfo input format, LaTeX input format, SGML or XML using a publicly available DTD, and standard-conforming simple HTML, PostScript or PDF designed for human modification. Examples of transparent image formats include PNG, XCF and JPG. Opaque formats include proprietary formats that can be read and edited only by proprietary word processors, SGML or XML for which the DTD and/or processing tools are not generally available, and the machine-generated HTML, PostScript or PDF produced by some word processors for output purposes only.

The "Title Page" means, for a printed book, the title page itself, plus such following pages as are needed to hold, legibly, the material this License requires to appear in the title page. For works in formats which do not have any title page as such, "Title Page" means the text near the most prominent appearance of the work's title, preceding the beginning of the body of the text.

A section "Entitled XYZ" means a named subunit of the Document whose title either is precisely XYZ or contains XYZ in parentheses following text that translates XYZ in another language. (Here XYZ stands for a specific section name mentioned below, such as "Acknowledgements", "Dedications", "Endorsements", or "History".) To "Preserve the Title" of such a section when you modify the Document means that it remains a section "Entitled XYZ" according to this definition.

The Document may include Warranty Disclaimers next to the notice which states that this License applies to the Document. These Warranty Disclaimers are considered to be included by reference in this License, but only as regards disclaiming warranties: any other implication that these Warranty Disclaimers may have is void and has no effect on the meaning of this License.

2. VERBATIM COPYING

You may copy and distribute the Document in any medium, either commercially or noncommercially, provided that this License, the copyright notices, and the license notice saying this License applies to the Document are reproduced in all copies, and that you add no other conditions whatsoever to those of this License. You may not use technical measures to obstruct or control the reading or further copying of the copies you make or distribute. However, you may accept compensation in exchange for copies. If you distribute a large enough number of copies you must also follow the conditions in section 3.

You may also lend copies, under the same conditions stated above, and you may publicly display copies.

3. COPYING IN QUANTITY

If you publish printed copies (or copies in media that commonly have printed covers) of the Document, numbering more than 100, and the Document's license notice requires Cover Texts, you must enclose the copies in covers that carry, clearly and legibly, all these Cover Texts: Front-Cover Texts on the front cover, and Back-Cover Texts on the back cover. Both covers must also clearly and legibly identify you as the publisher of these copies. The front cover must present the full title with all words of the title equally prominent and visible. You may add other material on the covers in addition. Copying with changes limited to the covers, as long as they preserve the title of the Document and satisfy these conditions, can be treated as verbatim copying in other respects.

If the required texts for either cover are too voluminous to fit legibly, you should put the first ones listed (as many as fit reasonably) on the actual cover, and continue the rest onto adjacent pages.

If you publish or distribute Opaque copies of the Document numbering more than 100, you must either include a machine-readable Transparent copy along with each Opaque copy, or state in or with each Opaque copy a computer-network location from which the general network-using public has access to download using public-standard network protocols a complete Transparent copy of the Document, free of added material. If you use the latter option, you must take reasonably prudent steps, when you begin distribution of Opaque copies in quantity, to ensure that this Transparent copy will remain thus accessible at the stated location until at least one year after the last time you distribute an Opaque copy (directly or through your agents or retailers) of that edition to the public.

It is requested, but not required, that you contact the authors of the Document well before redistributing any large number of copies, to give them a chance to provide you with an updated version of the Document.

4. MODIFICATIONS

You may copy and distribute a Modified Version of the Document under the conditions of sections 2 and 3 above, provided that you release the Modified Version under precisely this License, with the Modified Version filling the role of the Document, thus licensing distribution and modification of the Modified Version to whoever possesses a copy of it. In addition, you must do these things in the Modified Version:

A. Use in the Title Page (and on the covers, if any) a title distinct from that of the Document, and from those of previous versions (which should, if there were any, be listed in the History section of the Document). You may use the same title as a previous version if the original publisher of that version gives permission.

B. List on the Title Page, as authors, one or more persons or entities responsible for authorship of the modifications in the Modified Version, together with at least five of the principal authors of the Document (all of its principal authors, if it has fewer than five), unless they release you from this requirement.

C. State on the Title page the name of the publisher of the Modified Version, as the publisher.

D. Preserve all the copyright notices of the Document.

E. Add an appropriate copyright notice for your modifications adjacent to the other copyright notices.

F. Include, immediately after the copyright notices, a license notice giving the public permission to use the Modified Version under the terms of this License, in the form shown in the Addendum below.

G. Preserve in that license notice the full lists of Invariant Sections and required Cover Texts given in the Document's license notice.

H. Include an unaltered copy of this License.

I. Preserve the section Entitled "History", Preserve its Title, and add to it an item stating at least the title, year, new authors, and publisher of the Modified Version as given on the Title Page. If there is no section Entitled "History" in the Document, create one stating the title, year, authors, and publisher of the Document as given on its Title Page, then add an item describing the Modified Version as stated in the previous sentence.

J. Preserve the network location, if any, given in the Document for public access to a Transparent copy of the Document, and likewise the network locations given in the Document for previous versions it was based on. These may be placed in the "History" section. You may omit a network location for a work that was published at least four years before the Document itself, or if the original publisher of the version it refers to gives permission.

K. For any section Entitled "Acknowledgements" or "Dedications", Preserve the Title of the section, and preserve in the section all the substance and tone of each of the contributor acknowledgements and/or dedications given therein.

L. Preserve all the Invariant Sections of the Document, unaltered in their text and in their titles. Section numbers or the equivalent are not considered part of the section titles.

M. Delete any section Entitled "Endorsements". Such a section may not be included in the Modified Version.

N. Do not retitle any existing section to be Entitled "Endorsements" or to conflict in title with any Invariant Section.

O. Preserve any Warranty Disclaimers.

If the Modified Version includes new front-matter sections or appendices that qualify as Secondary Sections and contain no material copied from the Document, you may at your option designate some or all of these sections as invariant. To do this, add their titles to the list of Invariant Sections in the Modified Version's license notice. These titles must be distinct from any other section titles.

You may add a section Entitled "Endorsements", provided it contains nothing but endorsements of your Modified Version by various parties—for example, statements of peer review or that the text has been approved by an organization as the authoritative definition of a standard.

You may add a passage of up to five words as a Front-Cover Text, and a passage of up to 25 words as a Back-Cover Text, to the end of the list of Cover Texts in the Modified Version. Only one passage of Front-Cover Text and one of Back-Cover Text may be added by (or through arrangements made by) any one entity. If the Document already includes a cover text for the same cover, previously added by you or by arrangement made by the same entity you are acting on behalf of, you may not add another; but you may replace the old one, on explicit permission from the previous publisher that added the old one.

The author(s) and publisher(s) of the Document do not by this License give permission to use their names for publicity for or to assert or imply endorsement of any Modified Version.

5. COMBINING DOCUMENTS

You may combine the Document with other documents released under this License, under the terms defined in section 4 above for modified versions, provided that you include in the combination all of the Invariant Sections of all of the original documents, unmodified, and list them all as Invariant Sections of your combined work in its license notice, and that you preserve all their Warranty Disclaimers.

The combined work need only contain one copy of this License, and multiple identical Invariant Sections may be replaced with a single copy. If there are multiple Invariant Sections with the same name but different contents, make the title of each such section unique by adding at the end of it, in parentheses, the name of the original author or publisher of that section if known, or else a unique number. Make the same adjustment to the section titles in the list of Invariant Sections in the license notice of the combined work.

In the combination, you must combine any sections Entitled "History" in the various original documents, forming one section Entitled "History"; likewise combine any sections Entitled "Acknowledgements", and any sections Entitled "Dedications". You must delete all sections Entitled "Endorsements."

6. COLLECTIONS OF DOCUMENTS

You may make a collection consisting of the Document and other documents released under this License, and replace the individual copies of this License in the various documents with a single copy that is included in the collection, provided that you follow the rules of this License for verbatim copying of each of the documents in all other respects.

You may extract a single document from such a collection, and distribute it individually under this License, provided you insert a copy of this License into the extracted document, and follow this License in all other respects regarding verbatim copying of that document.

7. AGGREGATION WITH INDEPENDENT WORKS

A compilation of the Document or its derivatives with other separate and independent documents or works, in or on a volume of a storage or distribution medium, is called an "aggregate" if the copyright resulting from the compilation is not used to limit the legal rights of the compilation's users beyond what the individual works permit. When the Document is included in an aggregate, this License does not apply to the other works in the aggregate which are not themselves derivative works of the Document.

If the Cover Text requirement of section 3 is applicable to these copies of the Document, then if the Document is less than one half of the entire aggregate, the Document's Cover Texts may be placed on covers that bracket the Document within the aggregate, or the electronic equivalent of covers if the Document is in electronic form. Otherwise they must appear on printed covers that bracket the whole aggregate.

8. TRANSLATION

Translation is considered a kind of modification, so you may distribute translations of the Document under the terms of section 4. Replacing Invariant Sections with translations requires special permission from their copyright holders, but you may include translations of some or all Invariant Sections in addition to the original versions of these Invariant Sections. You may include a translation of this License, and all the license notices in the Document, and any Warranty Disclaimers, provided that you also include the original English version of this License and the original versions of those notices and disclaimers. In case of a disagreement between the translation and the original version of this License or a notice or disclaimer, the original version will prevail.

If a section in the Document is Entitled "Acknowledgements", "Dedications", or "History", the requirement (section 4) to Preserve its Title (section 1) will typically require changing the actual title.

9. TERMINATION

You may not copy, modify, sublicense, or distribute the Document except as expressly provided for under this License. Any other attempt to copy, modify, sublicense or distribute the Document is void, and will automatically terminate your rights under this License. However, parties who have received copies, or rights, from you under this License will not have their licenses terminated so long as such parties remain in full compliance.

10. FUTURE REVISIONS OF THIS LICENSE

The Free Software Foundation may publish new, revised versions of the GNU Free Documentation License from time to time. Such new versions will be similar in spirit to the present version, but may differ in detail to address new problems or concerns. See http://www.gnu.org/copyleft/.

Each version of the License is given a distinguishing version number. If the Document specifies that a particular numbered version of this License "or any later version" applies to it, you have the option of following the terms and conditions either of that specified version or of any later version that has been published (not as a draft) by the Free Software Foundation. If the Document does not specify a version number of this License, you may choose any version ever published (not as a draft) by the Free Software Foundation.

ADDENDUM: How to use this License for your documents

To use this License in a document you have written, include a copy of the License in the document and put the following copyright and license notices just after the title page:

```
Copyright (C)  year  your name.
Permission is granted to copy, distribute and/or modify this document
under the terms of the GNU Free Documentation License, Version 1.2
or any later version published by the Free Software Foundation;
with no Invariant Sections, no Front-Cover Texts, and no Back-Cover
Texts.  A copy of the license is included in the section entitled ''GNU
Free Documentation License''.
```

If you have Invariant Sections, Front-Cover Texts and Back-Cover Texts, replace the "with...Texts." line with this:

```
with the Invariant Sections being list their titles, with
the Front-Cover Texts being list, and with the Back-Cover Texts
being list.
```

If you have Invariant Sections without Cover Texts, or some other combination of the three, merge those two alternatives to suit the situation.

If your document contains nontrivial examples of program code, we recommend releasing these examples in parallel under your choice of free software license, such as the GNU General Public License, to permit their use in free software.

Program Index

Option Index

Variable Index

PO Mode Index

Autoconf Macro Index

General Index